Ace the IT Résumé

About the Author

Paula Moreira is currently the global IT training manager at a large financial services organization. She and her team support an IT team of about 2,000. She began her career as a techie and has spent the last 15 years working in IT education and career development.

About the Technical Editor

Tim Sosbe is an editorial and events director at Brandon Hall Research. Prior to joining Brandon Hall Research, Tim was the editorial director at MediaTec Publishing where he created editorial plans for *Certification Magazine*, *Chief Learning Officer* magazine, and *Talent Management* magazine. Earlier in his career, Tim was a newspaper journalist covering education and a magazine columnist covering human resources.

The McGraw·Hill Companies

Cataloging-in-Publication Data is on file with the Library of Congress

McGraw-Hill books are available at special quantity discounts to use as premiums and sales promotions, or for use in corporate training programs. For more information, please write to the Director of Special Sales, Professional Publishing, McGraw-Hill, Two Penn Plaza, New York, NY 10121-2298. Or contact your local bookstore.

Ace the IT Résumé, Second Edition

1 2 3 4 5 6 7 8 9 0 QPD QPD 0 1 9 8 7

ISBN-13: 978-0-07-149274-4
ISBN-10:   0-07-149274-7

Sponsoring Editor
Megg Morin

Editorial Supervisor
Patty Mon

Project Manager
Samik Roy Chowdhury (International
Typesetting and Composition)

Acquisitions Coordinator
Carly Stapleton

Technical Editor
Tim Sosbe

Copy Editor
Marcia Baker

Proofreader
Shruti Pande (International
Typesetting and Composition)

Indexer
Valerie Perry

Production Supervisor
George Anderson

Composition
International Typesetting and Composition

Illustration
International Typesetting and Composition

Art Director, Cover
Jeff Weeks

Ace the IT Résumé

Second Edition

Paula Moreira

New York   Chicago   San Francisco   Lisbon
London   Madrid   Mexico City   Milan   New Delhi
San Juan   Seoul   Singapore   Sydney   Toronto

To Maryann Lucania, Rosemary Botelho, and Paul M. Forbes—
great teachers and great human beings!

Contents

Acknowledgments   xi

Introduction   xiii

Part I   Creating a Winning IT Résumé

Chapter 1 Standing Out from the Crowd   3
   The Basics of Getting Noticed   4
   Marketing the Ten Hottest Skills   10
   Getting Past the HR Recruiter to the Hiring Manager   13
   Reading the Hiring Manager's Mind   16
   The Hidden Challenges for IT Managers   19
   Summing It Up   21

Chapter 2 The Anatomy of a Technical Résumé   23
   The Sections of Your Résumé   24
   The Layout of Your Information   33
   Other Information You Think You Want to Include   36
   The Technicalities   37
   Summing It Up   41

Chapter 3 The Online Résumé World   43
   Finding IT Jobs Online   44
   Job Sites that Don't Waste Your Time   44
   Creating an ASCII Résumé   45
   Online Résumé Forms   46
   Scannable Résumés   47
   Optimizing Your Online Résumé   48
   Summing It Up   52

Chapter 4 Uncovering Your Hidden Talents   53
   Discovering Yourself   54
   Summing It All Up   72
   Tailoring Your Résumé   74
   Using the Right Words   88
   Summing It Up   92

Chapter 5 The Cover Letter   93

The Purpose of Your Cover Letter   94
The Content of Your Message   95
Fatal Mistakes of a Cover Letter   97
E-mailing Cover Letters   98
Types of Cover Letters and How to Write Them   98
Sample IT Cover Letters   102
Summing It Up   110

Chapter 6 Common Résumé Dilemmas   111

Recent College Graduates   112
Paper Certifications   121
Career Changer   123
Problem History   130
Summing It Up   134

Chapter 7 Creative Ways to Get Hands-On Experience   135

Getting Experience at Your Training Center   136
On the (Unpaid) Job Training   136
Blogging and RSS Feeds   137
Hands-On Experience at Home   137
Online Labs   139
Beyond Hands-On Experience   139
Summing It Up   141

Chapter 8 How to Network When You Don't Know Anyone   143

Tell Everyone You're Looking for a Job   144
The Networking Interview   145
IT Professional Groups   147
Online Networking   147
Summing It Up   147

Chapter 9 Résumé Faux Pas: Why You Are Not

Getting Any Phone Calls   149

The Résumé Faux Pas Checklist   150
How Did You Do?   156
Summing It Up   157

Chapter 10 The Interview   159

What Really Happens in the Interview Process?   160
Skills to Demonstrate   161
How to Prepare   162

Common Questions for Different Areas of IT   164
Questions to Ask the Interviewer   168
Other Situations   168
Following Up after the Interview   171
Summing It Up   172

Part II   Résumé Encyclopedia

Chapter 11 A Résumé Encyclopedia   175
Application Developer   176
Architect   181
Business Analyst   184
Consultant   188
CIO   188
Database Administrator (DBA)   193
Helpdesk/Desktop Support Specialist   193
IT Manager   196
Infrastructure Specialist/Network Engineer   201
Multimedia Specialist   210
Project Manager   211
Quality Assurance Specialist   216
Security Analyst   220
Technical Writer   223
Telecommunications Specialist   223

Index   231

Acknowledgments

I'd like to thank the publishing and editorial team at McGraw-Hill and International Typesetting and Composition; and my family and friends for the encouragement and support. Special thanks to my husband, Pete, for his patience in answering all my techie questions and most of all, for being a great listener and my biggest fan.

This book is for all the talented IT professionals out there who are so talented but need a little help to put their experience and knowledge on paper.

Introduction

Top 10 Reasons Why You Should Buy This Book

1. You still list MS-DOS as a technology on your résumé.

2. You've sent out 100 résumés and haven't received a single call back.

3. Your résumé is four pages long.

4. Your résumé still includes your high school GPA.

5. You have no experience but you are trying to get a $60K+ job.

6. You are a career changer and realize that getting an IT job is not as easy as all those advertisements say.

7. You have been at the same job for so long that you have no résumé.

8. Your résumé begins with the line "I want to get a job in IT . . ."

9. You have been to all the career sites on the Web and they haven't helped you improve your résumé at all.

10. You want to get your dream job and make the big bucks.

Who This book Is For

All kidding aside, the IT job market has evolved over the last five years. Getting a career in IT isn't as easy as it once was. The market is more competitive, the jobs more demanding, and hiring managers more picky about the people they want on their teams. This is true for entry level positions as well as those positions at the top.

This book is about helping you differentiate yourself. It includes the topics specifically relevant to IT professionals—things like paper certification, lack of hands-on experience, how to present technical skills and qualifications. It also provides relevant examples for today's jobs including web programming, security specialists, and helpdesk technicians. Each job is different, so the book includes résumé strategies targeted to specific IT jobs. These résumé strategies will help you in tailoring your résumé and making sure you include key information that hiring managers are looking for.

This book is for any IT professional who is looking at a career in IT as an opportunity to do meaningful work in a career that will be around for a long time—a way to provide for their families, and to afford a comfortable lifestyle.

To the thousands of job seekers out there—good luck and I hope that this book will play a small part in your success.

—Paula Moreira

Ace the IT Résumé

Part I

Creating a Winning IT Résumé

In This Part

CHAPTER 1 Standing Out from the Crowd

CHAPTER 2 The Anatomy of a Technical Résumé

CHAPTER 3 The Online Résumé World

CHAPTER 4 Uncovering Your Hidden Talents

CHAPTER 5 The Cover Letter

CHAPTER 6 Common Résumé Dilemmas

CHAPTER 7 Creative Ways to Get Hands-On Experience

CHAPTER 8 How to Network When You Don't Know Anyone

CHAPTER 9 Résumé Faux Pas: Why You Are Not Getting Any Phone Calls

CHAPTER 10 The Interview

Chapter 1

· ·

Standing Out from the Crowd

Want to dramatically increase your earning potential, improve your lifestyle, and multiply your over-all net worth—all without diet and exercise? Get a job in Information Technology (IT).

The fast-paced, constantly changing IT world is an exciting place. The continuous introduction of new technologies and processes means endless opportunities to focus on what you really like and the chance to make a great living doing it. But, to keep on top of the seemingly boundless prospects out there, you've got to keep on top of your most important tool: your résumé. It's your passport to all these adventures, within and outside your company. Whether the changes around you are the result of "going e" (e-business, e-learning, e-everything), a new chief information officer (CIO) being hired, downsizing, or just looking for a new challenge, a résumé that can make you stand out from the crowd is a critical part of achieving your career goals.

Résumé writing is not the fun part of looking for a new job. Unless you are a professional writer, you will probably dedicate more time to writing your résumé than any other writing project in your career. An IT résumé has to have the right blend of technical skills and business *acumen* (the buzzword for business sense these days) whether you're applying for a tech support position or for the role of CIO.

Your résumé is your letter of introduction to the job you seek—your ticket to high-tech success. Keep it current even when you're not actively looking for a job, and you'll make the entire process easier when the right opportunity comes along. When a high-paying job opens up at a company you've always dreamed of working for, you can get your résumé into the hiring manager's hands while your competitors are still sharpening their pencils. Your dream job is out there. But, hundreds of other professionals may think it's *their* dream job. This book is your secret weapon. It offers proven steps for writing a winning IT résumé, explanations even your mother can understand, and plenty of examples you can refer to for inspiration.

This chapter offers a high-level perspective on what it takes to get noticed. We go into much more detail later on. For now, these are skills to remember throughout the résumé writing and interviewing processes.

In this chapter, we cover:

▶ The basics of getting noticed

▶ Getting past the HR recruiter and to the hiring manager

▶ Reading the hiring manager's mind

▶ Marketing the ten hottest skills

FACT *IT employment currently accounts for approximately 7 percent of the U.S. total workforce (Information Technology Association of America [ITAA]).*

The Basics of Getting Noticed

At the core of getting noticed is a firm belief in yourself and your abilities. Yes, Mom always taught you not to brag, but unless she wants to keep doing your laundry and providing you with rent-free housing, she'll adjust to your new, confident manner.

IT fuels a competitive spirit in a way that just doesn't seem to be there with accountants. Who cares if hundreds of candidates are applying for a single position? You deserve it, because you can solve the company's problem in your sleep. They're darn lucky you happened upon their ad and had a spare copy of your résumé.

But here's the rub: where does this self-assuredness and competitiveness go when you start to put your accomplishments down on paper? All too often, it gets lost in translation. Telling your friends how terrific you are is one thing. But, setting words to paper makes them seem more *real*, and that can be terrifying.

Confidence plays the most important role in getting noticed. You *must* genuinely believe two things (read them aloud if you need to):

▶ The right opportunity with the right company and the right team is out there for me.

▶ I have skills employers need.

Your job is to keep believing in yourself while you work through this book. Once you acknowledge your accomplishments, we'll show you how to make employers notice them.

By the time we get through with your résumé, you won't believe the masterpiece you've created. That's right—you will create a high-impact, attention-grabbing résumé. This book can act as your coach in providing you with trade secrets on how to shine. Once you compile your new résumé, you may not believe it describes you. You may even think you are being dishonest about your capabilities. No one could possibly be this good, you may think to yourself. Before you press DELETE in panic, let your new image grow on you. Try it out for size by sending it out. See the response. And, as you start getting responses back and you go on interviews, your confidence will increase. Presenting a strong image on paper will get you in the door.

Let's take a look at how to make yourself stand out as the perfect candidate for the job of your dreams.

Controlling Your Image

Presenting a strong image of yourself through your résumé is important, regardless of the position you seek. Most IT professionals, especially recent graduates or career changers, are uncomfortable walking in and demanding high-paying, influential positions. They know they can troubleshoot PC hardware and write Visual Basic (VB) code, but they don't quite know how to express in words how these skills can benefit an organization, much less how to promote themselves above other job candidates with similar skills.

To get noticed, you need to convey a strong image. In interview situations, this means how you physically present yourself. On a résumé, it's the words you use, the examples you provide, and the impression you create in the recruiter's mind. To convey a strong image, you must begin with a positive attitude.

In many situations, modesty is appropriate and becoming. Regardless of how many years you have been in the IT industry, it's difficult to brag about experience and accomplishments. Face it, IT professionals are rarely salesmen or marketers, and with good reason. While marketers like to embellish and sell the features and benefits of a product (including themselves), most IT professionals stick to facts and analytical data (hence, the binary nature of computers and computer languages). Marketers are comfortable making larger-than-life claims about their products. Techies tell you everything that works and doesn't work about their products. This is not a good idea when the product is you and *you want that job*. So, follow this crash course in self-marketing.

The goal is to help you get your dream job, the one that best fits your talents, knowledge, and lifestyle. This book can show you how to turn your skills and accomplishments into highly desirable competencies that enable you to command top dollar. It provides detailed examples of exactly what you need to say and how to say it. Your job is to adapt these examples to your own set of skills, and then watch the magic of a powerful résumé go to work for you.

The Importance of Your Job Title

How can you possibly keep up with all the different IT job titles out there? Does anyone really know the difference between a network administrator and a network support specialist level I? How about a PC technician and a PC specialist? If you're confused, pity the employers wading through stacks of inaccurately titled résumés.

The reality is that titles are assigned by Human Resources (HR) professionals who may be a little out of touch with what happens in the IT department. Don't get hung up on what your HR records say. We can help you master the art of the job title. The job titles you use on your résumé are important because they are used in three different ways by recruiters and employers:

▶ Job titles project your image

▶ Job titles are scanned for fit with the available positions

▶ Job titles show promote-ability

Image Projection

Of these two job titles, which sounds stronger: programmer or software engineer? The *software engineer* title instills greater confidence by projecting more experience, knowledge, and quality of work. In reality, the titles are interchangeable and can be used to describe the same person with one to two years of software development experience in VB. In actuality, employers will pay more for the software engineer applicant than they would for the programmer. The same with *helpdesk technician* vs. *helpdesk analyst*. The lesson is many similar job titles are out there that project a stronger image. Whenever possible, use the recommended titles in Table 1-1, which can help you project a stronger image.

TABLE 1-1 Powerful IT Job Titles

These titles ...	Are synonymous with ...
Infrastructure engineer	Network engineer
	Network administrator
	Systems administrator
	LAN manager
	MCSE
	Systems engineer
Software engineer	Applications developer
	Programmer
	Developer
	Software developer
	Web developer
Information architect	Content specialist
	Webmaster
	Copy editor
	Copy writer
Data architect	Database administrator
	Data warehouse manager
	Database analyst
Documentation specialist	Technical writer
User interface designer	Web designer
	Graphic artist
Helpdesk analyst	Helpdesk technician
	Helpdesk specialist
	Helpdesk support
	Helpdesk level I/II

TABLE 1-1 Powerful IT Job Titles (*continued*)

These titles ...	Are synonymous with ...
Messaging Systems Engineer	E-mail administrator
PC maintenance technician	Desktop technician
	Helpdesk
Quality assurance specialist	QA tester
	Testing specialist
Technical trainer	Instructor
Telecommunications analyst	Phone technician
Security analyst	Security engineer
	Information Security specialist
	Information security architect
	Security administrator
Infrastructure architect	Network planner
	Network designer
	Network architect
Development manager	Team leader
	Supervisor
	IT manager
Storage architect	Storage engineer
	Storage administrator
	SAN engineer
	Storage Area Network engineer
	Systems storage engineer

Hit Rates

Employers receive hundreds of résumés for every available position. Somewhere in the pile is your résumé. Research shows that recruiters typically spend about five seconds glancing at each résumé. Talk about a short amount of time to make a first impression!

FACT *The most in-demand positions in IT these days are network and Web-related (ITAA). The hottest positions are for web developers, which according to CNC Global (Canada's leading provider of IT staffing and contact center staffing services), accounts for 25 percent of all open positions.*

A no-brainer, yet effective, way to make sure you get at least your five seconds of fame is to use the job title being recruited for as the title of your résumé. Remember, many job titles are interchangeable. So if you're a network engineer, don't hesitate to answer ads for system engineers, network administrators, systems administrators, LAN managers, or MCSE, and use the title the company uses. Simple and effective—and it gives the impression that you understand the company's way of thinking.

If you can't fit the job title into your work experience, find a way to work it into your career objective statement or your cover letter. It's crucial that the hiring manager see the exact phrase he's looking for if your résumé is going to make the cut.

TIP *We do not recommend listing certifications like CNE or MCSE as job titles. Most job ads include these as qualifications, rather than as job titles. There are fewer hits on these as job titles vs. more generic titles, such as network engineer.*

Unless you're applying for a position with a company-specific title, it is also important to select the most common job title for the type of work you do. For example, if you are a Microsoft certified systems engineer posting your résumé on the Web, think like an employer. On job boards, the title "network engineer" returns more job postings than "network manager," "network administrator," or "LAN administrator." In other words, employers use the title "network engineer" more often than all the others, so that's how you should title your résumé.

Not sure which title to use? Go to an IT-job search engine, such as Dice.com, to find out which titles have the most number of positions posted. We cover web job boards in more detail in Chapter 3.

TIP *A quick search on a job board reveals the most popular titles to use.*

Skill and Career Progression

Unless you're new to planet Earth, you know companies don't like risk. Companies consider new hires a big risk—a risk that hiring managers try to minimize. Are you going to require a lot of ramp-up time? Do you have experience in similar positions using similar skills? List your skills in easy-to-read bullet points, and title each job appropriately. At least one of your previous positions should have the same title as the position you want. That way, you match the hiring requirements at a glance.

All that "a rose by any other name" stuff is good if your experience is fairly close to what you want to be doing, but what if you're reaching? Focus on the part of your job that's closest to what you want to be doing. If your official title is Tech Level 1, you might be responsible for database administration, PC support, and web site duties. If you're hoping to move into DBA, list "database administrator" as the job title and, as the first bullet, describe your responsibilities in this function. Other bullets would describe additional responsibilities. For a final bullet, you might consider "Additional duties associated with Tech Level 1 position."

Does this mean you should lie about your job title? Not unless you like the feel of egg on your face. Changes in job titles should be made after a careful self-assessment. Certainly, you should be qualified for the position you're seeking. Otherwise, you are wasting everyone's time (including your own) and sullying your reputation. By all means, use the resources in this book to find a stronger title, but be sure you are qualified for the position. Your goal is this: *to increase the likely match between what the employer is looking for and the skills you possess.*

If what the employer is looking for was only a part of your overall responsibilities, it is acceptable to put down the stronger job title as the primary descriptor of your role, but you will also want to include your other job responsibilities as part of the job description. The key is to find a job title that is interchangeable with your actual job title. The title should represent at least 50 percent of your job duties and should match, or be a stepping stone, to the position you most seek. Demonstrate a growth in responsibilities, product knowledge, and skills.

If you are like most job seekers, the idea of replacing your actual job titles with more impressive job titles may scare you. Some job seekers fear they will be discovered when employers check their references. No need to worry.

Before you list anyone as a reference, give them a recent copy of your résumé and tell them you are currently exploring employment opportunities. Never offer a person as a reference who hasn't agreed beforehand.

Remember, HR recruiters contact previous employers for employment verification, not to gather details on previous job responsibilities. It is highly unlikely that either the HR manager performing the reference checks or the HR manager at your previous employer will have any detailed understanding of your job responsibilities.

FACT *The greatest demand increase for IT positions is for senior infrastructure architects and analysts, according to CNC Global. The hardest skills to find are senior-level web developers, project managers, business analysts, and QA specialists, especially those with industry-specific experience.*

Selling the Benefits of Your Skills

Most people experience writer's block when they first sit down to write their résumé. They get caught up in the mechanics of how the résumé should be laid out, what font to use, what type of paper to print it on, and so on. Chapter 2 covers the particulars of formatting a professional-looking résumé. But beauty is only skin deep—if your résumé lacks substance, it'll be out of fashion faster than a failed dot-com.

Chapter 4 helps you identify and articulate your hidden traits and skills. It teaches you how to present your skill set as benefits for employers by asking yourself, "Why would an employer care?"

Bad hires cost employers tens of thousands of dollars in time invested, recruitment costs, training cost and effort, and lost productivity. You need to demonstrate minimal risk. Grab employers' attention by focusing on the benefits your skill set can provide their company. And, remember, the biggest benefit for employers of IT professionals is reducing technical ramp-up time and quick assimilation into the corporate culture.

Most people have a hard time identifying their skills, let alone understanding how those skills benefit employers. Your résumé, cover letter, and thank you letter should all explain and market the benefit of your skills. Your job is to make the employer feel good about your present skills and future potential.

Some of the things employers are looking for (without even knowing it) when hiring IT professionals are:

Experience   Because it saves them time and money

Trainability   Because it provides flexibility and opportunity for advancement

TABLE 1-2   Selling the Benefits of Your Skills

Benefit to Employer	Example for Résumé
Same industry expertise means increased productivity	More than ten years back-office software development experience for medical services industry.
	Five years experience managing a centralized helpdesk supporting 20,000 weekly incoming calls.
Easiest to train	Certifications include MCSE, Cisco CCNA, and CISSP.
Problem solving	Decreased customer-hold time by 20 percent by evaluating, selecting, and implementing a call-tracking system.
	Saved $1 million in annual procurement costs by centralizing computer systems, and purchasing and implementing an online-ordering system.
Growth and promotion potential	Recognized by management for increasing profitability by 12 percent within a one-year period of being hired.
	Managed departmental operations and staff of 25 with an annual operating budget of $1 million.

Problem-solving abilities   Because such employees are extremely efficient

Same industry experience   Because it translates to faster time to productivity

Growth and promotional potential   Because it minimizes employer risk

Table 1-2 provides examples of how your skills and experience can translate into benefits for a new employer.

Marketing the Ten Hottest Skills

You might expect the ten hottest skills for an IT professional would include technical skills, certifications, programming languages, and/or proficiency in application programs. Think again. An IT development manager can command a higher salary than a CIO!

IT systems have gotten more complex as ever-greater numbers of users expect more from their applications, become more self-sufficient, and require more data analysis to make business decisions. On top of that, new technology emerges *every day*, requiring new product knowledge, as well as legacy integration knowledge. Development managers are expected to know how to manage projects to time and budget constraints, provide leadership and motivation, and have complete understanding of business issues and processes.

The top IT positions go to candidates with great customer service, stellar project management, and effective teamwork-skills, which are classic soft skills. They can mean the difference between you and the next technically qualified candidate applying for your next promotion or job. Why? Because today's IT world isn't just about being technically savvy. With the increased shortage of IT professionals, the best jobs go to seasoned professionals who have a great combination of technical knowledge, general business skills, and great communication skills.

Soft Skills Defined

Simply put, *soft skills* are the ability to communicate with people. They are the skills that make customers feel happy. They are the skills that keep customers, make individuals valuable. So, if you're wondering what the incentive is to brush up on this skill set—it's money, baby!

To a techie, anything outside of product and development skills could be considered soft skills, but here's an unofficial list of soft skills for techies and why they're important.

Project management Project management goes beyond learning Microsoft Project. Success as a project manager depends on your ability to define, plan, organize, control, and complete a variety of complex and interdependent tasks.

Communication Whether answering the phone, writing an e-mail, or putting together a proposal, how well you put your point across affects others' perceptions of your abilities. Make sure each interaction paints an intelligent picture.

Presentation Forget the horror of high school oral-communications classes. These skills are a must for any situation—from running a meeting to pitching a product or solution, or justifying why you should get that raise. It doesn't matter how many are in the audience; every time you open your mouth, you are using these skills. Make sure you're presenting the image you want by mastering this skill set.

Selling Face it, regardless of whether your title includes "sales," you're always selling. Whether it's yourself, your project, or your next position, you're always asking people to buy in on something. Learn how to do it more effectively.

Running meetings Learning how to facilitate meetings and manage group interactions is an important first step to becoming a team leader.

Leadership Successful projects have many keys, including organizational buy-in, good project management, and proper resourcing. A strong leader understands these dynamics, harnesses the diverse energies within an organization, and pulls everyone together.

Problem-solving This is the skill you are probably most familiar with. To some, problem-solving comes instinctively. To others, it's not so natural. The key is to find a process that works and apply it.

Customer service Yes, people are difficult. But, when they're customers, they come first and they're always right. They need to feel valued and important. Just remember: if you don't treat them right, someone else will.

Self-direction This is the ability to do your job without having to be told how to do your job. It's extremely important, because by the time your manager gets through telling you how to do it, she could have probably done it herself.

Teamwork No man is an island, certainly not in IT where there isn't room for egos. With so many different operating systems (OSs), servers, networks, databases, and other things that need to be coordinated, no one can do it alone. Here's where those skills you learned in kindergarten come in: sharing, saying "please," and—more importantly—saying "thank you." Play nicely with others or take a time-out.

Unfortunately, as any five-year-old can tell you, knowing how to share isn't the same as doing it. You can't learn soft skills unless you practice them. And this top-ten list is worth more than a few quick laughs—it can be your ticket to a highly successful IT career. Take a look at your current situation and see how you've managed to put these skills into practice. On your résumé, demonstrate how you use these soft skills—and you can earn cold, hard cash.

 TIP *Online courses offer a great way for IT professionals to be introduced to soft skills. Some of the leading web sites offering soft skills training include http://www.skillsoft.com. Here's a sample list of the great topics on the market:*

▶ How to excel at customer service

▶ Call center frontline skills

▶ Fast-tracking your career

▶ Problem-solving and decision-making in business

▶ Managing yourself through change

The best place to feature these skills is as a part of a skills and qualifications summary section at the top of your résumé. Check out Figure 1-1 as an example.

Jon Doe

34 Orchid Avenue

San Diego, CA 98455

(555) 555-5555

Qualifications

- Personable and articulate, skilled in handling customers with professionalism and courtesy.

- Highly perceptive, with proven ability to pinpoint problems, provide creative solutions, and follow through to resolution in a timely and cost effective manner.

- Exceptional communication and presentation skills, ability to interrelate with people at all levels.

FIGURE 1-1   Sample skills and qualifications summary

Getting Past the HR Recruiter to the Hiring Manager

Your résumé is your calling card for an appointment to interview with a hiring manager. But, like a king in his castle, the hiring manager is surrounded by gatekeepers: recruiters, HR managers, even the hiring manager himself, as he sorts through stacks of résumés sent by his subjects. Your objective is to make it to the top of the stack that gets invited to an interview.

The trick here is to make it so easy for them to pick you as a natural choice that not choosing you won't even be an option.

Reading between the Lines: Tailoring Your Résumé to the Job Ad

The job ad can tell you a lot about what the hiring manager is looking for from candidates. Depending on where the ad is posted, you can get the details you need to target your résumé. Ads posted on job boards usually provide more information than newspaper ads, and they allow you to do a better job of targeting your résumé.

When you read a job ad, look for the following information about the position:

▶ Job title

▶ Responsibilities

▶ Industry

▶ Years of experience required

▶ Software/hardware experience required

▶ Education required

Obviously, you need to review this information to determine whether you meet the company's criteria. If you do, the information they've given you should tell you exactly how you should target your résumé to the specific skills the company needs.

The process is simple. Through the power of using interchangeable words, you turn yourself into a highly desirable candidate. Here's a quick summary of the steps:

1. Print the original job listing.

2. Underline the job title. Rephrase your career objective, so it includes the job title as your desired position.

3. Underline the industry. If you have experience in this industry, make sure you call out experience in this industry (and, possibly, in other industries) in the description of your past positions.

4. Underline the particular job skills and responsibilities. Review your own résumé to see whether a direct match occurs. If the employer calls for particular tasks that you may have rolled up into more general descriptors, break these tasks out again in your résumé. Also, note when the employer is looking for additional experience that you may already possess, but have not specifically listed on your résumé. Add it to your résumé. The goal is to have as

many matches as possible with what is included in the job posting because job search engines are keyed off the original job description. The more exact matches, the better.

5. Look for any acronyms listed in the job description. Incorporate these acronyms in parentheses in your résumé.

6. Reread your résumé to ensure it has not lost some of its power as a result of the edits. Chapter 4 includes examples of how to perfect the art of tailoring your résumé.

Filling in the Gaps: What's Implied in the Job Ad

When you pick up a job posting out of a newspaper, it may not have all the information you need to properly target your résumé. You need to fill in some of the information based on common industry knowledge. Shorter job ads list job titles and assume certain skills and qualifications. They may simply list years of experience as a measure of competency. Make sure you meet these criteria. Tables 1-3 and 1-4 help you assess what skill levels are assumed for various IT positions. More detailed job descriptions are available in Part II of this book.

TIP *Before responding to a newspaper job ad, visit the company's web site. You can often find a more comprehensive ad for the same position there.*

TABLE 1-3: What's Expected Based on Years of Experience

Experience	Expectations of Skills
Under 1 year	Knows commonly used concepts, practices, and procedures in the field or with the technology.
	Relies on instruction manuals, outside resources, and preestablished guidelines to perform the job.
	Works under immediate supervision and, generally, requires little independent thinking.
1–2 years	Familiar with standard concepts, practices, and procedures to get the job done.
	Can work independently on assigned duties and can make decisions about what needs to happen.
	Able to multitask to accomplish multiple projects at the same time.
	Works under general supervision; typically reports to a project leader or manager.
2–4 years	Has worked on projects "outside the box."
	Has been the team leader on a variety of projects. Usually a point of escalation for junior team members.
	Considered relatively knowledgeable on best practices.
	Is comfortable with accountability of results.
4 years +	Plans, directs, and manages the daily operations of a computer operations department.
	Establishes department policies and procedures.
	Generally manages a team. Relies on experience and judgment to plan and accomplish goals.
	Typically reports to a senior manager.

TABLE 1-4   What's Expected, Based on Job Titles

Network Engineer	Desired Skill Level
Level I	A+ certification desirable.
	Proficient in PC troubleshooting and basic network troubleshooting.
	Handle daily operations of networks, including troubleshooting user access, software installation, printer setup, and system backup.
Level II	Network+ and Server+ certification desirable. MCSE or CNE certification a plus.
	Install servers and software applications.
	Analyze, design, develop, support, and troubleshoot networking issues.
	Work with users; manage basic file, print, and application services; perform backups; install and upgrade software of all kinds; and do what it takes to keep networks working.
Level III	Manage multiserver environments.
	Manage a variety of hardware platforms.
	Administer security, troubleshoot to the protocol level, and perform network capacity planning.
Database Administrator	**Desired Skill Level**
Level I	Has knowledge of commonly used concepts, practices, and procedures within database administration.
	Has worked with common commercial database products, including Oracle, Microsoft SQL Server, and Access.
	Relies on instructions and preestablished guidelines to perform the functions of the job.
Level II	Design and build relational databases.
	Develop strategies for data acquisitions, archive recovery, and implementation of a database.
	Clean and maintain the database.
	Has a working knowledge of designing, developing, and manipulating Oracle databases, data warehouses, and multidimensional databases.
Programmer	**Desired Skill Level**
Level I	Work on existing applications, enhancements, debugging, and documenting.
	Proficient in at least two common programming languages (VB, C++, and so on).
	Familiar with database structures and understands the fundamentals of programming, including conditional statements and loops.
	Has practical experience through real-world application development or college work.
	Has knowledge of commonly used concepts, practices, and procedures, but relies on instructions and preestablished guidelines to perform job functions.
Level II	Has 2–5 years of work experience.
	Has a strong understanding of programming fundamentals and object-oriented programming.
	Works with customers to create system specifications.
	Follows the development process from conception to deployment, including initial specifications, development, quality assurance, revisions, and deployment.
	May serve as project leader in small- to medium-sized projects.

Reading the Hiring Manager's Mind

While the job ad can tell you a lot about the hiring manager's immediate needs, it doesn't reveal his deep, dark secrets. Relax—there's nothing illegal or illicit about this. We're just going to take a closer look at the dynamics of an IT environment.

IT departments are, almost by their very nature within the company structure, always short staffed. IT managers are constantly in recruiting mode for technicians, helpdesk staff, programmers, and project managers. There's a never-ending stream of projects to deploy, an always-full inbox, too much work, and not enough people to do it. And, just when the poor guy has a handle on things—BAM! New technologies, new business directives, new management—heck—even a new flavor of coffee can throw a frazzled IT manager for a loop.

Change constantly influences an IT department's priorities. The dot-com crash is a direct example of how even a change in the economy can affect the priorities of an organization. For you, this change is good. Learn to view this as an opportunity to position yourself better, based on the known and hidden needs of an IT manager.

Challenges for Employers

Employers are always at risk every time they make a new hire. Will the person be truly competent or did they just interview well? Will they stick around long enough for the company to receive a return on investments (ROIs) in training, company benefits, and so on? You can alleviate some of these worries. Let's take a closer look at how.

Reducing the Time to Productivity

You know that downtime you have when you start at a new job? You don't know where the bathroom is, you don't have the password for your e-mail, you can't even remember your phone number, and, oh yeah, you have a job to do. Well, while you view ramp-up time as an inconvenience, your employer sees it in terms of dollars down the drain.

Every moment you take to learn your way around the company and its technology is money lost for the company. Clearly, IT managers favor candidates who bring with them industry experience, as well as advanced systems and software skills. This isn't rocket science—the more experience you demonstrate having, the higher your résumé will rate. Your résumé should include a list of all the networking technology, OSs, database systems, applications, processes, and procedures you can support.

If you do not have experience in a specific industry, you should include your transferable skills. *Transferable skills* are those skills that are important to employers, regardless of the industry. Many times, IT professionals think to include only their technical skills. But, just as important are the soft skills they have mastered through their careers. When presenting transferable skills, you should be specific with how you exhibited these skills, so the hiring manager can see how they would apply within their organization.

TRANSFERABLE SKILLS

Transferable skills help round out your experience. They hint at what you are capable of without being specific to an industry or job. These skills work well in a qualifications summary section, open possibilities for promotion, and position you as a better-balanced and experienced professional. Try these out for size when you are building your list of skills:

▶ Learns technical information quickly

▶ Proven history of improving operations and increasing profitability

▶ Success-driven team player who continually meets and exceeds goals

▶ Able to handle challenges, with proven history of increased productivity

▶ Detail-oriented with excellent analytical and project-tracking skills

▶ Able to coordinate many tasks simultaneously

▶ Strong communication skills

▶ Team player interested in achieving overall department goals

▶ Enjoys working as a team member, as well as independently

▶ Proven skills resolving problems and tense situations

▶ Willing to do whatever it takes to get the job done

▶ History of flexibility; able to handle constant change and interruption

▶ Eager to perform work to maximize customer satisfaction

▶ Able to lead others in high-demand situations

▶ Self-motivated, hardworking team player

▶ Able to motivate staff to meet project deadlines

▶ Deals effectively with culturally diverse customer base

▶ Excellent interpersonal, verbal, and written communication skills

▶ Able to prioritize and work proactively

▶ Quick learner

▶ Proven ability to work in a fast-paced, challenging environment

▶ Exceptional ability to quickly master new software/hardware and apply its full range of capabilities

▶ Infectious enthusiasm for computers; gifted and inspiring PC trainer

▶ Expert troubleshooter and problem solver

▶ Team player with the ability to effectively coordinate; devoted to excellent service and customer satisfaction

▶ 14+ years experience with numerous software and personal/business computers of various manufacturers

Training Means Growth and Promotional Opportunities

IT managers like to make safe choices—it keeps their own jobs intact. So, they look for clues that a candidate will be a good fit for the company. One of these clues is training history. It's evident that you're willing to invest in your own self-improvement. Also evident is that you're open to change and working with new technology. Remember, IT departments are change agents within corporations. If you're not flexible, you're in the wrong field.

Your résumé should include a list of all the certifications you have achieved. In addition, you should also include a list of well-respected seminars, workshops, and full-length courses you have taken. This is not to be confused with a full historical transcript of your educational history, though. The following examples demonstrate how to incorporate your educational history with certifications earned and seminars attended. A short listing is sufficient to demonstrate you take your career seriously and are open to additional training.

TIP *To stay current with the latest IT certifications, visit http://www.certmag.com or http://www.comptia.org.*

TIP *One caveat: If you're a recent grad with a lot of experience, you may want to leave dates off your résumé because most companies try to offer lower salaries to college hires.*

The more advanced training you include on your résumé, the higher the hiring manager's comfort level in selecting you as their ideal candidate. Continuous learning demonstrates to the employer that you believe in improving your skills and will continue to develop yourself to become a more knowledgeable and productive employee.

TIP *Be sure to keep your résumé updated as you recertify your skills and take additional professional development courses. Résumés should always be works in progress, even if you're not actively looking for a job.*

The following are samples of educational history sections.

Sample 1

Pamela has earned advanced degrees in computer science and is applying for a consultant position with a worldwide consulting firm.

Education and Professional Development

2005	M.S. Computer Science, Brigham Young University, Utah
1997	B.S. Computer Science, Lewis-State College, Idaho
	Project Management Institute (PMPI) Certification
	Microsoft Certified Engineer (MCSE) Certification

Professional Seminars:

2004	Developing the Leader in You, Dale Carnegie
2000	Franklin Covey Project Management

Sample 2

Jason has a two-year degree, is in the process of completing a networking certification, and has completed coursework online.

EDUCATION

A.S. Computer Science, Cypress College, Orange, CA 1999–2001
MCSE Certification (four out of six courses completed)
A+ Certification

Additional coursework in:
Customer Service (online course), Element K
Call Center Frontline Skills (online course), SkillSoft

Sample 3

Hank has an undergraduate degree in computer science, has earned several networking certifications and is working on a high level certification.

EDUCATION

B.S. Computer Science, Rutgers University, Newark, NJ   1999

Certifications:

CISSP	(in progress)
CCIE	2006
CCNP	2005
CCNA	2004
Network+	2003
A+	2003

The Hidden Challenges for IT Managers

IT managers have a tough job. On top of the normal hiring managers' dilemmas, IT managers face unique challenges because of the importance of their departments in today's organizations. Imagine having to remain customer-service driven, while constantly being told what a terrible job you're doing and you'll begin to understand the mindset of the IT manager.

To build an immediate rapport with a hiring manager, all you need to learn is how to read his mind. Relax, there's a trick here: empathy. Understand the challenges the manager faces. How does it work? Like this.

Remember that big project you spent every moment on for six months? Remember how it didn't get the results your company had hoped for? Think about why. From an outsider's perspective, what were the issues the organization had to contend with? What was being asked of the CIO and his IT manager? What were the expectations and deliverables, and how closely did the outcome come to meeting these?

If you had been the CIO or IT manager, how would you have managed the projects better? Of course, you have the luxury of 20/20 hindsight, but this exercise provides you with insight into the challenges of IT managers—and that can help you create a connection with the person who can give you your next job.

Top Management Challenges

The top five management challenges are quite simple. They may be challenges you've faced yourself, in which case you'll be able to address these with personal recounts of lessons learned. These challenges include:

▶ Understanding business requirements

▶ Managing development teams

▶ Project managing for timely deliverables

▶ Managing outsourced vendors

To truly stand out from the crowd, you need to master the fine art of translating your understanding of and experience with these issues into result-oriented entries on your résumé. Here are some examples of how to address the top five IT manager's challenges:

Project-managed the development of the company's customer web site, coordinating among the internal marketing department, information services, and an outsourced development company

Wrote detailed product specifications document based on results of company-wide joint application development sessions

More than five years in web design and consumer marketing experience

Consulted with Fortune 100 companies on network design, implementation, and management using Novell and other vendor products

Published best-practice methodologies for knowledge-sharing with customers and partners

Introduced a new revenue stream with sustained 30 percent revenue growth by implementing an e-commerce system

Managed outsourced development team, created new team, and brought development services in-house

Designed and implemented corporate network/intranet,satellite office connectivity, and integration of technologies across acquired companies

Implemented a client management process focusing on more profitable customers

Cross-functional IT experience in areas of web administration, IS systems analysis, technical support, and computer training

Developed standards for desktops, servers, notebooks, and PDA devices

Summing It Up

Hey, it's not natural for a techie to be a self-marketer, but that's what it takes to get noticed and get the job. Pull out all the stops. You have to be confident. You have to know how to read the job ads, adapt your skills to what employers are looking for, and truly be able to present yourself in a way that makes employers sit up and take notice. The tips and tricks included in this chapter can get you started on the path to getting the job you want.

And speaking of that job you want. Plenty of jobs are out there, but they're going to those who make finding them a full-time job. Now, more than ever, is the time of opportunity for techies. But, if you want to get ahead, you've got to take control of your career. Look for opportunities, and be prepared when they come. The best jobs go to the candidates who have the sharpest skills, know what they're worth, and have their résumés ready to go.

Chapter 2

• •

The Anatomy of a Technical Résumé

Your experience and education will not make your job hunt easier if you don't nail the essential elements of your résumé. Your résumé is the showcase for your skills and, if your showcase is not attractive, it will not get the attention it deserves. Fortunately, understanding how to best present your information is not that complicated.

First, evaluate what you bring to the table and remember this as you lay out your skills and past experience. Begin with the basics: evaluate how your résumé looks (this can be almost as important as what your résumé says). The formatting and layout may come easier for a graphic artist than to a systems engineer, but by analyzing the components of your résumé, you can identify the prime factors of your résumé's appearance.

In this chapter, we cover:

▶ The sections of your résumé

▶ Writing a powerful objective statement

▶ Saying you are a "people person"

▶ Using honest terminology

▶ Presenting your education and experience

▶ The differences between chronological and skill-based résumés

▶ Laying out your résumé

▶ Other information you *think* you want to include

▶ Choosing paper type, font size, and all the technicalities

▶ Presenting your references

The Sections of Your Résumé

The following are the standard sections of a résumé:

▶ Header

▶ Key Qualifications and Profile

▶ Education

▶ Experience

▶ Computer skills and certifications

We are going to attack these sections one at a time.

Header

This is the easiest part of your résumé. It is essential for you to have all this information correct and complete, or don't expect too many calls. Include the following information:

Line 1 Name (bold and a few points larger than the other lines)

Line 2 Street address

Line 3 City, state, and ZIP code (you can also combine your complete address on one line)

Line 4 Phone number and/or cell phone number

Line 5 E-mail address

You can center the header at the top of the page, or place it flush to the right or left column. Listing a phone number where you can be reached during daytime hours is ideal. By including a cell phone number, you may open opportunities that you would otherwise miss. If you are currently employed, you probably cannot talk openly at work. Prospective employers understand this and are usually considerate of this fact. Try to check your cell phone or voice mail messages regularly throughout the day and return phone calls during your lunch or break time.

TIP *Please make sure you have a professional e-mail address. If possible, use an e-mail that reflects your name. Now is not the time to flaunt personal attributes or nicknames like sexybeast78@yahoo.com or bigguy@gmail.com. For more tips on résumé faux pas, check out Chapter 9.*

Key Qualifications and Profile Statement

This is the new name for what many folks would consider the *objective statement*. It's the first section of your résumé right below your header. This section is *key*. This is one of the first things an employer reads, and it's your best opportunity to grab their attention and announce you are perfect for this job. Unfortunately, many people do not use this opportunity.

Somehow, the standard was set that the objective statement is used to explain the job you would like. What a waste of time and space! When you are applying for a job, you usually state the position in the cover letter. Why waste the prime location on your résumé to repeat it?

Not a believer? Look at the following two statements and decide which is more likely to catch a hiring manager's eye:

To obtain a challenging position as an infrastructure specialist that uses my experience and knowledge of networking systems.

Or,

Infrastructure Specialist with experience in design, implementation, and support for WAN/LANs, wireless networks, DNS, DHCP, and Active Directory. Additional experience includes disaster recovery, capacity planning, and business continuity. Excellent problem-solving skills and interpersonal skills.

I hope you agree that the second example is a more powerful statement to begin your résumé. Yet so many people still opt for the traditional objective statement. Isn't it obvious that every applicant would like to obtain a challenging position that uses their experience and knowledge? You may not want to list a specific job for other reasons. That position may have been filled or you may be qualified for several openings. You would be limiting yourself if you listed a specific job title. Instead, an employer can view your résumé, see your area of expertise through your alternative objective statement, and find you ideal for a job you did not even know about.

What if you are applying with a large company that has several positions to fill? Couldn't it be confusing if you didn't state the job you would like on your résumé? You are in a unique situation because you are applying for an IT job. Your field of study is usually specified and your skill set reflects that directly. Your résumé is technical and will be directed to the IT department more easily than in other fields of work.

Writing a Powerful Statement about Yourself

Think of this space on your résumé as a commercial about yourself. Television commercials are brief, direct, and to the point, with a specific purpose in mind. Your commercial needs to be the same way, emphasizing your strong points in a few concise sentences to sell your skills and experience to a potential employer. In your objective statement, you can effectively paint a picture of your personality and skills. The following are some guidelines for writing your profile statement:

▶ Use adjectives to describe qualities that are important to employers in the IT field, such as motivated, driven, results-oriented, and detail-oriented.

▶ Highlight skills you have that are listed in the job description or advertisement, using slightly different wording.

▶ Make sure to avoid clichés such as "I am a hard worker" or "I am a nice person."

▶ Be creative with your descriptions of yourself, but do not lie.

► Include at least one sentence that describes your personal characteristics.

► Keep the length to three to four short sentences.

► Do not use the word "I."

► Do not sell yourself short.

You can write this as a paragraph or a list, whichever best serves your purposes. Here are two examples that show both styles:

Example 1: The Paragraph Profile Statement

Energetic, self-motivated Microsoft certified professional, skilled in Windows XP/Vista, Windows Server, and Macintosh environments with SUSE Linux experience. Possesses knowledge of LAN and WAN technologies, infrastructure capacity planning, and disaster recovery. A quick learner skilled in delivering to service-level agreements, effective interpersonal communication, and efficient problem resolution.

Example 2: The List Key Qualification Statement

KEY QUALIFICATIONS

► Results-oriented professional with 17 years experience in IT, customer service, and finance

► Ability to create a shared vision and translate vision into a workable business strategy and governance model

► Excellent communication skills, interfacing well with management, coworkers, and clients

► Comfortable working in a fast-paced environment, building and leading cross-departmental integration teams, and working with cutting-edge technologies

The list format in Example 2 is especially beneficial when quantifying your experience. By leading the statements with a number of years, your background is exemplified at a glance. For those who don't have a lot of experience, leave the number of years' experience out.

How to Say "I Am a People Person"

Even though you are searching for a technical position, your technical skills may not be your biggest asset. Hiring managers want someone who can work well with the team to achieve objectives. A position where you would be working solely on your own at all times is extremely rare.

For example, in infrastructure and helpdesk positions, you are in the business of customer service, whether it is for internal or external users. With programming and database design, you need to work closely with team members to plan and implement projects. As a project manager, you may interact with other IS members or even other departments, such as client groups.

Employers might not only be looking for the necessary technical skills, but also the personality and the people skills to fulfill this role. So, what are some of the terms you can use that signify these characteristics?

Approachable	Personable
Conflict management skills	Positive motivator
Customer service driven	Professional
Effective communicator	Receptive
Interpersonal	Sales and marketing skills
Leadership	Strong soft skills
Outgoing	Team player, team leader, team worker

Honest Terminology

The Politically Correct movement increased the likelihood of *spin doctoring* a job title or job responsibilities. While it is OK to rephrase some of the details of your experience, remember to keep it honest or else it might come back to bite you later—either in the interview or on the job.

Compare this to explaining your knowledge of a foreign language. You can be *fluent*, meaning you can speak, read, write, and comprehend the language in its entirety. You can be *conversational*, which means you can carry on a basic conversation, but are not necessarily able to read or write the language. Or, you can be *familiar with* the language and capable of recognizing phrases or words. Now, translate this analogy into the IT world. Let's use Microsoft Office as an example. To what degree do you know the applications?

Basic understanding or familiar with   You can use the basic functions.

Well-versed or proficient in   You know and can use every major function.

Expert in or master of   You know every feature and function of the program inside and out, possibly possessing the ability to train others on the application.

When you describe your knowledge or abilities, make sure you portray them accurately.

Technical Skills

After your profile section, no other section matters as much on your résumé as your skills section. This is what most recruiters and hiring managers skip before they start reading about your experience. Luckily, it's not a hard section to create, but the formatting may be a bit tricky because it's a laundry list of your technology experience.

You can list your technical skills in two primary formats: paragraph or columns. You may want to use the paragraph-style format for categorizing your skills. Column-style is easier on the eye and a good way make it easier to scan for technology. Look at the examples shown in Figure 2-1 and Figure 2-2.

Of course, the challenge is when you don't have a lot of experience, so you don't have much to list. In this case, you may not have much of a choice, except to use the paragraph style, so you don't attract any more attention to this.

Regardless of your preferred method for displaying your technical skills, avoid two important faux pas:

▶ Outdated technology: If it's not the latest or the next-to-latest technology, don't list it.

▶ Proper spellings: Because it's usually an alphabet soup of company names and acronyms, skipping over this section is easy when you're spell checking your résumé, but make sure you double- and triple-check it manually. Nothing is worse than claiming you're an expert in J23E.

TECHNICAL PROFILE

Languages:	Java, C++, HTML, SQL, PL/SQL
Technologies:	J2EE, Servlets, JSP, JDBC, EJB, Hibernate, RMI, JavaBeans, Spring, JSF, MQ Series
Script Languages:	JavaScript
Java IDE'S:	RAD (Rational Application Developer), WebSphere Studio Application Developer (WSAD), NetBean, MyEclipse and BEA Workshop
Methodologies:	OOAD, UML, Rational Rose 98/2000, Rational RequisitePro, RUP
Application Server:	IBM Websphere, Weblogic Server, Tomcat
Other Tools:	Rational ClearCase, ClearQuest, Microsoft Visio, Visual Source Safe, Borland StarTeam, StarTrack
Software Testing:	Test Plan/Test Cases/Test Suite, Unit Test, Component Test, Regression Test, Junit
Framework:	Struts Framework, Spring Framework and MVC Framework
Database:	Oracle, DB2, MYSQL
Operating System:	AIX-UNIX, Windows NT

FIGURE 2-1 Paragraph-style technical skills listing

TECHNICAL SKILLS

Business Analysis

- Rational Unified Process (RUP)
- Unified Modeling Language (UML)
- Software Development Life Cycle (SDLC)
- Object Oriented Analysis and Design Concepts (OOAD)
- Business Process Re-engineering (BPR)
- Test Lifecycle
- Multi-tier Web Applications
- Data Warehousing
- Business Intelligence (BI)
- Data Modeling (ORDBMS)
- Service Oriented Architecture (SOA)
- Prototyping
- Agile and eXtreme programming methodologies

Business Documentation

- Documented Business Requirement
- Use Case Specification
- Funotional and Nonfunctional Specification
- System Requirement Specification
- UML diagrams (Use Case, Class and Sequence)
- Traceability Matrix
- Project Estimate
- Change-Version Control
- Training and User Manuals
- Master Test Plan Review (Integration, System and Acceptance)

FIGURE 2-2   Columns-style technical skills listing

Education

If you attended a prestigious college, list the name of the college first, as shown here:

Harvard University, B.S. in Computer Science, 1999—3.7 GPA

If you did not, list the degree first, as shown here:

B.S. in Computer Information Systems, University of Kentucky, 2000—Cum Laude

If your GPA was not 3.5 or above, then leaving it off is best. If you graduated several years ago, you can also drop the mention of your GPA.

If your education history falls into another scenario, you can present it on your résumé, as follows:

If you attended college, but did not receive a degree Present this by categorizing your studies that are applicable to the job, but do not include courses unrelated to the field. For example, the following:

Web Programming and Design, Essex Community College, 2002–2004
is more impressive than:

Essex Community College, 2002–2004

- ▶ Java Programming
- ▶ Web Fundamentals
- ▶ Adobe Photoshop
- ▶ Communications
- ▶ Political Science
- ▶ Biology

College with no degree, many years ago When it has been more than ten years since graduation, listing the number of years, rather than the specific years, is better—for example, "three years" instead of "1965–1967."

Attended several colleges Only list the most recent college you attended or the institution you graduated from. An exception may be if you attended a prestigious university and want to include this in addition.

Master's degree List this prior to undergraduate education.

High school education This should only appear if you did not attend college, do not have certifications, and recently graduated from high school. With these exceptions, most individuals seeking an IT position do not place their high school education on their résumé. If you do, use the same format as when presenting college education.

Studies in progress These are appropriate to list in your résumé, along with your education. List the information the same as you would with completed college education or certifications along with the anticipated finishing date. This is common practice, as many people start to look for jobs prior to finishing school or taking a certification exam.

Certifications

Here is one place where abbreviations are appropriate, and even preferred, but make sure you are using the correct ones. (If you have the certification, let's hope you know the proper abbreviation.) Sometimes these abbreviations are crucial.

If an HR manager is evaluating the résumés, they may have been instructed only to pass along a candidate who is PMI-certified. If those letters are not on your résumé, it may not go anywhere. You hope everyone in that position would know that a "Project Management Institute" is PMI-certified, but you never know who is dealing with your résumé. This is especially true if the company is not a technology company, but another type of industry looking for a project manager.

Using the proper terminology for your certifications is also imperative when companies use online résumé posting, internally or through Monster.com. Electronic searching will look for specific phrases or terms, such as A+ or Java.

If you do not have many certifications and would like to write out the certification titles to take up space, it is a good idea to include the abbreviation in parentheses.

Experience

When displaying your work experience, what do you include? How long should your work history go back? As a rule of thumb, only include experience relevant to the job you are applying for. Don't go back more than ten years unless a position from that time is directly relevant to the desired job.

You also don't have to list recent jobs that are irrelevant to the one you are applying for. If you were in a management role for ten years, and then took a part-time receptionist job to be home more with your children, don't feel you need to include it on your résumé. You can explain that in the interview.

REMINDER *For tips on how to explain gaps in employment or career changes, see Chapter 6 on common résumé dilemmas.*

One important factor to remember when writing your resume is consistency. If you are putting the names of companies in boldface, make sure you boldface every one. If you are abbreviating states, do it in every instance. You want to keep your writing style to the point, but do not over-abbreviate. Use standard abbreviations where appropriate, such as with states and dates, but don't assume that everyone knows HSI stands for Hightech Solutions International.

Chronological Order Is Not Mandatory

One résumé myth is that experience needs to be listed in chronological order, beginning with the most recent. This is not true. If you are in the industry, have a stable work history, and are searching for a similar job, this layout is ideal for you. But, if you are changing careers or changing industries, you don't need to adhere to that hierarchy.

Evaluate your experience and make judgment calls about your unique situations. If you performed similar job responsibilities in a past position and believe it will cast you as a more qualified candidate, list that job first. Simply deemphasize the dates in your job listings. This would be in the format of a skill-based résumé (see sidebar).

If you are a recent grad or a career changer, you may have several jobs that are inappropriate to the position you are applying for. If you were in a position of management, it is acceptable to keep that job on your résumé if you don't have other experience. This is because it demonstrates some of the other qualities a company may be looking for. If the non-IT-related job was not a management position, leaving it off is usually best. Focus on your skills more than your experience.

SKILL-BASED IT RÉSUMÉ

A skill-based résumé may benefit anyone in the following situations:

► Lack of experience in the industry

► Many technical skills acquired in a short amount of time

► Skills are more impressive than job titles or past positions

► Older job experience needs to be highlighted

► Gaps in employment history

This format is appropriate for many job seekers in this relatively young IT industry. In this type of résumé, you focus on your computer skill set and, possibly, your certifications, more so than your experience. Several examples of skill-based résumés are in Part II. In the section "Candidate with Certifications Only," we also discuss formatting the layout, depending on your experience.

Job Titles and Locations

If your job titles are more powerful than the companies you worked for, present your title first. Then, remember to keep it consistent and format the rest of your experience the same way.

TIP *Don't make your résumé more difficult to read by switching the format from one listing to another.*

This is an excellent place to make judicious use of bold, italics, and regular fonts, as shown here:

Systems Engineer, *Competitive Enterprises,* January 2002–Present

Or, reverse the layout if you want to highlight your job title:

IBM, *Systems Engineer,* January 2002–Present

If you held several positions within the same company, list the company as a heading and the various positions below it, with bulleted points about each one. If you held many positions, don't list them all. This could appear as if you were unable to do any of the positions successfully and needed to be replaced. Instead, choose the most significant positions and only include them.

Listing the location of your past employment is optional, but it does not add anything to your employment history. This takes up space and makes your eye search more for the relevant information. If you moved around a lot, listing locations may hurt you. You do not want to give the employer the idea that you are a flight risk and will only be with their company until you are ready to move on. As part of an interview, you may need to fill out an application where you list your complete history and you would disclose that information then.

Dates and Gaps in Employment

When should you include dates? With employment and education history, include dates if they are profiling you appropriately for the job you are applying for. If you fear an employer may think you are too old or too young, omit dates all together or de-emphasize them.

Consistency is important here, too. If you are spelling out the month, followed by the year, use the same format throughout. Don't use March 2004, and then later use 4/06. And, there is no need to be exact, such as pinpointing the day you left your last job.

If you have large gaps in your employment history, using the year only is probably preferable. A comparison of the two styles is shown here.

Month-to-Month	Year-to-Year
8/2003–Present	2003–Present
2/1999–1/2003	1999–2003
2/1995–5/1999	1995–1999

Seeing those gaps is easier when you use the month-to-month format, but the year-to-year format makes this issue less obvious. Don't feel this is misleading, as it is commonly used in writing résumés. Again, those details will be disclosed in the interview or if you are required to fill out an application. Your goal now is to get the interview, and then make the employer realize those gaps are not a deciding factor.

Volunteer and Internship Experience

If you have volunteer or internship experience *that is relevant* to the job you are applying for, list this in the same format you would use for work experience. Give yourself a title and support it with your list of accomplishments. Don't downplay this experience just because you did not get paid. Instead, use it as a stepping stone to obtain a better position.

Salary History

Do not include your salary history on your résumé. Sometimes an advertisement or job posting may request or require this. If so, you can put it in the cover letter, but never on the résumé itself. Even then, you will best serve yourself by stating your salary is negotiable.

The Layout of Your Information

A common dilemma—what information do I display first on my résumé? My experience, education, or certifications? It depends on your level of experience and varies case-by-case, but here are a few guidelines for recent graduates, candidates with certifications only, and experienced computer professionals.

Recent Graduate

After your objective statement, list your education, followed by your computer skills. If you have a computer degree, list courses related to the job.

Be sure to leave off skills that can be assumed. If you are a computer programmer, you likely know how to use Internet Explorer (IE), and a hiring manager is not going to want to see that. When do you this, it looks like you are trying to make your list of skills longer and, in the process, you look less credible.

With your list of courses, keep them relevant to the job. You may think because you took Controversial International Conflicts, this makes you a more well-rounded candidate, but the hiring manager will not.

The layout for recent graduates should be as follows:

▶ Education

▶ Computer skills

▶ Related courses

The following is an example of a layout for recent graduates:

EDUCATION
B.S. in Computer Information Systems
Hawaii University, Honolulu, HI, 2006

TECHNICAL SKILLS
Business Systems Analysis: UML 2.0, Rational Rose, ARIS
Programming: C#, .NET, J2EE, XML
Other: Windows XP, MS Access, MS SQL Server

RELATED COURSES
Object-Oriented Analysis and Design. Introduction to SQL, Business Systems Analysis, Defining Business System Requirements, Use Case Writing, Business Process Modeling, Introduction to Unified Modeling Language 2.0

Candidate with Certifications Only

If you do not have a computer degree and you do not have work experience, your certifications and your computer skills are definitely your strong points. If you have several certifications, list those first, followed by your technical skills and a section about your experience with computers. If you only have one or two certifications, lead with your skill set.

The following is the layout for several certifications and little experience:

▶ Certifications

▶ Technical skills

▶ Experience with computers

Here is an example:

CERTIFICATIONS
MCSE, A+, Network+

TECHNICAL SKILLS
Operating Systems: Windows 95/98/NT/2K/XP Pro and Home versions, Windows Server NT/2000/2003, workstations, Macintosh OS to OS X v.10.3.5, SQL Server installation
Databases: Microsoft SQL 7, Microsoft Access, FileMaker Pro, Crystal Reports
Networking: WAN/LAN protocols, administration and configuration, TCP/IP, FTP, DNS, SMTP configurations, VPN, NT/AD domain registration
E-mail: Outlook
Peripherals: Pocket PCs, printers (networked and local)
Hardware: Dell and HP servers, desktops and notebooks

EXPERIENCE
List experience

For one or two certifications and little experience, use this layout:

▶ Technical skills

▶ Certifications

▶ Experience with computers

Here is another example:

TECHNICAL SKILLS
Operating Systems: Windows 95/98/NT/2K/XP Pro and Home versions, Windows Server NT/2000/2003
Databases: Microsoft Access, FileMaker Pro, Crystal Reports
Networking: WAN/LAN, TCP/IP, FTP, and DNS
E-mail: Outlook
Applications: Microsoft Office 2003

CERTIFICATION
CompTIA A+ Certification

EXPERIENCE
List experience

Experienced IT Professional

You have many options for the layout and presentation of your information. Often, the most difficult part is summarizing the most relevant information to the job. Most important, you need to use the objective statement to summarize your qualifications for that specific job. Then, list the information emphasized in the description followed by your education, certifications, and, possibly, your skill set, if space permits. You can find several examples in Chapter 11.

Other Information You Think You Want to Include

You probably are thinking of including a lot of information in your résumé that we haven't discussed yet. Before you do, take the following recommendations into consideration:

Don't overdo it   You want to leave some surprises for the interview. Think of your résumé as the preview to a movie. You are showing the main plot, but you don't want to give away the entire storyline.

How does this relate to the job?   Before you add any additional information, ask yourself how this relates to the job you are trying to get. Does an IT manager care that you are CPR-certified? Probably not. But, if you are fluent in Japanese and applying to an international company, this is a definite asset. You not only need to look at the job, but also at the company.

Skills from the past   Be especially careful when you consider adding items that are too far in your past. If you took a weekend workshop on Photoshop 5 years ago and haven't touched it since, you probably don't want to list this program under your computer skills. If you get hired, your boss may ask you to use that skill at a later date. You won't look quite as impressive as when you wrote it on your résumé.

Extracurricular Activities and Achievements

Depending on where you are in your career, you may or may not want to include your extracurricular activities and achievements. If you are a recent grad, including leadership roles and honors received may be a good idea, as you don't have much experience to put on your résumé.

So, when should you take these items off? As your work experience becomes greater, this section becomes smaller and you will probably drop all references to being the chess club president. And, even as a new grad, keep this section to a minimum.

Some appropriate extra topics to include in your résumé are:

▶ Foreign languages

▶ Memberships in technical associations

▶ Recent leadership positions

▶ IT-related volunteer work, such as providing networking support for a charity organization

▶ Publications, if you have worked on any books, articles, or journals

▶ Recent awards and recognition for work related to the desired job

Now, you should think twice about including some things in this section because they may ignite hiring managers' prejudices. These include religious organizations, political volunteering, and animal-rights groups. Nothing is wrong with any of these, except in some people's perceptions.

The Technicalities

Today, we seem to have double the work when it comes to laying out your résumé. Not only do you have to worry about your online résumé, but you still need to make sure your paper résumé reads well. We talk more about your online résumé in Chapter 3.

The résumé layout essentials are as follows.

Paper

Keep it simple. With the proliferation of online résumés, you won't have to produce too many paper résumés, but bringing a few copies with you when you go on interviews is always good. Use white, off-white, or a light cream-colored paper. Do not try to impress with flashy paper or crazy combinations of colored font because this does not get you the positive attention you are shooting for. Plus, your résumé is likely to be faxed or photo copied, and colored paper does not reproduce well. A slightly thicker paper, such as 24-pound bond or résumé paper, will withstand the shuffling from desk-to-desk, but don't use anything heavier.

Number of Pages

If you are just beginning your career, try to keep your résumé to one page. Do not extend it to that second page to include your part-time waitress job or to list your ten college extracurricular activities. If you are trying to keep your résumé to one page, you are more likely to focus on precise skills and assets, keeping out the unnecessary details.

A two-page résumé may be appropriate for someone with more experience and expertise. If you go to two pages, make sure you mention your strongest points on the first page (or at least highlight them). If you don't, employers may not be motivated to turn the page. Going beyond two pages almost ensures your résumé won't get read.

Font

Times New Roman or Arial are two of the most-used fonts, and your résumé is not the time or place for creativity. Variation in fonts makes your résumé more difficult to read and doesn't impress anyone in the technical field.

Use either a 10-point or a 12-point font. Anything smaller is difficult to read and anything larger appears that you do not have enough experience to fill the page.

Avoid excess use of italics, as they are difficult to read. You may want to use them in a title or to distinguish one field from another.

Keep all text black. Black on white is most common for a reason: it has punch. Why else would every newspaper in America be written on white paper with black ink? Even changing to gray can lose some impact.

White Space, Margins, and Alignment

One of the most overlooked components of résumé layout is the use of white space. In the process of overloading a résumé, many people do not leave enough space between lines or sections, congesting their résumé more than the L.A. freeway. Make yourself look professional and organized, simply by allowing for more white space. Your résumé is easier to read and the main points stand out more.

Using smaller margins is OK, such as a three-quarters of an inch all around. This saves space and it looks fine, as long as you leave ample white space between sections.

Also make sure you use proper alignment. Do not center all the information on your résumé: left-align the main content. If you indent a section, be sure to indent the entire section to exactly the same place, and then use that indent as the standard for the rest of your résumé.

Let's look at the difference attention to such details can make. The résumé shown in Figure 2-3 is a good use of white space.

Nicole Ruhn

8142 Green Orchard Rd. Apt. 507
Grand Rapids, MI 37281
W (541) 547-3883, H (541) 746-6738
Nicole.Ruhn@hotmail.edu

Network Engineer with experience in design, implementation, and support for Ethernet and AppleTalk local and wide area networks. Additional experience includes purchasing, planning, and cost control. Background includes administration of Unix, PC, and Macintosh operating systems and software. Interpersonal skills with excellent problem solving skills.

TECHNICAL SKILLS

Operating Systems
Windows NT Server 4.0, Windows NT Workstation 4.0, Windows 95/98, DOS, Novell 3.12/4.11, SCO Unix 5.0.5, Novell 4.11.

Applications
SQL Server 7.0, Goldmine 4.0, MS Office 97/00, Unidata, Richter, Support Magic 3.31, Lotus Notes 4.6, Norton Antivirus.

Technical Knowledge
DHCP, WINS, routers, switches, PBX, POP3, TCP/IP, NetBIOS, NetBEUI, SNMP, and other networking protocols, HTML 4.

EXPERIENCE

Director of MIS, HealthNetwork.com   March 99 to June 00

- Engineered and supported a copper 10/100 switched Ethernet network, which included a Cisco 1720 router, T1, and managed switches.
- Integrated a Macintosh AppleTalk/TCP/IP network for a design department of 7 Macs and a Mac Server with OS 9.

FIGURE 2-3 This is a good use of white space

Now look at the same information presented without consistent indentation or additional line spacing, as shown in Figure 2-4.

Without making a good use of white space, your résumé becomes more difficult to read and the information gets lost.

To increase readability, use bullets wherever appropriate, especially when highlighting your experience. These bulleted statements stand out much more than a paragraph that includes all your accomplishments in prose format.

Presenting Your References

References should never be included in or attached to your résumé. Another great résumé myth is that the bottom of your résumé should contain the phrase "References available upon request." There is no reason for this—it does nothing for you except take up space. All employers assume you can provide them with references when it's appropriate. In addition, you cannot be sure who will get a copy of your résumé, and you don't want just anyone calling your references.

Prepare a list of references as a separate document (see Figure 2-5). Bring this with you to every interview. You can't predict when an employer will ask for them, and you don't want to be caught looking unprepared. If they don't make the request, offer your references when you are fairly advanced in the interview process.

Nicole Ruhn
8142 Green Orchard Rd. Apt. 507, Grand Rapids, MI 37281, W (541) 547-3883, H (541) 746-6738
Nicole.Ruhn@hotmail.edu
Network Engineer with experience in design, implementation, and support for Ethernet and AppleTalk local and wide area networks. Additional experience includes purchasing, planning, and cost control. Background includes administration of Unix, PC, and Macintosh operating systems and software. Interpersonal skills with excellent problem solving skills.
Technical Skills

Windows NT Server 4.0, Windows NT Workstation 4.0, Windows 95/98, DOS, Novell 3.12/4.11, SCO Unix 5.0.5, Novell 4.11, SQL Server 7.0, Goldmine 4.0, MS Office 97/00, Unidata, Richter, Support Magic 3.31, Lotus Notes 4.6, Norton Antivirus, DHCP, WINS, Routers, Switches, PBX, POP3, TCP/IP, NetBIOS, NetBEUI, SNMP, and other networking protocols, HTML 4.
Experience

HealthNetwork.com, Director of MIS   March 99 to June 00
- Engineered and supported a copper 10/100 switched Ethernet network, which included a Cisco 1720 router, T1, and managed switches.
- Integrated a Macintosh AppleTalk/TCP/IP network for a design department of 7 Macs and a Mac Server with OS 9.

FIGURE 2-4 This is a bad use of white space

TARA MASTERSON
101 Cross Road Drive
Atlanta, GA 93241
(634) 522-9134

_____ PROFESSIONAL REFERENCES _____

Ephrem Rufael, Director of MIS
Smart IT Solutions
Baltimore, MD
(410) 634-8121
ephrem.rufael@smartITsolutions.com

Bobbi Conley, IT Manager
Creative Publishing
Washington, DC
(202) 584-9910
bobbi.conley@creativepublishing.com

Dr. Chad Spence, Professor of Computer Science
American University
Denver, CO
(624) 512-5932
chad.spence@american.edu

_____ PERSONAL REFERENCES _____

Jessica Waxman
11 Bear Creek Parkway
Freehold, NJ 21201
(212) 443-7171
jwaaxman@excite.com

Andrea Sendroff
1877 Towson Drive
Newport Beach, CA 10332
(213) 884-5692
andrea.sendroff@newyork.edu

Jana Seifarth
1742 20th Street SE
Dundalk, MD 21034
(443) 574-9912
jseifarth23@hotmail.com

FIGURE 2-5 Sample references document

Include three professional and three personal references. First, list your professional references, and then your personal references. Mark them accordingly. Put them in order of your strongest reference first, as the employer may only contact the first person on your list.

Before you add someone to your list of references, make sure you get their permission. Also, make certain they will give you a favorable reference. Aside from your skills, a prospective employer may ask them about your work habits, punctuality, temperament, reliability, and weaknesses. If you feel comfortable with your reference, ask them what they would say when they are asked those questions. If their answer is unfavorable, remove them from your list.

When you are starting your job hunt, notify all your references. Ideally, letting them know just before they may be contacted is best, so they are prepared to give you a good recommendation.

As important as what you include in your résumé is what you should *not* include. Here are the highlights:

▶ Elaborate fonts, pictures, or outlandish paper stock

▶ Too much or not enough information; give enough, but not irrelevant, information

▶ Misspellings, typographical errors, or poor grammar

▶ Outdated information

▶ Unrelated experience or accomplishments

▶ References

▶ Names of past supervisors

▶ Past compensation

▶ Personal information, such as health, sex, marital status, weight, height, Social Security number, citizenship, date of birth, or race

▶ Unprofessional e-mail addresses or personal web sites

▶ Salary history

▶ Reasons for leaving past employment

By keeping these technical details of the anatomy of your résumé in mind, you can create one that is more likely to get noticed and get you results.

Summing It Up

Having a well laid out resume is critical. It's not just about your experience and education but how you lay it out on paper (or electronically). You need to ensure that hiring managers and recruiters will invest the time. Stick with the recommendations in this chapter to ensure you don't miss important details and catch their eye every time.

Chapter 3
The Online Résumé World

Recruiting and hiring new employees can cost a company hundreds of thousands of dollars and a ridiculous number of man-hours, especially when they become engulfed in paper résumés. To save money and time, most large companies use electronic methods to review candidates. These include: (1) accepting e-mail résumés, (2) having applicants complete online résumé forms, and (3) scanning résumés.

When you create your résumé, you need to consider how to submit it, as this will affect the layout and design you use.

In this chapter, we cover:

► Finding IT jobs online

► Job sites that don't waste your time

► Keywords and buzzwords

► Optimizing your online résumé

► Online résumé forms

► Creating your PDF résumé

► Scannable résumés

► The biggest mistake of electronic résumés

► Example of an electronic résumé

Finding IT Jobs Online

In this day and age, most companies use the Internet exclusively for their recruiting needs, so it's critical that you know where to look.

Job Sites that Don't Waste Your Time

When you start your job search online, you will find many sites are out there. You could waste hours, or even days, searching through the thousands of listings and hundreds of pages. How can you best use your time when looking online?

Using the top job sites can make your job hunt less of a monster (pardon the pun.) Luckily, the Internet bust has left us with a few reliable web sites you can count on. Here are some of the sites that won't waste your time:

Career Builder (http://www.careerbuilder.com/)

ComputerJobs (http://www.computerjobs.com/)

Computerwork (http://www.computerwork.com/)

Craig's List (http://www.craigslist.org)

Dice (http://www.dice.com/)

Hot Jobs (http://hotjobs.yahoo.com/)

IT Jobs (http://www.itjobs.net/)

Monster (http://www.monster.com/)

NOTE *If you don't live in the United States, be sure to check out whether these online job boards have a national version. For example, Monster has a version specifically for our Canadian residents (http://www.monster.ca).*

NOTE *You should also look for local job boards for specific regions. For example, Job Circle (http://www.jobcircle.com) is a good resource for IT professionals in the Northeastern U.S.*

Don't limit yourself to just one site. Post your résumé to as many sites as you can to increase the likelihood of getting it viewed. Although this takes extra time, be patient when searching for jobs online. Sorting through the many job listings and posting on multiple sites is time-consuming, but you need to cover all the bases to make sure you are doing an effective job. A cyclical popularity for different job boards has impacted companies' strategy for where they post jobs.

Creating an ASCII Résumé

Although the most popular job boards let you upload your résumé in Word or Adobe Acrobat format, plenty of employer web sites don't. So, after spending how many hours creating the most beautiful résumé on the planet, in the online world, that may not matter! Gone is the fancy formatting. Gone are line breaks, columns, and different fonts. Now what?

Regardless of whether you're submitting your résumé to a job board or on an employer's web site, having a well-formatted, ASCII text résumé is always best. This means cleaning up special characters, adding line spacing, and creating white space, so people can read it.

Before you go any further, you need to create your text.

The following is an exercise to create an online-friendly résumé in ASCII format:

1. In your word processor document, set your margins so you have 6.5 inches of text displayed.

2. Open your existing résumé or create a new one.

3. Select all the text, and then select a font that is fixed-width 12 point, such as Courier 12. This gives you 65 characters per line.

4. Save your résumé as a text-only file with line breaks. If you were instructed to use hard carriage returns at the end of paragraphs, instead of at the end of lines, save as text-only without the line breaks.

5. Open this new file in Notepad or any other text editor you have on your system.

6. If your traditional résumé is longer than one page and contains your contact information or page numbers on every page, remove that information. On the computer screen, your résumé will read as one continuous page.

7. Review the appearance of your résumé in the text editor. This is exactly how most recipients will see it.

8. Replace all characters not supported by your text editor. For example, bullets may appear as question marks in Notepad. You can replace the bullets by using asterisks or dashes. You can create a horizontal line for effect by using a series of hyphens or other characters.

9. If long lines of text are in your editor, use Notepad's Word Wrap feature under the Edit menu. This feature inserts hard returns, letting you format the résumé to meet your specified margins.

10. Copy-and-paste the text of the résumé into the body of an e-mail when you are satisfied with the way it looks.

11. Create a short cover letter using the same steps previously described. Insert the cover letter above the résumé within the e-mail message.

12. Make sure you preview your online résumé whenever you submit it to ensure that formatting is what you expected.

Online Résumé Forms

Many of the popular job-seeker sites let you post your résumé using an online form, which can then be searched by employers or e-mailed out to job postings that interest you. Some individual companies also have an online form on their web site that you can use to submit your information.

Sometimes, the form is a simple, open field where you cut-and-paste your entire résumé. In electronic online forms, the data is automatically converted to ASCII and entered into a searchable database.

When completing an online résumé form, you can make this process easier by using your online résumé to extract what is appropriate. The power of your résumé is in the words you use. An employer can search on different criteria, so you want to make sure you cover all the bases.

Forget trying to keep your résumé to one page! The new challenge is getting in all those keywords (in a way that still makes sense) and not running out of character space. Most online forms have a maximum character limit of 3000. That's about three pages of a printed résumé. Also, caution about adding special characters line "-" and "_" for effect. These take up more characters than simply adding paragraph returns. So, if you run out of characters, try deleting the formatting using these characters and simply add paragraph returns.

Résumés as Attachments

The standard for e-mailing résumés is either a Microsoft Word format or an Adobe Acrobat PDF version. When sending out your résumé in Word format, make sure you stay with the standard Arial or Time New Roman fonts. This helps to ensure the end result prints according to how you originally designed it. If you've used different nonstandard fonts, then create a PDF version of your résumé. These days, you can create a PDF version without having to purchase Adobe Acrobat Professional by using the online version of Acrobat.

Do More than Just Post Your Résumé

After you post your résumé, the phone calls will start pouring in, right? Don't bet on it. With the millions of résumés posted online, you can't count on a leap of faith. You need to do more than just post your résumé.

Automate your job search using search agents to notify you of new job postings and help you search for those positions that meet the criteria you denote. You can receive e-mail as new jobs that meet your criteria are posted. The job sites are getting even more competitive. It's fun to see how they're offering some Amazon-like features to differentiate themselves. These cool new features include:

▶ *People who applied for this job also applied to . . . feature for finding similar jobs*

▶ *See recommended job . . . feature for displaying your search agent results*

Keywords and Buzzwords

In today's Google age, keywords are king! When it comes to online résumés, your goal is to include as many keywords as possible to increase the odds that your résumé ends up at the top of the search-results screen.

When employers search their online databases, they enter keywords to narrow the search of qualified candidates. *Keywords* are used as search terms to narrow the field of candidates for a position. Imagine receiving 100 résumés a day for IT positions! By the end of the month, that's about 3,000 résumés. Employers can't possibly scan each individual résumé, so they search through their database for applicants that match exactly what they're looking for—like the specific technology the company uses. This means, the more detail you put into your online résumé, the more hits you'll receive.

For online résumés, maximize the use of industry jargon and abbreviations. You can logically assume recruiters will instruct the search-engine dictionary to look for all the buzzwords in your field. You may want to both write out terms and abbreviate because you do not know what search will be done—for example: MCSE (Microsoft Certified System Engineer). The clearer you can be with your qualifications, the more often your résumé will be hit in searches.

One way to identify keywords is to underline all skills listed in the job description, and then incorporate those words into your résumé.

Scannable Résumés

Prior to the widespread availability of HR-recruiting software, such as *BrassRing*, larger companies scanned your résumé on receiving it. This does not mean they read it super-fast! Scanning a résumé transforms a paper résumé to electronic data that can be read, searched, and tracked by a computer system.

What Is Résumé Scanning?

Your résumé is placed on the scanner and an optical character reading (OCR) program reads the résumé. All your information is converting into text files, stored in a database, and then graded by your qualifications.

When an employer is ready to hire someone, they can specify the type of experience, skills, or education needed for a particular position, and then sort all the résumés in their database. Any résumés that match are selected and printed.

If the employer uses this technology, a computer reads your résumé before a human does. When applying for a job with a mid-size to large company, a good idea is to ask them if they would like both a scannable and a traditional résumé. It is not as common for a small company to make the investment in a résumé-scanning system, but try to check with HR before you send your résumé.

Tips for Creating a Scannable Résumé

The main difference between a traditional résumé and a scannable résumé is the latter is much simpler. To make your résumé scannable, use standard fonts, dark type, and plenty of facts for the computer to extract.

The following are some tips on how you can enhance your résumé's scannability:

▶ Use white or light-colored paper, 8.5" by 11", printed on one side only.

▶ Provide a laser-printed original, not a photocopy.

▶ Use a large font size (10 to 14 points) and a standard font style, such as Times New Roman.

▶ Left-align all information in your résumé.

▶ Avoid italics, underlining, vertical and horizontal lines, graphics, and boxes.

▶ Use boldface and/or capital letters for section headings as long as the letters don't touch each other.

▶ Avoid compressing space between letters, as it becomes unreadable when scanned.

▶ Avoid two-column formats that look like a newspaper because many scanners read left to right across an entire page.

▶ Put key information in the top third of the résumé. That corresponds to one screen on a computer.

▶ Do not fold or staple the paper.

▶ When faxing, set the fax machine to "fine mode" or "detailed mode," so the recipient receives a better quality copy.

Optimizing Your Online Résumé

When posting your résumé, remember, the formatting issues related to electronic résumés. These guidelines help make your résumé stand out from those who simply cut-and-paste their paper résumé and press SUBMIT.. But, how else can you make your résumé pop to the top of search results?

1. **Spell check it** There's no excuse for typos in today's wired world. It's sloppy and inexcusable when job boards have spell checkers right on the site. But don't be too trustful of spell checkers when it comes to technical abbreviations. Make sure you go back and triple-check all those certification abbreviations.

2. **Maximize your keywords** If you're in IT, you know how search engines work. Research the jobs you're looking for, pick out the keywords that describe that job, and make sure you build them into your résumé. Spell out acronyms for double points. For IT folks, your skills or technology section provides plenty of opportunities to quadruple your key-word score.

3. **Optimize your job title Do:** Write out your complete job title. Ensure that it's descriptive of the position rather than a generic technical position title. Include any acronyms for the title in parentheses. Make sure that it's current. Make sure it's spelled correctly. **Don't:** Abbreviate it. It's all about increasing those search hits and some software only allow searching on job titles.

4. **Renew your résumé often** If you want to keep showing up at the top of search results, make sure your résumé isn't more than 30 days old. Employers see new résumés first. This means updating every few weeks. Keep refining how you present yourself. Post multiple versions of your résumé targeted to different jobs.

5. **Check out your hits** Most job sites tell you how many times your résumé has come up in job searches and how many times it's been read. If the numbers aren't increasing, then something's wrong. If you're not getting enough hits, add more keywords. Elaborate on your job responsibilities, so there is an opportunity to add those keywords. If your résumé is getting hits, but it's not getting read, think about tailoring your résumé title. Is it too generic? Is it not grabbing the right amount of attention?

At the risk of sounding cliché, it is the little things that make the difference, such as alignment and spacing, the use of special characters and capitalization, and the inclusion of keywords. The information is basically the same in these two examples, but by modifying the format and layout, your qualifications and skills are more easily noticed.

Transforming your traditional résumé into one that is going to be a showstopper online is just that easy, as you can see in Figure 3-1 and Figure 3-2.

Nicole Ruhn
8142 Green Orchard Road, Apt. 507
Grand Rapids, MI 3281
W (541) 547-3883
H (541) 746-6738
Nicole.Ruhn@hotmail.com

Infrastructure Engineer with eight years experience
in design, implementation, and support for local and
wide area networks, including administration of PC,
Mac, and Linux operating systems. Ability to work
closely with teams across the business and to work
on project teams involved with implementations,
upgrades, migrations, and deployments. Knowledgeable
on change management and configuration management
procedures. Excellent interpersonal and problem-
solving skills. Attention to detail, well-organized,
and thrive under deadlines.

TECHNICAL SKILLS

Operating Systems - Windows 95 / 98 / NT / 2000 / XP /
Vista workstations, Windows NT / 2000 / 2003 servers,
Macintosh OS to OS X, SUSE Linux 9.x / 10.x

Applications - SQL 7 / 2000 / 2005, Citrix, MS
Office 2000 / XP / 2003 / 2007, Internet Explorer,
Oracle 8i / 9i / 10i, VMWare Server, Crystal Reports
X / XI, Remedy, HP OpenView, Netbackup

Networking - Administration and configuration of
WAN/LAN protocols, TCP/IP, FTP, DNS/ SMTP, VPN,
NT/AD domain registration, VLAN, Access Lists, PIX
firewalls, routers, switches, terminal services

CERTIFICATIONS

Cisco CCNA, 2005 / MCSA, 2003 / Network +, 2002

EDUCATION

B.S. in Computer Science - University of Hawaii,
Honolulu, HI, 2002

EXPERIENCE

Infrastructure Engineer - HealthNet Corp. March 04 to
June 07

^Provide incident management for desktop/workgroup-
 related problems in a 500-user environment.
 Troubleshoot, research, diagnose, document, and
 resolve technical issues for Windows 2000 / XP and
 MS Office applications.

^Escalation point and mentor to junior technicians.

FIGURE 3-1   Example 1. Comparison of bad and good formatting with online résumés

Nicole Ruhn
8142 Green Orchard Road, Apt. 507
Grand Rapids, MI 32812
W (541) 547-3883
H (541) 746-6738
Nicole.Ruhn@hotmail.com

INFRASTRUCTURE ENGINEER - KEY QUALIFICATIONS

* Eight years experience in design, implementation, and support for local and wide area networks, including administration of PC, Mac, and Linux operating systems.

* Ability to work closely with teams across the business and to work on project teams involved with implementations, upgrades, migrations, and deployments.

* Knowledgeable on change management and configuration management procedures.

* Excellent interpersonal and problem-solving skills. Attention to detail, well-organized and thrive under deadlines.

TECHNICAL SKILLS
Operating Systems
   Windows 95 / 98 / NT / 2000 / XP / Vista workstations, Windows NT / 2000 / 2003 servers, Macintosh OS to OS X, SUSE Linux 9.*x* / 10.*x*

Applications
   SQL 7 / 2000 / 2005, Citrix, MS Office 2000 / XP / 2003 / 2007, Internet Explorer, Oracle 8*i* / 9*i* / 10*i*, VMWare Server, Crystal Reports X / XI, Remedy, HP OpenView, Netbackup

Networking
   Administration and configuration of WAN/LAN protocols, TCP/IP, FTP, DNS/ SMTP, VPN, NT/AD domain registration, VLAN, Access Lists, PIX firewalls, routers, switches, terminal services

CERTIFICATIONS

* Cisco CCNA, 2005

* MCSA, 2003

* Network +, 2002

FIGURE 3-2   Example 2. Comparison of bad and good formatting with online résumés

```
EDUCATION
B.S. in Computer Science
University of Hawaii, Honolulu, HI, 2002
EXPERIENCE
Infrastructure Engineer
HealthNet Corp.                    March 04 to June 07
* Provide incident management for desktop/workgroup-
  related problems in a 500-user environment.
  Troubleshoot, research, diagnose, document, and
  resolve technical issues for Windows 2000 / XP and
  MS Office applications.
* Escalation point and mentor to junior technicians.
```

FIGURE 3-2 *Continued*

Summing It Up

Today, its all about your online resume. Just because you don't have to print it out on fancy paper doesn't mean that its appearance isn't important. Online resumes make it even harder to stand out so pay attention to the details we discussed in this chapter to ensure that your resume gets seen.

Chapter 4

Uncovering Your Hidden Talents

Evaluating your own skills honestly is tough. If you yammer on and on about the things you're great at, it sounds too much like bragging. If you harp on what you're not good at—well, really, who wants to do that? But, an honest evaluation of your skills is a crucial step in résumé writing. Skip this step and you could be stuck in the same dead-end job forever, or never even land that first job in your field.

Once you accept the inevitability of a self-evaluation, the process can seem overwhelming. Not to worry—this chapter breaks it down into several manageable steps for you.

In this chapter, we cover:

▶ Identifying your technical skills and accomplishments

▶ Plugging information you've gathered about yourself into your résumé in three sections: summary, technical skills, and work experience

▶ Tailoring your résumé to *any* job posting—including the one for the job of your dreams

Discovering Yourself

Self-discovery can be grueling work. In many IT jobs, daily deadlines mean you barely have time to breathe, let alone time to reflect on the job you've done and what a terrific person you are. But, you *have* to make time to reflect on your accomplishments if you want to better your situation. Think of it as an incredibly cheap alternative to therapy.

To identify your skills and abilities, we follow a three-step formula:

1. Identify technical skills and operational abilities.

   Our goal is to end up with a concise list of operating systems (OSs), applications, hardware systems, and other technical capabilities. (Managers will list operational experience, rather than technical skills.) Why a list? It's an effective, eye-catching way to present a lot of information clearly. Skim through this book and you'll see what we mean!

2. Create a complete work/experience history.

   Here, we gather the information that will make up the bulk of your résumé. We identify your job responsibilities and accomplishments. This is the section that can make Mom proud, even if she still doesn't have a clue what you do.

3. Work the magic.

   This is the crucial step that sets you apart from every other candidate. We show you how to turn run-of-the-mill IT skills into highly sought-after performance-impacting skills. The result? You stand out as the leading candidate for any position.

Set aside about two hours for this task. It doesn't have to be all at once—break it up into four 30-minute sessions if that's easier. But, do put in the necessary time if you want to have a résumé that stands out from the crowd.

Step 1: Identify Your Technical Skills

Your résumé should start with an overview of your technical skills. A bulleted list is an effective way to present this information. It lets recruiters and hiring managers quickly scan your skills, and then match them with the position they need to fill. If a hiring manager has a stack of résumés, he won't waste time trying to dig out hidden information. Make it easy for them to choose you.

Use Worksheet 4-1 as a jumping-off point for listing your skills. You may have skills not covered here; if so, add them. Be sure to note software versions where applicable, as well as your level of expertise and when you last used the product, according to the key that follows this list.

WORKSHEET 4-1 Technical Skills Inventory

Skill	Version	Self Rating	Years Experience	Last Used
Hardware				
____ PC				
____ MAC				
____ Sun				
____ IBM mainframe/mini				
____ HP				
Operating Systems				
____ Microsoft Windows				
____ NetWare				
____ DOS				
____ UNIX				
____ Linux				
____ Solaris				
____ MAC OS				
____ VMS				
____ VM				
PDA				
____ PalmOS				
____ RIM Blackberry				
____ Windows Mobile				
Networking				
____ Directory Services				
____ LAN Protocols (TCP/IP, IPX/SPX, DNS, DHCP, NFS)				
____ WAN Technologies				
____ Web protocols (SSL)				
____ Messaging protocols (SMTP)				
____ BridgingRouting				
____ Network Management				
____ Ethernet				
____ Fiber Distributed Data Interface (FDDI)				
____ Frame Relay				

WORKSHEET 4-1 Technical Skills Inventory (*continued*)

Skill	Version	Self Rating	Years Experience	Last Used
Networking (*continued*)				
___ High-Speed Serial Interface (HSSI)				
___ Integrated Services Digital Network (ISDN)				
___ Point to Point Protocol (PPP)				
___ Switched Multimegabit Data Service (SMDS)				
___ Dial-Up Technologies				
___ Synchronous Data Link Control (SDLC)				
___ Virtual Private Networks (VPNs)				
___ Voice/Data Integration Technologies				
___ Wireless				
___ Digital Subscriber Line (DSL)				
___ Cabling				
___ Transparent Bridging				
___ Mixed Media Bridging				
___ Source-Route Bridging (SRB)				
___ LAN Switching				
___ Asynchronous Transfer Mode (ATM) Switching				
___ MPLS				
___ Data-Link Switching (DLSw)				
___ Open Systems Interconnection (OSI) Protocols				
___ Internet Protocols (IP)				
___ IPv6				
___ Xerox Network Systems				
___ NetWare Protocols				
___ Apple Talk				
___ IBM Systems Network Architecture (SNA) Protocols				

WORKSHEET 4-1 Technical Skills Inventory *(continued)*

Skill	Version	Self Rating	Years Experience	Last Used
Networking *(continued)*				
____ Enhanced Interior Gateway Routing Protocol (EIGRP)				
____ IBM System Network Architecture (SNA) Routing				
____ Interior Gateway Routing Protocol (IGRP)				
____ Internet Protocol (IP) Multicast				
____ NetWare Link-Services Protocol (NLSP)				
____ Open Systems Interconnection (OSI) Routing Protocol				
____ Open Shortest Path First (OSPF)				
____ Routing Information Protocol (RIP)				
____ Resource-Reservation Protocol (RSVP)				
____ Quality of Service (QoS)				
____ Simple Multicast Routing Protocol (SMRP)				
____ Security Technologies				
____ Directory-Enabled Networking				
____ Networking Caching Technologies				
____ IBM Network Management				
____ Remote Monitoring (RMON)				
____ Simple Network Management Protocol (SNMP)				
____ Border Gateway Protocol (BGP)				
____ Multiservice Access Technologies				
____ Tag Switching				
____ Microsoft Exchange				
____ Lotus Notes				
____ Lotus Domino				
____ Novell GroupWise				
____ Legato				

WORKSHEET 4-1 Technical Skills Inventory (*continued*)

Skill	Version	Self Rating	Years Experience	Last Used
Networking (*continued*)				
____ EMC				
____ SMS				
____ Active Directory				
____ Cisco IOS				
____ Citrix MetaFrame				
Development				
____ HTML				
____ DHTML				
____ ColdFusion				
____ ASP				
____ ASP.NET				
____ Java				
____ J2EE				
____ JavaScript				
____ VBScript				
____ XML				
____ C++				
____ C#				
____ J#				
____ Visual C++				
____ Visual Basic				
____ VB.NET				
____ XML				
____ XAML				
____ Servlets				
____ Applets				
____ Active X				
____ XAML				
____ MFC				
____ COM				
____ ADO				

WORKSHEET 4-1 Technical Skills Inventory (*continued*)

Skill	Version	Self Rating	Years Experience	Last Used
Development (*continued*)				
____ADO.Net				
____ATL				
____CORBA				
____VBScript				
____WebLogic				
____Visual Studio				
____.NET				
____NEON				
____BEA Tuxedo				
____MQSeries				
____COBOL				
____Perl				
____PHP				
____UNIX Shell Scripts				
____MS Access				
____Business Objects				
____SMS				
____UML				
____Glipper				
____WPF				
____Windows Workflow				
Web Designer/New Media				
____HTML				
____Dreamweaver				
____Adobe Photoshop				
____JavaScript				
____SMIL				
____RealText				
____RealPix				
____Flash				
____FrontPage				

WORKSHEET 4-1 Technical Skills Inventory (*continued*)

Skill	Version	Self Rating	Years Experience	Last Used
Web Designer/New Media (*continued*)				
____ Adobe Illustrator				
____ Macromedia Fireworks				
____ Macromedia Flash				
____ Macromedia Director				
Database Development				
____ Oracle				
____ SQL				
____ SQL Server				
____ Sybase				
____ MS Access				
____ MySQL				
____ FileMaker				
____ PL/SQL				
____ CA-Easytrieve Plus				
____ DB2				
____ Visual FoxPro				
____ PowerBuilder				
____ JDBC				
____ Crystal Reports				
____ OLAP				
____ Informix				
____ ADO				
____ OLE DB				
Telecom				
____ Octel				
____ PBX				
____ ISDN				
____ VoIP				
____ VoFR				
____ CTI				
____ IVR				

WORKSHEET 4-1 Technical Skills Inventory *(continued)*

Skill	Version	Self Rating	Years Experience	Last Used
Telecom (*continued*)				
___ WAN				
___ Voice				
___ Video				
___ Definity				
___ Cable				
___ DSL				
___ IVR				
___ Mosaix				
___ Telephony systems				
Applications				
Windows desktop				
___ Microsoft Office				
___ Microsoft Access				
___ Microsoft FrontPage				
___ Internet Explorer (IE)				
___ Lotus Notes				
___ Microsoft Outlook				
___ GroupWise				
___ Microsoft Project				
Hardware				
___ Installation				
___ Troubleshooting				
___ Repair				
___ Maintenance				
___ PC support				
___ Remote administration				
Operating Systems				
___ Installation				
___ Troubleshooting				
___ End-user training				
___ Beta test				
___ Rollout product				

WORKSHEET 4-1 Technical Skills Inventory *(continued)*

Skill	Version	Self Rating	Years Experience	Last Used
Operating Systems (*continued*)				
___ Customer support				
___ Field service maintenance				
Network Operating Systems				
___ Administration				
___ Installation				
___ Supporting				
___ Planning				
___ Security administration				
___ Configuration management				
___ User management				
___ Administer print services				
___ Security planning				
___ Protocol analysis				
___ Systems backup				
___ Security management				
___ System troubleshooting				
___ Client configuration				
Development				
___ User requirements gathering				
___ Process modeling				
___ Product specifications				
___ Application development				
___ Interface design				
___ Product development				
___ Program debugging				
___ Quality assurance				
___ Program testing/analysis				
___ Developing algorithms				
___ Data storage techniques				
___ Logic structures				
___ Structure programming methodology				

WORKSHEET 4-1 Technical Skills Inventory (continued)

Skill	Version	Self Rating	Years Experience	Last Used
Development (continued)				
____ Object-oriented programming (OOP)				
____ CPU memory addressing				
____ Client/server programming				
____ Event-driven programming				
____ Advanced access programming				
____Design Patterns				
____ OLE automation				
____ ODBC integration				
____ Integration				
____ Dynamic data exchange				
____ System analysis				
____ JAD				
Database Administration				
____ Transact–SQL				
____ Server administration				
____ Database programming				
____ Performance and optimization techniques				
____ Transactions and record locking				
____ Database design				
____ Relational database design				
____ Database permissions				
____ Database migration				
____ Data analysis				
____ Report creation				
Web Development				
____ Web page development				
____ E-commerce				
____ Searching				
____ Web site management				
____ User interface development				

WORKSHEET 4-1 Technical Skills Inventory *(continued)*

Skill	Version	Self Rating	Years Experience	Last Used
Web Development (*continued*)				
____ Graphic design				
____ Information architecture				
____ HTML development				
____ Scripting				
____ AJAX				
____ Database integration				
Applications				
____ Antivirus security management				
____ User support				
____ Installation				
____ Configuration				
____ Optimization				
____ Training				
Helpdesk				
____ Internal customer support				
____ Escalation support				
Technical Writing				
____ Documentation				
____ Technical manual development				
____ User training				
____ Help support				
Infrastructure Engineering				
____ Resource planning				
____ Infrastructure design and planning				
____ Capacity planning				
____ Disaster recover				
____ Business continuity				
____ IT planning				
____ Architecture				

WORKSHEET 4-1 Technical Skills Inventory (*continued*)

Skill	Version	Self Rating	Years Experience	Last Used
Infrastructure Engineering (*continued*)				
____ Standards planning/compliance				
____ Integration				
Systems Analysis				
____ JAD				
____ Project management				
____ Team leader				
____ Develop system specifications				
____ Systems analysis life cycle				
____ Development methodologies (SCRUM, Agile, waterfall, and so forth)				
Quality Assurance				
____ Product testing				
____ Scalability testing				
____ UI testing				
____ Quality control				
____ User assessment				
Management				
____ Departmental coordination				
____ Team leader				
____ Project management				
____ Contractor managing				
____ Project leader				
____ Quality control				
____ Resource allocation				
____ Scheduling				
____ Service-level agreements				
____ Site supervision				
____ Product specifications				
____ Strategic planning				
____ Systems design				

WORKSHEET 4-1 Technical Skills Inventory (*continued*)

Skill	Version	Self Rating	Years Experience	Last Used
Management (*continued*)				
____ Technical presentations				
____ Technical staff supervision				
____ Vendor management				
____ Budgeting				
____ Staff supervision				
____ Interfacing with upper management				
____ Asset management				

Self-rating Key

0   Heard of the product (doesn't really count)

1   Know what the product does (covered it in a college course or read about it in a magazine) and have seen a demonstration of the product (do not list this as a skill)

2–3   Use the product occasionally (basic functions; not a primary job responsibility), or have not used the product in the last year

4–5   Continue to use the product/skill on a daily basis

6–7   Can provide frontline support for the product

8   Have trained others on how to use the product

9   Am the person people turn to for help when they can't figure it out

Last Used Key

<6 months

6–12 months

1–2 years

2+ years

As you go through the list, take a moment to jot down major projects you have completed using a particular software package, hardware setup, or operating system (OS). Get everything down on paper at once, while it's all fresh in your mind. Otherwise, you risk forgetting something important.

Don't worry about presentation as you fill out the table—we'll pretty it up later. For now, all that matters is creating a written record of your skills.

Look at the following examples to see how the checklist translates to a robust, easy-to-read experience section.

Software Engineer

TECHNICAL EXPERIENCE:
REPORTING TOOLS
    Crystal Reports, SQL Reporting Services
DATABASES
    Sybase, Oracle , SQL Server
GUI TOOLS
    PowerBuilder, X-PATH, ObjectSmith, Data Junction
LANGUAGES
    C, SQR, SQL, SQL*Plus, PL/SQL, PowerShell
HARDWARE
    PC, Sun, MAC
OPERATING SYSTEMS
    Windows Server 2003/NT, UNIX, Sun Solaris, MAC OS, Windows XP/95

QA Tester

TECHNICAL SKILLS:
Testing Tools: WinRunner, TestDirector, LoadRunner, QAPartner/Silk Test, SQA Suite, PVCS Tracker (bug reporting and analysis)
Software: SQL, PL/SQL, C, C++, VB , Java, JavaScript, VBScript, HTML, 4Testscript, TSL (Test Script Language)
Databases: Oracle, MS Access, FoxPro, MS SQL Server
ERP: SAP
Applications: MS Office, MS Word, MS Excel, MS PowerPoint
Internet: Java, JavaScript, VBScript, ASP, JSP, HTML, JDK, JDBC, Internet Explorer
Operating Systems: Windows 95/98/XP, Windows NT/2003, HP/Sun Solaris-UNIX

SPECIAL CONSIDERATIONS FOR IT MANAGERS

When you make the move to management, the rules change a bit. Your technical skills take a backseat to your experience with managing policies, procedures, forecasting, budgeting, space planning, vendor relationships, team building, documentation, infrastructure design, and resource planning. Employers do still want to know about the technical environments you've worked in previously, but not in the amount of detail you're used to giving.

When you apply for a management position, your Technical Skills section evolves into a Qualifications section. We show you how to showcase your expertise in the section "Summary of Qualifications," and provide you with examples you can see and put to work for you in Part II of this book.

Step 2: What Have You Accomplished?

Once you define your areas of expertise, it's time to get specific. As before, we break things down into manageable bits of information and rebuild it in a results-oriented, benefits-loaded format.

Start by simply listing your previous employment experience. Use the form provided in Worksheet 4–2. List employers (and relevant information), the positions you've held, and the dates of employment. Next, using the skills checklist from the previous section, note specific skills used in each position. Also jot down special responsibilities and other projects that really gave you a chance to shine.

WORKSHEET 4-2 Employment History

Job Title: _____

Employer:_____

Employment dates: _____

Skills: _____

_____

_____

_____

_____

_____

TIP Take your time on this section. Look for documentation to help jog your memory—were you given written performance evaluations? Read them over and excerpt any information you can.

Uncovering Your Special Talents and Skills

Do you want to really shine? Use the following questions to uncover your own special talents and skills. You'll be surprised by just how much you have to contribute to your next organization.

▶ Your boss always counts on you for something you're especially good at. What does your boss always counts on you for?

▶ Think of a problem that came up that had other people stumped but you were able to resolve. What did you do? What does that say about your abilities?

▶ What's your best trick of the trade? What do you do better than anyone else in your organization? What keeps you successful?

▶ When did you go above and beyond your job description and more than earn your pay that day?

▶ If your friends were to praise your skills, what would they say?

▶ If you felt totally comfortable bragging about yourself, what would you brag about? What are you most proud of?

▶ List ten qualities other people have that you most respect or admire. Go through the list and apply each of these qualities to some aspect of yourself or your work.

▶ If you suddenly had to leave the area for a while, how would your coworkers' jobs be tougher or less enjoyable when you're not there to help?

▶ What professional award would you most like to receive? For what? How close are you to getting it?

▶ How many of your professional goals have you achieved so far? Five years ago, did you think you could be where you are today?

Step 3: Making Magic Happen

If you properly completed the previous section, you probably have a straightforward list of skills, tasks, and responsibilities. Here's where the magic comes in. But, our magic gives you much more than a rabbit in a hat. Used correctly, our magic can land you the opportunity of a lifetime. We're going to take your résumé and turn it into reasons why an employer should choose you over any other candidate who applies for a position.

So, how does our magic work? We follow a three-step procedure to create a résumé guaranteed to generate results.

PAR

PAR—problem, action, and results—is a widely used method for quantifying your skills. *PAR statements* are powerful because they show clear examples of you making a difference for your past employers. Job seekers who develop achievement statements and use them almost always find work faster than those who don't.

Why? It's simple, really: achievement statements give potential employers a chance to see your professional competencies, strengths, and skills. This is almost like giving them a sneak preview of what you can do for them. They'll want to interview you—and make you an offer—quickly, before someone else takes advantage of your skills.

Remember, it's all about presentation. We're taking *skills you already possess* and marketing them in an entirely new way to get you the best opportunity possible. Here's how it works:

▶ What **problem** did you solve for your employer?

▶ What **action** did you take to resolve the problem or situation?

▶ What were the beneficial **results** of your action?

Having trouble determining how your skills fit into this model? Run down the following list of questions to help jog your memory as you begin writing your career achievements:

▶ Did you solve a recurring problem for your department?

▶ Did you suggest any new procedures or programs for your company?

▶ Did you make your job easier or more efficient?

▶ Did you train anyone?

▶ Did you implement a new procedure or system?

▶ Did you do a job with fewer people or in less time?

▶ Did you help increase sales?

▶ Did you save the company money?

Here are some examples of PAR statements:

Developed scripts to replace outdated backup system and automated backup processes, saving the company over $10,000.

Cut requisition costs by 20 percent, saving the company $100,000 for the fiscal year.

Reduced the cost of purchased computer systems by 40 percent by finding alternative suppliers.

Worked extended hours when the company experienced a shortage of resources.

Implemented configuration control standards to streamline helpdesk center operations.

Ideally, you'll be able to come up with several PAR statements for each job on your résumé. They can be presented in a bulleted list beneath your job description to allow employers quick, easy access to the information they need.

Recognition

In this section, we seek out the work you've done that has been recognized—the stuff that sets you apart from the rest of the crowd.

▶ Were you asked to take on more responsibility?

▶ Were you asked to lead or participate in a special project?

▶ Did you create or assume new responsibilities?

▶ Did you receive any rewards or special recognition?

▶ Did you receive a bonus for exceeding your goals or objectives?

▶ Did you do anything for the first time at your company?

▶ Were you promoted?

▶ Were you praised or acknowledged by customers, coworkers, or vendors you worked with?

▶ Did you receive perfect scores on standard industry or college examinations?

The following examples are recognition statements:

Invited to head the product development division for a new company product created in response to customer demand.

Served as technical consultant to a committee formed to assess customer satisfaction.

Created a new tracking system to monitor response time on customer calls.

Selected as the spokesperson by the American Association for the Advancement of Science for Engineers and Software Developers.

So What?

The "So what?" technique, when properly applied, is what makes your résumé a true winner. Too many people fill their résumés with boring job descriptions. Potential employers are busy people. They don't have time to sift through endless terminology and long-winded language. They want to know what you can do for them.

To get at that information, you need to explain not only what you did, but *why it mattered*. After each statement written in response to the previous questions, ask yourself "So what?" This can help you come up with the difference your action made.

Think of this as the difference between features and benefits, for example:

Microsoft Word has macro functionalities.

So what?

Microsoft Word offers users macro functionalities that enable quick, easy customization of documents and reports.

See the difference?

Now, we look at some of the statements just mentioned and apply the "So what?" method to strengthen them.

Before	After
Worked extended hours when the company experienced a shortage of resources	Preserved customer response time by working extended hours when the company experienced a shortage of resources
Implemented configuration control standards to streamline helpdesk center operations	Implemented configuration control standards to streamline helpdesk center operations; reduced manpower needs by 20 percent and improved overall customer satisfaction levels
Served as technical consultant to the committee formed to assess customer satisfaction	As technical consultant to the committee formed to assess customer satisfaction, provided technical expertise in creating and implementing automated online helpdesk functionality
Invited to head product development division for new company product created in response to customer demand	Headed product development division for new company product; brought product to market ahead of schedule and under budget

Summing It All Up

The Summary or Qualifications section of your résumé is designed to give hiring managers a "big picture" view of who you are. If you are applying for your first management position, you must get inside the employer's head. Think benefits, not features. You want the employer to recognize and become interested in the competitive advantage you bring to the position.

The job posting itself is your best clue. Use it to your greatest advantage: pick out the keywords and focal points, and stress those in your summary. Include keywords likely to be entered in a searchable database.

Although it sounds simple, this is a difficult section of your résumé to write. Do not attempt it until the rest of your résumé is complete. It's a summary, and you can't summarize information you haven't yet written or seen.

Some additional tips:

▶ Aim for about five bullet points, using nouns and adjectives, not action verbs. Save your action verbs for the body of your résumé.

▶ Draw on your work experience, volunteer time, and/or extracurricular activities in terms of duration, scope, accomplishments, and so on. If you lack relevant experience, emphasize interpersonal, organizational, and supervisory skills you have developed.

▶ The first statement summarizes the experience you related to your job objective (for example, one-year experience in helpdesk support).

▶ The second statement describes your working knowledge of the various components or aspects of the position, such as customer service, troubleshooting, or project management.

▶ The third statement outlines the various skills you possess to do the work effectively, such as problem solving, customer service, or project management.

▶ The fourth statement may refer to any academic background you have that complements your practical experience, such as machine design, resource assessment, or marketing.

▶ The fifth statement lists your personal characteristics and attitudes as required on the job, such as reliable, able to work under pressure, and creative.

▶ Not sure how to put it all together? The following is an example of a project manager's qualifications:

Holly Smith, Project Manager

Qualifications

▶ *18+ years experience in IT-supporting technologies in the oil and gas, financial, banking, medical, insurance, legal, government, education, and telecom (GSM) sectors*

▶ *Excellent project management, business analysis, and technical writing skills*

▶ *Sound understanding of application development methodology from the perspective of a user, designer, and developer*

▶ *Experience includes five years of programming/analysis/QA with financial applications*

▶ *Effective communication skills with all levels of management, customers, development team members, and vendors*

Of course, the Qualifications section is still relevant even if you're not yet at the management level. The following example gives you a look at how a programmer's summary might appear:

Sam Gill, Programmer

Summary of Qualifications

▶ *Extensive experience of six years in business systems analysis, database, and applications design*

▶ *Experienced in different business systems, including credit card systems, insurance, banking, public utilities, warehouse maintenance systems, manufacturing, human resources, and technology groups*

▶ *Experienced in database designs and performance tuning of DB2 applications*

▶ *Excellent communication and interpersonal skills*

Obviously, people at different levels need to stress different skills. An IT manager could follow the example shown next.

Henry Rocks, IT Manager

Qualifications

▶ *Accomplished IT professional with over ten years experience in financial and banking industries*

▶ *Broad knowledge and experience in matching appropriate technologies, designs, and systems development techniques with organization needs, capabilities, and resources*

▶ *Ability to plan and implement information technology strategies and develop user teams for large-scale technology implementations*

▶ *Keen ability to develop operational plans to meet organization goals*

▶ *Detail-oriented with a commitment to high standards*

Tailoring Your Résumé

Once you invest a significant amount of time perfecting your résumé and cover letter, you may be tempted simply to send it off again and again, without changing a word. Resist the urge. We'll show you just how to tailor your résumé perfectly to each individual job posting. With a small amount of effort, you can maximize your results and snag multiple offers.

Why is tailoring your résumé to specific job postings important? In general, people are lazy and set in their ways. A hiring manager who has to replace an employee who is leaving or who needs to fill a new position typically has a prepared job description. The first thing this person does when considering the stack of résumés that pour in within minutes of placing the job posting is to compare the information presented by the candidates against the specific skills needed for the job.

Remember, the hiring manager may not be a technical person and they may not realize your seven years of SQL experience mean you are obviously a database expert. You want to use terminology *from the job ad* in your cover letter or résumé (or both) to maximize your chance at getting the interview.

Sample Job Listings and Résumés Made to Fit

Following are several sample résumés tailored to specific job ads. Notice that even when a candidate doesn't have all the required skills, as many matches as possible are made between the résumé and the ad text.

Director of IT Position

Figure 4-1 is a sample job posting for a director of IT position, and Figure 4-2 is an example of a résumé optimized for this position.

Director of IT

As Director of IT, ensure technology leadership in the marketplace and provide internal support to drive quality, productivity, and innovation.

TECHNICAL DUTIES AND RESPONSIBILITIES

- Responsible for the development and oversight of business applications, which run on Digital Equipment Corporation (now Compaq) Alpha computers running the OpenVMS operating system.
- Responsible for overseeing the design and development of software applications. The development language is Synergy.
- Provide oversight of the Technical Services group, which manages the local area network (LAN). The LAN employs NT servers.
- Provide oversight of the Technical Services group, which manages desktop applications. The applications are standard Microsoft products.
- Negotiate contracts, determine future capacity, and manage telecommunications equipment, which is a PBX switch, "Definity" model G3R.
- Provide oversight of the Technical Services group, which manages the wide area network (WAN). The WAN communicates with 6 remote sites and supports approximately 50 remote users.
- Provide oversight of the Operations group, which includes helpdesk, EDI transmissions, and disaster recovery.
- Bring innovative ideas and systems to support business strategies.

OTHER DUTIES AND RESPONSIBILITIES

- Provide oversight of Computer Operations, Technical Services, and Programming areas within the IT department needed to support the 24/7/365 organization.
- Manage the day-to-day activities, relationships, and resources necessary for the continued support of the division's business information system.
- Coordinate with the Web Services group to ensure that the web applications integrate with mainframe applications.
- Assist the Business Planning team to ensure that all IT services (equipment, data, phone services) are coordinated and managed.
- Responsible for developing and maintaining disaster recovery plan.
- Provide oversight for all data and network security.
- Responsible for developing and maintaining a corporate-approved IT operating budget.

COMPETENCIES

- Leadership skills
- Communication skills
- Project management
- Analysis and reporting skills
- Customer focus
- Interpersonal skills

EDUCATION AND/OR EXPERIENCE

College degree in computer sciences (or related academic field) and a minimum of ten years of progressively responsible and diverse IT experience, or equivalent education and experience in a service environment. Ability to communicate with all levels of the organization is critical. Demonstrated leadership and problem-solving skills. Familiarity with numerous aspects of the computing environment, including applications development cycle, PC operating systems, PC architecture, network architecture, voice/data communications environment, and EDI processes.

FIGURE 4-1 Job listing for the director of an IT position

Thomas Banks
2343 High Road
Catonsville, MD 23433

(410) 455-5678
tbanks@aol.com

Summary of Qualifications

- Innovative and dynamic Director of IS with 13 years of diversified IT experience, including applications development, network architecture and operations, security, voice/data communications, and EDI processes
- Responsible for an IS operations team of 20 with a $10 million operating budget
- Direct oversight of computer operations, technical services, and development departments to support a 24 x 7 business environment
- Responsible for proper capacity and disaster recovery planning as well as all data and network security
- Proven success in solution providing, project management, systems analysis, designing, development, pre-sales technical support, implementation and post-implementation support and maintenance
- Customer focused, with excellent communication and interpersonal skills

Experience

Director of IS
Data Processing Institute, Baltimore, MD

11/1998–Present

- Outsourcing systems consulting company supporting client network infrastructure, voice communications, security management, email, VPNs, and web sites. Serviced 50 clients with typical installations of 200–500 distributed users. Services provided included:
  - Hosting and maintenance of global web sites
  - Intranet and VPN installations to support partners and remote users
  - MS Exchange email services supporting corporate and remote users
  - Network security (Checkpoint firewall/VPN)
  - Ecommerce transactional capabilities
- Managing procurement and lease programs for all desktops, laptops, servers, and networking equipment (Dell, GE Capital, Cisco) on behalf of all clients in order and leveraged aggregate buying power for deeper discounts.
- Managing 18 full-time staff members, an outsourced helpdesk, in-house and consultant development groups to support a 24 x 7 operations environment.
- Responsible for business recovery and capacity planning for internal and client systems and networks.

IT Manager, Development Services
Blue Streak Utility Services Inc., Baltimore, MD

8/1997–10/1998

- Managed outsourced development team, created new team, and brought development services in-house for overall cost savings and increased productivity.
- Assisted in logical application development and systems architecture of online energy management and profiling service.
- Managed all Internet-based systems and equipment, including Web, email, ftp, application, SQL, ColdFusion, SMS servers, and all routers, switches, and redundant connectivity.

FIGURE 4-2 Director of IT résumé

- Designed and implemented corporate network/intranet and satellite office connectivity and integration of technologies across companies that were acquired.

QA Consultant   1/1997–7/1997
OptiMark Technologies Inc., Jersey City, NJ

- Developed the test plan and test script to allow the QA department to validate a new market data interface (DEC Alpha, HP Unix).

Manager, Development   6/1990–12/1996
Dow Jones Markets, New York, NY

- Member of a cross-functional team (12 people) set up to assist a strategic partner (OptiMark Technologies Inc.) develop and deploy a new automated order match and trading system.
- Responsible for development, operations, and networking interfaces between OptiMark and Dow Jones' systems (ActiveX, Java, CORBA, TCP/IP, NT4.0, Web Server, Lotus Notes).

Education

B.S. in Computer Science, University of Maryland, Baltimore, MD   1988
Minors: Math and Business

FIGURE 4-2 *Continued*

IT Manager

Figure 4-3 shows a posting for an IT manager position, while Figure 4-4 demonstrates how to target a résumé based on this posting.

IT Manager

- Responsible for planning, administering, and reviewing the acquisition, development, maintenance, and use of local computer and telecommunications systems within the Dallas offices.

- Responsible for the overall scheduling, controlling, and directing of resources, people, funding, and facilities for IT projects. These projects may involve major modifications to existing systems or the implementation of discrete new IT facilities, systems, or subsystems.

- Reports to the Senior Director of Administration.

- Consult with personnel across all organizational levels to determine current and future IT needs and to identify areas for improvement.

- Analyze the information needs of the company and develop technological solutions to satisfy those needs.

- Prepare and direct IT policy and plan strategy regarding security aspects of IT systems and overall IT growth.

- Oversee planning and implementation of all systems within company's overall IT framework. This includes interface with the on-site US SAP team.

- Direct activities to select and install technology as approved by management.

- Oversee the provision of training for internal users.

- Direct the integration of IT operations, computer hardware, operating systems, communications, software applications, and data processing.

- Establish priorities for systems development, maintenance, and operations.

- Provide advice to senior managers regarding IT-related issues.

- Prepare guidelines and evaluate IT systems against given standards and performance criteria.

- Provide day-to-day product or system support to users via the helpdesk.

REQUIRED SKILLS

- MCSE and CNE certification.

- Advanced Novell and Windows NT installation and administration skills.

- Lotus Notes and Domino Server Admin.

- MS product certifications.

- TCP/IP, VPN, and firewall working knowledge.

FIGURE 4-3 Job listing for IT manager

Jon Duffy   jon@yahoo.com
11 Cardinal Place
Reading, PA 19610

SUMMARY

- Six years experience managing IT projects and systems, development teams, and customer service centers using in-house and outsourced resources.
- Experienced network infrastructure and capacity planner.
- Internet technology skills, including TCP/IP, VPN, and firewall setup and administration.
- Excellent communication and interpersonal skills, including helpdesk skills.
- Detail oriented, with very strong organizational and planning skills.

TECHNOLOGIES

Windows 2000/NT 3.1–4.0 Server Administration
Internet Information Server 3.0+ Administration
Microsoft Project
Microsoft Office 97, 2000, and XP
IBM Netfinity Manager
Visual Studio 6.0
Networking/IP Technologies
Internet Technologies (DNS, FTP, POP3, SMTP, WWW)
Windows 3.1, 3.11WFW, 95, 98, ME

EXPERIENCE

Blue Streak Utility Services Inc., Concord, Ontario   1/2000–7/2001
Manager, Technology Division

Managed outsourced development team, created new team, and brought development services in-house. Outsourced web design and e-branding. Assisted in logical application development and systems architecture of online energy management and profiling service. Managed all Internet-based systems and equipment, including web, email, ftp, application, SQL ColdFusion, site minder servers and all routers, switches and redundant connectivity. Designed and implemented corporate network/intranet and satellite office connectivity and integration of technologies across companies that were acquired.

YourHome.com Inc., Toronto, Ontario   9/1998–5/2000
IT Manager

Project and technical management of a large home-based web portal. Included logical design and systems/network architecture. Managed development staff of 6 (DBA, Programmer x 2, Web Developer, Web Designer, HTML coder). Acted as technical liaison representing the organization to investors and clients.

Interlog Internet Services Inc., Toronto, Ontario   10/1996–9/1998
Manager, On-Site Support

Helpdesk/call center management covering telephone and on-site support with a staff of 20 employees.

EDUCATION

Humber College, Canada-Ontario-Rexdale   1996
Certified Electronics Engineering Technician, two-year program

FIGURE 4-4 IT manager-targeted résumé

Security Analyst

Primary Responsibilities

- Performs daily network and host security monitoring, traffic analysis, and intrusion detection
- Conducts daily review of all firewall and IDS logs
- Provides weekly security analysis reports to the security manager
- Assists in the development of network and systems security architecture
- Assists in conducting system-vulnerability scanning
- Maintains proactive, consistent communications with the management team on system or network security issues, status, and projects
- Assists the senior security analyst and the security manager in security incident investigations
- Provides technical security assistance to network and helpdesk personnel in the areas of password management, e-mail security, and firewall/IDS configurations
- Assists in documenting information security policies and procedures
- Assists in providing information security training to all employees, contractors, alliances, and other third parties
- Assists in conducting internal information-security audits
- Assists in performing information security-risk assessments

Job Requirements

Experience & Knowledge

- Two+ years of professional experience in security architecture, including designing, implementing, and configuring secure perimeters, including routers, firewalls, VPNs, remote access, and overall network design
- Experience in firewall and intrusion-detection systems analysis
- GIAC GCFW, GCIA, and GSEC or SSCP preferred
- College degree or equivalent combination of education, experience, and/or training preferred

Other Competencies

- Supports Security Manager and team in changes in direction
- Adjusts personal priorities to meet changing organizational objectives
- Able to handle multiple priorities
- Monitors and identifies changing risk-management requirements
- Demonstrates ability to communicate clearly, and articulate ideas to security and various IT staff

FIGURE 4-5 Job listing for an Internet security analyst

- Facilitates interviews, records, and interprets responses, and makes sound judgments based on information available
- Succinctly organizes thoughts and information in easily understood formats
- Ability to identify and escalate security issues to the appropriate management staff in a timely basis
- Ability to interact with both technical and nontechnical staff
- Demonstrated understanding of threat, vulnerability, and risk as it pertains to the network and various systems
- Analyzes newly discovered threats and vulnerabilities, and effectively organizes methods to mitigate them

FIGURE 4-5 *Continued*

Internet Security Analyst

Figure 4-5 shows a job ad seeking an Internet security analyst. In Figure 4-6, we targeted the résumé to meet its required qualifications.

Systems Administrator

Figure 4-7 gives an example of a job listing for a systems administrator with four years experience. Figure 4-8 is a sample résumé targeted to those requirements.

Shawna Kvislen

1632 Prairie Drive, Sioux City, IA
67543 / 550-787-9089
Shawna_kvislen@hotmail.com

KEY QUALIFICATIONS

- Networking specialist with over nine years experience in designing, implementing, and configuring secure networks with four years of experience in implementing, troubleshooting, and supporting advanced IDS systems
- Well-versed in current published attack methodologies. Experienced in the use of automated host-based intrusion detection and response systems, firewalls, proxy servers, strong certificate-based encryption, and router and switch access control lists.
- Skilled in developing effective relationships with management, coworkers, customers, and vendors. Team player with solid communication skills. Detail-oriented individual in time-sensitive situations.
- CCSP and CISSP certified

TECHNICAL SKILLS

Operating systems: Windows NT/95/98/XP, NetWare, Linux, SunOS, Solaris, FreeBSD, OpenBSD, MacOS, OpenBSD, NetBSD, AIX, HP-UX

Security systems: Snort, AlertLogic, Enterasys Dragon, AirMagnet, ISS, Trend Micro Viruswall, Symantec Security Information Manager, ServGate Edge Force M Series, Blue Coat SG, AV, RA appliances, Check Point Firewall-1, Cisco PIX, Net Ranger, Black Ice

Tools: Encase, Symantec Forensic Utility, TCT Forensic Tool

Web servers: Websphere, MS IIS, Netscape Enterprise Server, Netscape FastTrack Server, Apache Webserver

Devices: Cisco routers, Juniper NetScreen, Nortel devices, Nbase Xyplex terminal servers, AlertLogic

Protocols: TCP/IP, IPX/SPX, ATM, OSPF, RIP, EIGRP, IGRP, BGP, MBGP, HSRP, IKE, IPSec, PPP, IGMP, DCP, L2TP

CERTIFICATIONS

MCSE, CCSP, CISSP

EXPERIENCE

Network Security Analyst, Tricon Manufacturing   6/2003 – Present

- Consulted with and advised senior management of current and future security threats and appropriate security countermeasures to combat against unauthorized access to IT assets.
- Responsible for system administration of over 30 Cisco and AlertLogic IDS sensors, including the configuration, installation, and auditing of PIX and Netscreen firewalls.

FIGURE 4-6 Internet security analyst-targeted résumé

- Conducted evaluations of existing technical documents for accuracy and complete-ness, and developed a penetration testing and vulnerability analysis plan.
- Responsible for the importing and maintaining proxy logs for a 30,000+ enterprise user-wide reporting solution.
- Research, evaluate, test, recommend, and implement new security products and releases.
- Additional responsibilities include troubleshooting security-related problems, inter-faces with internal and external audit requirements in compliance with SOX.

Internet Security Analyst, Vistainfo   4/2000–6/2003

- Maintenance of the firewall rule-base, overall network security, development of VPN connections between company and customer locations, firewall monitoring and alert, and monitoring the corporate network for possible network intrusion.
- Extensive knowledge of firewall setup and administration using Checkpoint Firewall-1, Linux iptables, NATs, and VPNs.
- Experienced in bandwidth management, monitoring, and ensuring quality of service.
- Addition responsibilities included administering and creating secure UNIX (Solaris, Linux, OpenBSD, FreeBSD) and Windows NT environments
- Project included centralizing 70+ company domain names hosted at different ISPs to the company's own name servers running Open BSD and BIND 8.*x*/BIND 9.*x*.
- Also migrated 20+ company nationwide locations to one namespace. Configured DNSSEC, multiple views, zone delegation, multiple nameservers, DHCP and host registration with DNS via dynamic updates and TSIG signed zone transfers. Tested interoperability with Microsoft DNS servers.

Network Administrator, Trinity College   10/1998–4/2000

- Managed and performed the statistical and tactical aspects of disaster recovery and auditing, and security policies, procedures, and guidelines.
- Performed security administration functions (maintaining users, groups, IDs, and passwords) for HP, UNIX, and FileNet systems at corporate and field locations.
- Implemented and oversaw the installation and configuration of Windows (95/98/NT), Novell, and UNIX operating systems.
- Worked with other network administrators in troubleshooting and maintaining the network with over 2,000 client computers, while ensuring top security.

EDUCATION

BS in Computer Science, California Technical University, 1997

FIGURE 4-6 *Continued*

Senior Systems Administrator

EDUCATION

Bachelor's degree in Computer Science or equivalent technical certifications

EXPERIENCE

- Minimum four years experience administering and maintaining optimized secure Windows Server networks.
- Capable of installing complete network operation environments, including the operating system, service packs, server products, and supporting companion products

JOB SUMMARY AND MAJOR RESPONSIBILITIES

- Duties include, but are not limited to: installing and administering Microsoft line of server products; developing, documenting, and maintaining server software configuration and standardization; providing workstation assignments, remote dial-up, e-mail, printer services; assisting network engineers in evaluating software, patches, and fixes for security bugs and networking degradation; providing remote storage for data security and integrity; restricting unauthorized access of network resources; reviewing server loads and recommending load balancing for optimization.
- Provides 24/7/265 ownership of all server infrastructure gear.
- Provides complex tier III troubleshooting and support services.

BREADTH AND DEPTH OF SKILL LEVEL AND PROJECT ROLES

- Senior-level professional.
- Provides leadership for their systems administrators.
- May direct work of others.
- Leads medium-to-large projects.
- Acts as role model to other systems administrators within the group.
- Provides technical guidance and training to other systems administrators.
- Possess and applies in-depth and specialized server administration skills.
- During system failures and outages, devises game plan and resolution.
- Coordinates the team to resolve issues and information managers of situation and steps to be taken.

FIGURE 4-7 Job listing for systems administrator

119 N. 12th Street, Guelph, MI 58447 ▪ (701) 522-8591 ▪ sgerman@hotmail.com

Scott German

Summary of Skills	• Certified system engineer with broad experience in IT systems management and infrastructure planning. • Ten years experience administering, maintaining, and supporting secure networks. • Solid track record for the implementation of technology solutions for optimizing operational efficiency. • Experienced team leader focused on meeting business needs by delivering excellent service, effectively prioritizing multiple mission critical tasks and working well under pressure. • Excellent work ethic, interpersonal skills, solid critical thinking and problem-solving skills.	
Technical Skills	**Systems**	Windows NT/2000/2003 Server, Solaris 8, Redhat Linux 7.x, Cisco IOS
	Networking	IPX/SPX, TCP/IP, IPv6, IPSec, FTP, SMTP, HTTP, HTTPS, POP3/IMAP4, DHCP, DNS, WINS
	Server Applications	Exchange 5.5/2000/2003, SQL 7.0/2000 Server, BIND 8.x (DNS), IIS 5.0/6.0, Oracle 8i/9i/10g, Active Directory, MS ISA Server 2002/2004, RightFax Server 8.7, McAfee Groupshield for Exchange, Veritas Backup Exec, PowerQuest Deploy Center, Veritas NetBackup, SMS 2003, Citrix Metaframe XP, Live Communication Server 2003, WebLogic 8, ColdFusion, HP OpenView, Microsoft Cluster Services, Veritas Storage Foundations, Veritas Cluster Services, F5 BigIP Load Balancer
	Network Hardware	HP ProLiant Servers, Dell PowerEdge Server, Dell Power Connect Switches, Lucent Pipeline router, EMC CX700, Brocade SAN Switches, 3Com switchers/hubs, HP SureStore Backup drives, Cisco VPN Concentrator, Cisco Catalyst, APS UPS
	Desktop Applications	MS Office 2003, MS Project 2003, MS Visio 2003, Norton Antivirus, McAfee Virus Scan, Symantec Ghost, Clearcase

FIGURE 4-8 Systems administrator-targeted résumé

Employment History	**Infrastructure Engineering Supervisor,**
	First American Title Co., Santa Ana, CA 9/2006- Present

- Manage a team of five systems engineers responsible for the daily implementation and maintenance of Microsoft Exchange, Active Directory, SQL Server, and BEA Weblogic. Team served as tier II & III escalation support.
- Streamlined operations and optimized environment through automation and standardization including:
  - Automation of application deployments for testing, production, and disaster recover environments, resulting in the reduction of deployment time from one hour to under 15 minutes.
  - Automation of server operating-system builds and postbuild software installation and configuration, reducing the amount of time spent performing manual operations.
  - Eliminated manual system administrative tasks with the use of scripting techniques and third- party applications.
  - Implemented a change management process for patch management across development, testing, staging, and production environments increasing environment consistency and reducing overall system deployment time. Deployed Microsoft SMS for server and desktop patch management.
  - Centralized all systems documentation in using Clearcase.
  - Implemented HP Systems Insight Manager to support monitoring of production environment.
  - Successfully implemented weekly maintenance windows via a change management process.

Sr. Systems Engineer,
Twinn Software, Aliso Viejo, CA   6/2003–9/2006

- Successfully led the migration team responsible for upgrading the corporate network from Windows NT, Exchange 5.5, and SQL 7.0 to Windows 2000 (Active Directory), Exchange 2000, SQL 2000, ISA 2000, and IIS 5.0. This included the migration of 250 servers and 2,000 desktops. Team consisted of server administrators and desktop support specialists in five U.S. sites.
- Part of the business continuity/disaster recovery team. This effort included designing and building out the technical infrastructure for the corporate data center in CA. Responsible for the specification and procurement of network software/hardware for the project.

FIGURE 4-8 *Continued*

- Additionally, authored and implemented the Network Operational Procedure Manual to meet business continuity needs.
- Responsible for hiring, mentoring, and training new engineering team members.
- Maintained VPN and security infrastructure including:
  - Implemented and configured a remote VPN solution for developers using Microsoft RRAS
  - Implemented a firewall solution using Microsoft ISA 2000 Server
  - Maintained corporate web site and host web sites running on IIS 5.0
  - Maintained external DNS services (BIND and MS DNS Services)

Systems Administrator,
SystemsPro Corp., Mission Viejo, CA   2/2000–5/2003

- Designed, implemented, and supported LAN, WAN, and wireless networks of more than 1,000 systems.
- Configured and maintained Cisco switches, routers, and CiscoWorks.
- Installed and administered Active Directory and provided technical support services for servers (Win2K/2003/Solaris/Linux), clients (Win NT/2000/XP) and client/server applications, including backup and restoration of data, OS upgrades, and security patches, and user account creation and maintenance.
- Installed, configured, and maintained domain controller, SQL, Exchange, DNS, DHCP, WINS, and IIS.
- Created and managed user accounts and groups, and set up trusts among the domains.
- Provided support for corporate security initiatives, such as intrusion detection, virus protection, and firewall administration.
- Documented and tracked calls using Remedy and solved trouble tickets daily.
- Design and supported storage area network (SAN) and performed backups using Veritas NetBackup.

Education	**B.S. Information Technology,** California State Polytechnic University, Pomona, CA 2000

FIGURE 4-8 *Continued*

Using the Right Words

You may not be a professional writer, but you need to learn the importance of choosing the right word if you want your résumé to make an impact. Whenever possible, write your job description with strong action words. Instead of the long-winded "Was responsible for maintaining database . . ." try the more concise—and powerful—"Maintained database. . . ." In general, whenever you see an "-ing" construction, ask yourself if you could jazz it up a little if it were rewritten.

Short bullet points pack a punch and leave the hiring manager with important details they can find in a hurry and remember later.

Here's a list of action words you can use to replace "-ing" constructions in your résumé.

achieved	acted	adapted
addressed	adjusted	administered
advised	altered	analyzed
arranged	assembled	assessed
audited	balanced	broadened
budgeted	built	calculated
calibrated	catalogued	categorized
chaired	changed	charted
checked	classified	coached
collated	collected	combined
communicated	compared	compiled
completed	composed	computed
conceived	concluded	conducted
configured	considered	consolidated
constructed	contracted	contrasted
controlled	converted	coordinated
corrected	corresponded	counseled
created	critiqued	cultivated
cut	decided	decreased
defined	delegated	delivered
demonstrated	described	designed
detected	determined	developed
devised	diagnosed	differentiated

directed	discovered	dispensed
displayed	dissected	distributed
diverted	documented	doubled
drafted	drew	edited
eliminated	empathized	encouraged
enforced	enhanced	enlarged
ensured	established	estimated
evaluated	examined	expanded
expedited	explained	expressed
extracted	facilitated	filed
finalized	financed	fixed
followed	forecasted	formulated
founded	gathered	gave
generated	guided	hired
hosted	identified	illustrated
implemented	improved	improvised
incorporated	increased	informed
initiated	inspected	installed
instituted	instructed	integrated
interacted	interpreted	interviewed
introduced	invented	investigated
itemized	judged	launched
learned	lectured	led
liaised	listed	located
maintained	managed	marked
marketed	measured	mediated
met	minimized	modeled
moderated	modernized	modified
monitored	motivated	narrated
navigated	negotiated	observed

obtained	opened	operated
ordered	organized	oriented
originated	oversaw	painted
patterned	performed	persuaded
photographed	piloted	planned
predicted	prepared	prescribed
presented	printed	processed
produced	programmed	projected
promoted	proofread	proposed
protected	provided	publicized
published	purchased	raised
received	recommended	reconciled
recorded	recruited	redesigned
reduced	referred	refined
rehabilitated	related	rendered
reorganized	repaired	reported
represented	researched	resolved
responded	restored	restructured
retrieved	reviewed	revised
revitalized	saved	scheduled
searched	secured	selected
separated	served	serviced
set	sewed	shaped
shared	showed	simplified
sized	sketched	sold
solved	sorted	specified
spliced	split	spoke
started	streamlined	strengthened
studied	summarized	supervised
supplied	talked	taught

tended	tested	traced
trained	transcribed	transformed
translated	traveled	treated
trimmed	troubleshot	tutored
uncovered	unified	updated
upgraded	used	utilized
verified	weighed	welded
widened	wired	won
wrote		

In addition to the use of action words, you should also consider the adjectives that you use to describe your personal qualities.

Accelerated	Keen	Resourceful
Accomplished	Knowledgeable	Responsible
Analytical	Major	Solid
Capable	Mature	Specialist
Competent	Motivated	Stable
Consistent	Nationwide	Substantial
Doubled	Outstanding	Successful
Driven (that is, customer-service driven)	Positive	Talented
	Powerful	Thorough
Dynamic	Productive	Trained
Effective	Proficient	Versatile
Efficient	Profitable	Vigorous
Excellent	Proven	Well-educated
Exceptional	Qualified	Well-rounded
Global	Quick-thinking	
Highly	Rated	

Consider the combination of the adjectives and your action words to create powerful descriptors, such as:

- ▶ Effectively contributed to . . .

- ▶ Diligently assisted with . . .

- ▶ Consistently supported . . .

- ▶ Thorough attention to detail . . .

- ▶ Goal-oriented . . .

- ▶ Technically skilled . . .

- ▶ Proven ability . . .

- ▶ Solid knowledge . . .

- ▶ Highly versatile . . .

- ▶ Expert planner . . .

 NOTE *Here's a brief word about the use of adjectives in your résumé. While some adjectives can enhance and punch up your experience, others can kill your credibility. Avoid these adjectives.*

- ▶ Visionary strategist . . . (when you're applying for a helpdesk position)

- ▶ Demonstrated excellence . . . (a little over the top for a systems administrator)

- ▶ Projected unprecedented growth . . . (when referring to hardware-growth rates of 15 percent)

Summing It Up

Starting to get your skills down on your résumé is the hardest part. The worksheets and samples in this chapter should provide a shortcut to uncovering your hidden talents. You won't get it all the first time, so make sure you keep refining how you present yourself. Once you have everything down, let others provide feedback. Running your résumé by impartial parties can help you continue to refine and improve it.

Chapter 5

The Cover Letter

When seeking out cover letter advice, you can find a lot of cute, overly imaginative, amusing, and arrogant examples. Some begin with a quote about Kermit the Frog, and some close with "I will come to your office next Friday to take you to lunch." What are these people thinking?

That does not get employers to bite. Most IT hiring managers are going to throw that letter in the trash. Not only will they be unimpressed that you are making their lunch plans, but they also will only remember your name because they think you're behaving in a ridiculous manner. Some of those stunts might work when you apply for a position in marketing, sales, or advertising, but you need to take a different approach in the technical arena.

In this chapter, we cover:

- ▶ The purpose of your cover letter
- ▶ Hooking the employer
- ▶ Getting to the point
- ▶ The content of your message
- ▶ Fatal mistakes of the cover letter
- ▶ Types of cover letters and how to write them
- ▶ Sample IT cover letters

The Purpose of Your Cover Letter

The purpose of your cover letter is to get your résumé read. The purpose of your cover letter is not to summarize all your skills and experience—that's what your résumé is for. Your cover letter is to introduce you and direct the reader to your enclosed résumé.

So, how can your cover letter accomplish its main goal? By enticing an employer and making a dynamite first impression. Your cover letter needs to show a little about who you are and why you are the best person for the job. It is the warm handshake that puts a "face" to your name, highlights your strong points, and presents nonrésumé details that set you apart from the next closest candidate.

For this to happen, you need to do three things:

▶ Hook the employer into reading your résumé

▶ Get to the point quickly and concisely

▶ Reveal some of the positive aspects of your personality

Hook the Employer

Your cover letter can capture the interest of the employer by telling them specifically what you can do for their company. Your letter needs to be personalized—not generic—and it needs to demonstrate why you are going to make an impact on their company in particular.

To hook the employer, you need to find out as much about the company as possible, starting with the name of the hiring manager.

Addressing Each Letter

If the job posting does not list the name of the hiring manager, you may want to do some research:

▶ If a phone number is given, call and ask for the name of the hiring manager for that position. You may need to use some investigative skills and turn on the charm!

▶ If only an e-mail address is listed, try to figure out the company from that address, and then contact them by phone.

If you are unable to find a specific name to address your cover letter to, the best alternatives are "Dear Hiring Manager" or "Dear Recruiting Manager." Avoid more formal salutations, such as "Dear Sir" or "Madam." It's especially important not to assume the hiring manager is a he or a she. In today's world, the hiring manager could easily be either or both, if multiple managers are involved. Also, for what it's worth, the phone calls wouldn't win points with me . . . even if the detective work is impressive!

Next, you want to do some research on the company. The easiest way is to visit its web site or talk to someone you know who works there. Try to get an idea of what the company is all about, its motto, and its history, and take that into consideration when you write your cover letter. If you can incorporate some of their philosophy into your cover letter without sounding cheesy, go for it.

Get to the Point

Your cover letter needs to be less than one page. Any longer and you are lessening your chances of having it read. Remember, an employer usually spends less than 30 seconds reading a cover letter. If you fill the entire page, you may already be saying too much. Condense, condense, condense. Long sentences with colorful, obscure words are unimpressive in a cover letter.

Reveal Positive Aspects about Yourself

Showing some personality in your cover letter is acceptable, but you don't want to cross the line and come off as unprofessional. If you checked out books about writing cover letters, you have probably seen many examples of this.

To be effective, you want to use positive action words and keywords to reflect your positive aspects. And, you want to write in a tone that projects confidence, professionalism, and experience.

On the other hand, here are some examples that indirectly reveal *negative* points:

Lose the attitude   *If you are looking for the best programmer you could possibly hire, look no further, because here I am! My unbelievable skill set and ability to work with others far exceed that of anyone you have employed before.*

Get some confidence   *Although I don't have the experience you are asking for, I can probably step up to the challenge. I would just need some time to adjust to the work environment and develop my skill set further.*

Don't be so blunt; they do not have to know this from the get-go   *I was recently laid off and am looking to get into the work force again.*

The Content of Your Message

The body of a traditional cover letter basically covers these areas:

▶ Introduction

▶ Self-promotion

▶ Call to action

▶ Thank you

Introduction

In the first paragraph, you need to state why you are writing. A hiring manager or recruiter does not want to waste time trying to figure out the purpose of this letter. Be direct, concise, and to the point. State the title or type of the job you are applying for and why the position interests you.

Stay away from the common "I am writing in response to the posting on your company web site for a ...," but there is no need to try to come up with a catchy quote or crazy introduction. Just get to the point.

The following are some examples of effective opening statements:

I have been closely following the progress of leading communications companies like yours and am impressed with the growth of your organization over the last year.

I have five years experience as an IT project manager working on large systems implementations and am PMI working toward my PMI certification.

Sharon Bymers recommended that I contact you regarding the infrastructure specialist position within your IT management division.

As a C++ programmer of four years, I have worked with all aspects of the language and I find this field stimulating and challenging.

If your staff could benefit from the addition of an eminently qualified software testing professional, we should meet to discuss my credentials.

Self-Promotion

The next section needs to outline why you alone are ideal for this job. If you are responding to a job posting, you know what the company wants, so exploit that. Use the main points of the job description to explain how you could best satisfy their needs, incorporating your relative skills, experience, and training. Use the keywords listed in their ad and hone in on specifics related to them.

Remember, no one likes a pushy salesman. Be careful not to exaggerate your skills or sound too boastful. No one wants to hear that you are the greatest person ever, and most employers do not want to hire someone with that attitude.

In addition, your résumé needs to be an *overview* of your relevant qualifications and experience, not a paraphrased summary of your résumé. For example, if the company is looking for someone with networking experience, don't write the whole letter about your last job doing this. Just introduce the fact that you have this experience, with a supporting fact or two. Further details are contained in your résumé.

Call to Action

This closing paragraph requires some assertiveness, but not overaggression. As mentioned earlier, suggesting that you will see them on Friday when you pick them up for lunch is not a good idea. This is simply over the edge, arrogant, and inconsiderate of the hiring manager's schedule. Wouldn't you be offended if someone said this to you?

That said, you do want to make a call to action at the conclusion of your cover letter. Although you should make respectful follow-ups, you still want to prompt them to contact you. This would suggest a closing such as, "I look forward to hearing from you about my suitability for this position." This is less pompous than "I will call you on Thursday at 11:00 A.M."

Watch out for employers that state "no phone calls." You don't want to disregard these requests.

Thank You

Ending your cover letter with a gesture of thanks is proper job-hunting etiquette. If the Human Resources (HR) director or hiring manager is taking the time to read your correspondence, you want them to know you appreciate it. This ending can positively affect their impression of you.

Fatal Mistakes of a Cover Letter

After you write your cover letter, solicit the advice of others and proofread the letter.

The following are some fatal mistakes to avoid when writing your cover letter:

▶ Avoid grammatical, spelling, or formatting errors.

▶ Avoid salutations, such as "Dear Sir" or "To Whom It May Concern." If you can't personalize the letter with a name, which is best, then "Dear Hiring Manager" or "Dear Recruiting Manager" are acceptable.

▶ Avoid a handwritten cover letter. Some people think this is more personal, but that couldn't be more wrong.

▶ Avoid specific salary figures, even if they are requested. State that your salary is negotiable and can be discussed in the interview. You don't want to count yourself out before you have a chance to prove what you are worth. Even if an employer has a maximum dollar amount they want to spend, you might change their mind.

▶ Avoid summarizing your résumé. Don't be redundant.

▶ Avoid exaggerations of qualifications or experience.

▶ Avoid negative or controversial subject matter, such as political or religious topics, or insults to your previous employer or company.

▶ Avoid revealing too much about *why* you are looking for a job. That can come out in the interview.

▶ Avoid personal issues or feelings.

▶ Avoid an overly aggressive sales pitch about yourself.

▶ Avoid excluding the cover letter. Some HR personnel do not even accept résumés without cover letters.

▶ Avoid personal or cheesy closings, such as *Yours truly, Eagerly waiting,* or *Your next employee.*

E-mailing Cover Letters

When e-mailing your cover letter, use the same writing guidelines. Then, follow the formatting guidelines, as discussed in Chapter 3:

► Create your e-mailable cover letter using the guidelines for writing an ASCII résumé.

► Make sure all information is left-aligned.

► Use characters, such as asterisks and hyphens, to highlight information.

► You may want to shorten your letter slightly as it is more difficult to read from a computer screen than from a piece of paper.

► Paste the cover letter into the e-mail; do not send it as an attachment.

► Write a descriptive subject line, such as "My assets for desktop technician position" or "Software engineer résumé, referred by Larry Jones."

Types of Cover Letters and How to Write Them

You can use different types of cover letters, depending on the situation:

► Traditional cover letter

► T-letter

► Networking letter

► Thank you letter

► Recommendation letter

Traditional Cover Letter

The *traditional cover letter* accompanies your résumé when you are responding to an advertisement or a job posting. Figure 5-1 illustrates an outline of the sections of the traditional cover letter.

The T-Letter

The *T-letter* is a straightforward cover letter that lists the *employer's wants* in one column and *your qualifications* in the adjacent column. For busy hiring managers, this layout is a quick read and easily points out a great match.

A T-letter is perfect if your skills and experience match most or all of the employer's requested qualifications. If that is not the case, do not use this type of cover letter. You would be highlighting your weaknesses before the employer even has a chance to see your strengths. See Figure 5-2 for a sample of the body of a T-letter.

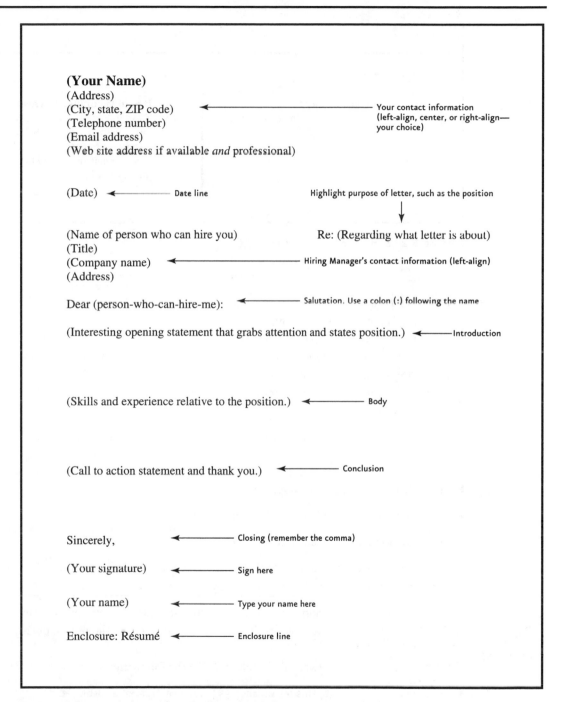

FIGURE 5-1   Sample layout for a traditional cover letter

You want:	I have:
• A computer degree • Basic understanding of Java and JavaScript • Attention to detail	• **B.S. in Computer Science** • Thorough knowledge of **Java** and **JavaScript,** as well as **SQL** • **Attention to detail**, as well as expert organization and logical thinking skills

FIGURE 5-2   Sample body of a T-letter

Networking Letter

Networking is not limited to asking the people you know if their company is hiring. You can send a letter to someone you do not yet know who could help you in your job search. By using a mutual friend or acquaintance, you can make connections with potential employers. In addition to asking for a job, you can use a *networking letter* to solicit advice and ideas, or job leads and referrals. A sample networking letter is shown in Figure 5-3.

Your networking letter can:

▶ Help you get a job by making a personal connection and establishing rapport.

▶ Prioritize you over applicants who don't have connections.

▶ Provide information on a target employer.

▶ Help you acquire referrals or recommendations.

▶ Help you gather advice on your course of action.

▶ Enable you to become familiar with an employer who may be hiring later. To save time with their recruiting efforts, they may contact you when that time comes.

Make sure your networking letter is well written and does not appear presumptuous or pushy. If the person does not know you or probably won't remember you, state that openly at the beginning of the letter.

When writing your networking letter, mention the following:

▶ How you came to write this letter, such as from a referral of another lead.

▶ The credentials you have in the field, such as your education or background.

▶ Your knowledge about issues the employer is facing. Be careful not to sound as if you are telling them how to do their job.

Melissa Spellman
11 South Ferry Way
Springfield, MI 91120
515-645-2727
spellmanm@excite.com

October 17, 2001

Matt DeWitt
Vice President of Technology
eBusiness International
2121 Broadway
St. Louis, MI 91343

Dear Mr. DeWitt:

I am not sure if you will remember, but we met when your department was attending IT training in Springfield this summer. I assisted you and your employees with their workstation setups and MCSE lab sessions at the Technology Institute. I was very impressed with you and your team, and have a small request.

I have been with my company for some time, and I am interested in leaving to further my career in the networking field. You seemed to know a lot about the industry as well as who's who in St. Louis, and I would like to ask your advice about corporations there. I am planning on moving to the area soon and would appreciate any insight you could provide.

I will call you next Thursday to try to set up a couple of minutes to talk. Don't worry, I only want some advice, and if you have the time I would love to take you to lunch. I am enclosing my résumé to remind you of some of my qualifications.

Thank you in advance for your time and assistance!

Sincerely,

Melissa Spellman

Melissa Spellman

Enclosure: Résumé

FIGURE 5-3   Sample of a networking cover letter

Thank You Letters

You may not necessarily sway an employer's decision with a thank you letter, but there are no disadvantages to sending one—pre- or postinterview

Before the Interview

You can send a note or an e-mail to thank the interviewer for the appointment, confirm the time and place, and add a selling point to increase the interviewer's anticipation of your meeting.

After the Interview

Send a thank you letter or an e-mail to immediately remind the interviewer of you, make another good impression, add information not covered in the interview, and provide another reason for the interviewer to contact you.

Although your thank you letter is more casual than an initial cover letter, do not forget about professionalism. Type and proofread it, just as you would other correspondence to potential employers.

Others Who Deserve a Thank You

If someone gives you a recommendation or refers you to a job opening, send that person a thank you letter (see Figure 5-4). Keep them in your good graces, as you may need their help again later.

Recommendation Letter

After meeting with the hiring manager, you may receive a request for letters of recommendation. While it is best to get letters of recommendation when you are directly involved with your references, don't panic if you do not have any when you are asked.

Contact your references and, if they are willing to praise you, offer to write a draft letter. Say you know they are busy, you would like to save them some time, and they can fine-tune the letter.

When you do get a recommendation letter, keep an electronic copy and a paper copy to ensure you have them for future reference.

Sample IT Cover Letters

Figures 5-5 through 5-9 are sample cover letters for several different IT positions and experience levels.

The following numbered list of points corresponds to the numbers in Figure 5-5, indicating the highlights of the cover letter.

❶ Todd researched the company and mentioned that in the first paragraph. This shows his interest in the organization, not just in the position. Todd then stated how he could help the company.

❷ Todd used headings to point out important qualifications from the job description. He did this because he is not experienced and he wants to draw attention away from that and toward his abilities.

Rebecca Fellows
13 Cherry Court
Freehold, NJ 71180
(213) 452-9900
rfellows32@hotmail.com

July 3, 2002

Nicole German
IT Manager
World Perks Inc.
52 Gallow Way, Suite 502
Aberdeen, SD 52009 **Re: Desktop Support Technician position**

Dear Ms. German:

Thank you for taking the time to speak with me yesterday about the exciting **Desktop Support Technician** opportunity with World Perks Inc. As I mentioned, I am extremely interested in working for an organization of this caliber.

(Insert a paragraph summarizing any strong points that were not discussed in the interview. If everything was covered, summarize the top qualifications of theirs that you meet.)

Thank you for your concise explanation of your needs. I know that my experience and knowledge of desktop applications and your networking system will be a great benefit to your organization.

I look forward to hearing from you soon to continue our discussion.

Sincerely,

Rebecca Fellows

Rebecca Fellows

FIGURE 5-4 Sample of a thank you letter

❸ Todd created "experience" by discussing work he has done for friends and family, such as setting up a network.

❹ Todd mentioned traits of his personality that would be beneficial in this position. He tied that into how this will help with nontechnical aspects of this position, such as training new employees.

Todd Hagen
3645 Lake Trail Road, Apt. 301
Grand Rapids, MI 30221
412-631-8802
toddlhagen@gmail.com

September 2, 2006

Harvey Jones
Director of IT Engineering
Accredited Communications
7712 Commerce Ave
Detroit, MI 31882

RE: Desktop support position

Dear Mr. Jones:

❶ I have been following your organization's growth over the recent six months and was pleased to see your recent expansion in the Detroit area. I was happy to see that this expansion also included new openings for desktop support technicians. I am interested in demonstrating how I can be part of a team dedicated to supporting Accredited's growth through outstanding customer service.

Certified and Experienced ❷

I am **A+** and **Network+** certified and currently working toward my **MCSE** certification. As a part of my training, I have had ample hands-on experience, including installing and configuring PC and Macs, and troubleshooting and repairing small networks. In addition, I **❸** have also performed consulting work for a variety of small businesses in the community and belong to a number of local IT user groups to ensure that I keep my IT skills sharp.

Dedicated to Customer Service

❹ I pride myself on my attention to detail and service-oriented attitude. My outgoing and detail-oriented personality is particularly effective when training new hires on their system essentials and troubleshooting time-sensitive challenges.

Thank you for considering me for the desktop support position at Accredited Communications. I am interested in setting up a time to further demonstrate how I can bring the positive attitude and knowledge you need for your networking team.

Sincerely,

Todd Hagen

Todd Hagen

FIGURE 5-5 Sample cover letter for a PC technician with no experience

Helen Rufael
1900 Foxhill Court
Spokane, WA 55021
321-563-0091
hrufael2@excite.com

May 30, 2002

Scott Clausson
Technical Services Manager
IT Training Corporation
648 Battery Avenue
Seattle, WA 55762   **Re: Helpdesk Analyst**

Dear Mr. Clausson:

① Customer service is something that comes naturally to certain people, and I am one of those people. I excel as a **Helpdesk Analyst** because I have the technical skill set combined with the personality to deliver solutions and solve problems quickly, with an upbeat attitude.

② My experience at the General Electronics helpdesk included servicing 300 **③** franchise locations in desktop applications and proprietary software support. While there, I researched, implemented, and administered a call tracking system used by the helpdesk, development team, and training department. Within two **④** months the average call time went down by nearly 50 percent.

⑤
Statistically, **my average performance ranks number one** or two each week in regards to number of calls, average call time, percentage of closed calls, and customer appreciation rating.

⑥ Thank you for considering me as a top candidate. I would like the opportunity to meet with you to discuss my background further and share my ideas about making the helpdesk at the IT Training Corporation more productive and more successful.

Sincerely,
Helen Rufael
Helen Rufael

Enclosure: Résumé

FIGURE 5-6   Sample cover letter for a helpdesk analyst with minimal experience

Melissa Johnson
1463 19th Street SE
Newport Beach, CA 92384
713-444-4533
Melissa.Johnson@gmail.com

July 30, 2006

Julie Crown, IT Manager   RE: Web Page Designer position
Total e-Packages   Referred by Kevin McMahon
18 Technology Drive
Santa Ana, CA 92701

Dear Ms. Crown:

❶ Kevin McMahon recommended that I contact you regarding the design position with Total e-Packages. As a **web page designer**, I was impressed by your organization's wide-spread public visibility with recent design projects. I was especially interested when Kevin showed me the innovative work you are doing with FedEx and Wachovia Bank.

I want a role with Total e-Packages – and with me on your team, Total e-Packages can be even more successful in its ability to deliver **the total package for e-business success.** **❷**

My experience with Smyth and Turner Agency includes:

❸

- **Three years in graphic design** and layout for major accounts, including Burger Time and Hudson Bay Inc.
❹ - Utilization of my **B.S. in Web Design and Production** from the Baltimore Institute of Art.
- Assisting in the design of Smyth and Turner's recently launched web site, in addition to working on sites for various other **large national clients**.

My graphic design experience combined with my solid skill set has prepared me for handling large accounts such as those you service at Total e-Packages. I look forward to discussing how my contributions can assist in marketing your company for bigger profits and higher visibility.

Thank you for your consideration and for an opportunity to further demonstrate how I can help you deliver the total package for e-business success.

Sincerely,

Melissa Johnson

Melissa Johnson

FIGURE 5-7 Sample cover letter for a web page designer, including mention of a referral

Molly Skandalis
153 Rolling Avenue
Bel Air, FL 402213
878-777-3323

January 2, 2007

Ms. Paige Boyle
IT Manager
Raven Enterprises
176 Main Avenue
Ft. Lauderdale, FL 30232

Dear Ms. Boyle:

① As a **C# programmer** for the past three years, I've had the opportunity to work on a number of complex and challenging projects. Over this time, I've developed an excellent work ethic for producing quality, efficient, and bug-free code. **②**

Six months ago, I moved into a **team leadership position** and now supervise and mentor less-experienced developers on their own projects, while at the same time, continue to work on high-profile projects of my own. These projects allow me to continue to develop my **③** own application architecture skills and to continue to work with new technology. I enjoy the flexibility and adaptability that this allows me. **④**

I am enclosing my resume for consideration for the Sr. Applications Developer position listed with your company. I can be available for an interview at short notice and look forward to meeting you to discuss how the combination of my team management and technical skills can benefit your application development team at Raven Enterprises. Thank you for your consideration.

Sincerely,

Molly Skandalis

Molly Skandalis

FIGURE 5-8 Sample cover letter for an experienced application developer

Jeff Kloos
72 Guelph Avenue
Mound, MN 93225
605-523-9821
Jeff_kloos@gmail.com

February 26, 2007

Mindy Thompson
Quality Assurance Manager
Stanley Morgan Financial Management
5523 106th Avenue SE
Minneapolis, MN 93223

RE: Quality Assurance Specialist position

Dear Ms. Thompson:

I would like to submit my résumé in response to your Monster.com job posting for a quality assurance specialist. I believe a strong fit exists between the qualifications you are looking for and my experience.

① Your qualifications

- A computer science degree
- Basic understanding of Java and JavaScript
- Attention to detail

My experience

- B.S. In Computer Science
- Thorough knowledge of **Java** and **JavaScript**, as well as **SQL** ②
- Attention to detail, as well as expert organizational and logical thinking skills ③

In addition to meeting your primary qualifications, I also have knowledge of software testing tools, such as **Mercury**, and automated testing processes through my experience with **IBM**. ④ ⑤

I look forward to discussing how I can effectively contribute to the Quality Assurance team at Stanley Morgan. Thank you for your consideration.

Sincerely,

Jeff Kloos

Jeff Kloos

FIGURE 5-9 Sample cover letter for a quality assurance specialist with no experience

The following list points out valuable tips found in Figure 5-6 for writing a cover letter to reflect your personality and key accomplishments, even when your experience is minimal.

1 Helen used the first paragraph to demonstrate her understanding of the importance of customer service in the helpdesk profession.

2 She highlighted past experience in a similar position to create credibility.

3 Helen quantified past experience by using specific numbers to explain the size of the helpdesk in her last position.

4 She highlighted a major accomplishment to show initiative in improving the company, aside from performing normal duties.

5 Helen added bold highlighting to a fact about personal performance to show her dedication to job responsibilities.

6 She concluded by thanking the hiring manager for his consideration. She included a statement about helping the company.

The following details highlight the cover letter in Figure 5-7, illustrating an excellent way to write a cover letter that incorporates a referral.

1 Melissa name-dropped right away, by referring to the current employee who recommended the position.

2 She used the company's motto to draw attention to the message in the letter, as well as to show familiarity with the company.

3 She bolded key points, such as the company's motto, years of experience, and job title.

4 Melissa summarized key accomplishments in bulleted form as her qualifications closely matched the job description.

The following numbered list corresponds to the numbers in Figure 5-8, pointing out key examples of personal traits, work experience, and professional skills maneuvered into the cover letter.

1 Molly highlighted her key qualifications for this position: C# programming and management experience.

2 She plugged some of the other skills mentioned in the job description and highlighted her education.

3 Molly emphasized her teamwork abilities, as well as her independent work capabilities.

4 She included a personal statement about having an open mind and the ability to adapt to new projects easily, both valuable characteristics to an employer.

The following list of points refers to the cover letter in Figure 5-9, demonstrating how to project yourself as an ideal candidate, even though you have little experience.

1 Jeff is using a T-letter because the employer's qualifications and Jeff's profile match well. This format easily points out why Jeff deserves consideration.

2 The employer said SQL was a plus, but not a requirement, so Jeff only listed this in his column and presented this skill as a bonus.

3 Jeff added some personal characteristics that are relative to a quality assurance specialist.

4 He highlights IBM because of the credibility of the company.

5 His experience at IBM was a three-month internship, but Jeff is leveraging this to let the employer know that, even though he is just graduating, he does have some working knowledge.

Summing It Up

Remember, the purpose of your cover letter is to get your résumé read. Keep it simple but make sure you include a cover letter each and every time. Short and sweet every time—hook the employer, highlight your skills, and tell focus their attention on how your experience can really solve their business need. Guaranteed to work every time.

Chapter 6

· ·

Common Résumé Dilemmas

After reading this far, you're probably itching to write the perfect résumé. Well, we have a secret for you: it doesn't exist. Before you march off to the bookstore to demand your money back, let us clarify. We all have experience we want to highlight—and other experience we'd rather downplay. In this chapter, we show you how to handle four of the most common résumé dilemmas faced by IT professionals. We give you practical examples you can put to use immediately. Chapter 11 provides you with additional résumé samples that can teach you how to develop your own strategy for facing these challenges.

In this chapter, we cover:

▶ Recent college graduates

▶ Paper certifications

▶ Career changers

▶ Problem histories

Recent College Graduates

Do any of these statements describe your situation?

▶ Your résumé lists your college extracurricular activities.

▶ Your parent's address is listed as your permanent address.

▶ You list every job since you started working at 16.

▶ Your uncle is listed as a reference.

If you answered yes to even one of these, you're most likely a recent college grad, and the prospect of writing your first professional résumé may seem daunting. The biggest challenge is to fill the page so it doesn't only include your name, address, and college degree. (And increasing the font size to 16 points is not an option!)

As you sit down to draft your résumé, remember one thing: a lot of competition is out there for entry-level positions. If you are only 23 and just out of college, no employer expects you to have the track record of a 40-year-old. Don't worry about your lack of real-world experience. Instead, focus on the skills you've learned and the knowledge you've attained. Let's take a look at how to approach each section of your first résumé.

A special note for IT professionals-in-process: the final semester of your senior year is not the time to start on your résumé. Starting to build your resume as soon as you get into your heavy-duty IT courses is extremely important. Your projects are fresh in your mind then, and describing them will be easier when it's time to put them to good use. You never know when that great internship is going to come along—you want to be prepared!

Defining Your Career Objective

Forget the flowery language you find on most résumés. Simply put, recent college graduates need not include anything beyond the position they seek. Why?

▶ No one expects recent college graduates to know what they want in the long term from their career.

▶ Traditional career objective statements are usually ignored by employers scanning résumés in response to job ads.

No Plan Required

Employers know that most recent college graduates have spent the last two to five years earning their degree, taking general classes to provide the foundation for thinking logically and methodically (in theory, at least). They may be familiar with local college programs that offer more practical and hands-on programs, but they are primarily interested in finding candidates with working knowledge in IT systems and who appear trainable.

Your first postgraduation résumé is used to apply for your first "real" job in IT. College grads with a career plan are the rare exception. Truly, no one expects recent college graduates to know what their career will look like five to ten years out. Fortunately, a career is built one job at a time, and many of the most successful and rewarding careers take unexpected detours that no one could predict at age 22. So, define the type of job you want as your first entry-level position and *describe your qualifications for that job.*

Objective Ignored

If you've spent hours perfecting the career objective portion of your résumé, you may be disappointed to learn that most employers won't take the time to admire your carefully crafted sentences. But you should understand why employers don't bother to read this statement.

▶ This statement is so generic, it could apply to any position in the company.

▶ The statement describes every other candidate applying for the position.

▶ Employers are reviewing résumés for specific job postings.

There's a double-edged sword, though. Even though your objective statement will probably be ignored, you still need to include it. Look at it this way: the hours you've invested won't go to waste. You just need to learn to maximize the effectiveness of your objective statement. And, the next section shows you how to do just that.

I'm Trainable!

Employers are looking for candidates who have a base set of IT skills and who are trainable. The top of your résumé is precious real estate for effectively addressing the question "Why should you hire me?" This is space that should be devoted to selling your credentials—both your educational and practical experience. Use this space to *imply a job objective,* and *advertise credentials and strengths as a potential employee.*

Check out the example shown here:

Qualifications

▶ *Self-motivated, customer-focused, recent college graduate with an exceptional ability to quickly master new software/hardware*

▶ *MCP, A+, and Network+ certified as part of earning undergraduate degree*

▶ *Six-month internship, supporting a multiple server Windows Server 2003 environment, servicing 200 users for an accounting firm*

▶ *Hired full-time postgraduation as the network administrator*

▶ *B.S. in Computer Science, Montclair State University, 2005*

Jennifer recently graduated from college and has been working for the past six months as a networking technician. She earned A+ and Network+ certifications as part of her undergraduate work and has gained valuable experience with on-the-job training through an internship program with a local accounting firm. Most important for Jennifer is to highlight her capacity to handle multiple important projects simultaneously (completing her coursework and holding down a full-time job) and her readiness to keep her skill set current with industry demands.

Defining Your Experience

Many recent IT college grads obsess over describing relevant, interesting, and impressive background experience. Some are so intimidated by their lack of hands-on experience, they resort to exaggerating or fabricating their personal histories.

Don't give in to this temptation. Stretching the truth on your résumé is always a mistake, particularly with IT positions. Most IT hiring managers include peer interviews as part of the interviewing process to help assess candidates' experience. A few simple questions by an experienced IT professional easily uncover how much you know. Exaggeration can mean automatic disqualification.

Relax. You have learned quite a bit in college. And, once you write this section of your résumé, you can tell your parents they got their money's worth. The following section can help you uncover your relevant experience. This involves two steps:

1. Uncovering your knowledge

2. Uncovering and applying your practical experience

What Have You Learned?

Ever wonder exactly what you learned from those endless theoretical college courses? A lot, in fact. Theory, design, and analysis courses go a long way on your résumé. First, these classes show you are trainable. You can learn. Employers like this. They also like knowing you know the basics—logical thinking, decision trees, redundancy planning, or whatever.

A simple way of discovering how much you know is to make a list of all the IT, math, and business courses you took in college, and then look up the descriptions of these courses in your school's course catalog as a refresher of what you've learned. Luckily, most course catalogs are available online these days, so it's not hard to copy-and-paste the descriptions into an impressive list. Table 6-1 is an example of the information you should look for and list.

TABLE 6-1   Skills Learned from College Courses

Course Title	Skills and Knowledge Gained
Introduction to Computer Science	Computer operating system (OS) architecture
	Hardware interfaces and OS software of computers
	Software engineering methodologies, including initial system specification, development, quality assurance, revisions, and deployment
	Develops initial design and programming skills using a high-level programming language (primarily C++/Java)
	Data structures, arrays, records, files, pointers, linked lists, trees, graphs, stacks, queues, and heaps
Computer Science II	Abstract behavior of classic data structures (stacks, queues, priority queues, tables, trees), alternative implementations, and analysis of time and space efficiency
	Recursion
	Object-oriented and functional programming
	Models of computation

TABLE 6-1   Skills Learned from College Courses (*continued*)

Course Title	Skills and Knowledge Gained
Introduction to Software Engineering	Introduction to the concepts, methods, and current practice of software engineering
	The study of large-scale software production, software life-cycle models as an organizing structure, principles and techniques appropriate for each stage of production
UNIX Operating System	UNIX system administration, including tools and utilities, shells, and mail and news administration
C Programming	Structured techniques, pointers, structures, classes, declarations, tools and libraries, I/O and file manipulation, application compilation, and abstract programmer-defined objects
Java Programming	Java object-oriented programming (OOP) principles, graphical user interface programming, SQL databases, and client/server programming techniques
Operating Systems and Computer Architecture	Systems structure and systems evaluation
	Memory management and process management
Programming Fundamentals	C
	Java
	C++
Relational Databases	Relational algebra, views, queries, normal forms, optimization, and incrementality
	Other models for databases: hierarchical and network models
	The entity-relationship model, knowledge bases, and exceptions
	Distributed databases
	Applications
	Programming in SQL and Oracle
Software Engineering and Object-Oriented Development	Large-scale application design using entity-relation and object-oriented models
	Management of large-scale projects, including version control, document traceability, and distributed development
	Testing, validation, and verification
	Introduction to formal methods, simulation as a tool
	Large-scale, team-oriented project
Systems Analysis/Design Theory	Fundamentals of development of successful computer-based information systems, with an emphasis on the roles of systems analysts, programmers, users, and management
	Definition of user requirements
	Systems analysis life cycle
Database Theory	In-depth coverage of the content of database management systems (DBMS), including physical and logical database structures using Oracle
Introduction to SQL	Foundations of SQL commands for business applications
HTML Programming	Web design, HTML, FrontPage, Dreamweaver, JavaScript

TABLE 6-1 Skills Learned from College Courses (*continued*)

Course Title	Skills and Knowledge Gained
AS/400 Programming	Control Language (CL) for message handling, data queues, data areas, logic statements, program calls, and asynchronous jobs
Oracle	Database design, objects, data integrity, security, and performance tuning
Networking Essentials	Networking architecture, transmission concepts, and management
	OSI model
	TCP/IP, server installation, applications, user management, workgroup management, printing, and security
	Windows Server
	Client/server
	Network cabling
VB Programming	VB, database creation and access, inter-application communication, advanced printing techniques, and graphics
	Event-driven programs
	Advanced access programming
	Graphical user interface (GUI) design
C++ Programming	Object-oriented programming (OOP)
	Microsoft Foundation Classes
	GUI programs
	Pointers, memory management, and user-defined types
	Object linking and embedding (OLE) automation
	Dynamic Data Exchange (DDE)
	Large application design and development

Uncovering Your Practical Experience

Most computer science or MIS programs include hands-on projects. Some come in the form of course projects, others in senior projects and, best of all, internships.

Course projects and senior projects are practical applications of your theoretical knowledge. With the fast-paced IT environment out there, finding a computer science program that teaches the latest and greatest of the commercial applications and languages used in today's business environment is difficult. And, it is next to impossible to hire leading-edge developers to teach in a college environment or to find college professors who are truly involved in real IT business projects. Nonetheless, your college projects offer considerable experience that can be represented as practical experience on your résumé.

Make a list of the experience you accomplished. The things to pull out of this list include:

▶ Real-world application languages you can program in (C#, .NET, Java, HTML, XML)

▶ Use of commercial applications (Microsoft Excel, Microsoft Word, Macromedia Flash)

▶ Use of real-world processes for planning, design, and project management (Microsoft Visio, Microsoft Project, Microsoft Visual Studio)

▶ Management of networking systems (Windows Server 2003, Novell NetWare, Sun Solaris)

▶ Operation of computer operating systems (Windows XP, Windows 2000 Professional, UNIX, Linux)

▶ Development of databases using commercial software (Microsoft SQL, Oracle, Sybase)

▶ Understanding of ERP systems (SAP)

Internships are more common with IS degrees from business management schools. They offer an excellent opportunity to gain hands-on experience in a true business environment. Most last only a single semester, so you can't expect to get much real experience, but you do get a sense of what it means to work within a team of IS people.

If you've completed an internship, it shows you have initiative. Hiring managers value that more than the actual experience you may have gained. The key things employers look for from internships are:

▶ Application of basic skill set

▶ Introduction to real-world applications, programming languages, and development processes

▶ Accountability

▶ Ability to perform under a deadline

▶ Project planning and documentation experience

▶ Project ownership and responsibility

▶ Ability to work as part of a team

Pulling It All Together

The best way to describe the skills you pick up from course projects and internships is to use a skills-based résumé or functional résumé layout. A *skills-based résumé* works best when your skills are more impressive than your job titles. As the name suggests, this kind of résumé highlights skills, while deemphasizing actual employment dates by presenting a condensed work history at the bottom of the résumé. This is a great way to present significant skills gained from a position that lasted a short period of time—such as an internship.

A skills-based résumé organizes your skills into categories and lets you list your knowledge under these headings, such as the following:

▶ Programming and Analysis

▶ Database Design

▶ Computer System Administration

▶ PC Support and User Training

▶ Network Analysis and Documentation

▶ Customer Support

▶ Computer Math

▶ Data Integrity

▶ Computer Applications

▶ Systems Analysis

▶ Internet Development

▶ Business Management

▶ Operations Management

The next step is to review the job posting you're applying for. Identify the key skills they're seeking and pick out the relevant skill headings you should include. Any other knowledge and skills you feel would make you a better candidate for the position should be categorized under a functional heading of "Additional Skills." Practical experience should be interspersed with the knowledge and skills you have acquired. Look to include three to six supporting statements under each skills heading, including examples of your practical experience.

Figure 6-1 shows a sample résumé that doesn't maximize college experience well. Figure 6-2 shows the same information presented differently, to create a much more effective résumé. Without much editing, we were able to draw attention from the fact that Nick has only been working as a helpdesk technician for three months, has yet to earn his B.A. degree, and had previous unrelated experience. Here's what we did:

▶ Removed the objective statement. It had too many buzzwords and was too generic.

▶ Introduced the "Profile" section.

▶ Moved up and renamed the "Special Skills" section to "Technical Skills," and then listed skills in bulleted format.

▶ Added computer coursework information to provide more details around your major course of study.

▶ Eliminated "Interests" section, which is irrelevant to employers.

NICK RUHN
6109 Rosemont Street
Long Beach, CA 90888

Residence: (555) 555-6666   e-mail: nlruhn21@hotmail.com

OBJECTIVE   To obtain a challenging position in a progressive company, utilizing abilities developed through experience and education, with the opportunities for professional growth based on performance.

EDUCATION   California State University, Fullerton. B.A. degree expected 12/06
Major: Business Administration
Concentration: Management Information Systems
GPA in major: B average

EXPERIENCE   Cool Fuel Incorporated, Paramount, CA. 9/2000–Present
Position: Technical Support Intern
Duties: Assisted in the transition from Windows NT to Windows Server 2003. Performed administrative duties on the network, provided technical support on the network and user level, wrote programs for company reports in Visual Basic, Excel, and Crystal Reports.
CSU Business School Computer Lab, Fullerton, CA 2004–06
Position: Lab technician
Duties: Managed the school's computer lab facilities. Provided technical support to faculty, administrators, and students.
Trader Joe's, Long Beach, CA 2002–04
Position: Clerk
Duties: Customer service, order writing, stocking, and coordinating employees in distributing work duties.

SPECIAL SKILLS   Visual Basic, SQL, Microsoft Access, C++, Microsoft Office, Windows 95/98/XP, Windows NT/2003, knowledge of networking and TCP/IP, the ability to learn software, strong written and oral communication skills, strong organizational skills, and a team player.

INTERESTS   Snowboarding, surfing, mountain biking, running, and a lover for the outdoors.

FIGURE 6-1 An example of an ineffective résumé

Striking the Right Balance

As you can see, a recent college grad's résumé needn't appear skimpy or unimpressive. Draw on the knowledge you've acquired, the practical projects you've worked on, and your internships and part-time jobs. Demonstrate your ability and willingness to handle a responsible full-time position, even if it is your first such job.

6108 Rosemont Street, Long Beach, CA 90888 ▪ (555) 555-6666 ▪ nlruhn21@hotmail.com

Nick Ruhn

Profile	▪ Honors Management Information Systems major with extensive coursework and lab hours in programming (C#, .NET) and networking (Windows Server 2003)
	▪ Excellent communication and problem-solving skills for resolving user issues quickly and courteously
	▪ Seeking to leverage and apply existing history of strong academic achievement, problem resolution, and analytical skills in a corporate environment

Technical Skills	**Languages/ Databases**	VB 6.0, SQL, Access, C#, ASP, VBScript, HTML, Visual Studio 2005
	Systems	Windows 95/98/XP, Windows Server 2003
	Networking	IPX/SPX, TCP/IP, IPv6, FTP, SMTP, HTTP, HTTPS, POP3/IMAP4, DHCP, DNS, WINS
	Software	MS Office, Crystal Reports, Norton Anti-Virus

Education	California State University, Fullerton, CA Anticipated December 2006
	Major: Business Administration with a concentration in Management Information Systems
	GPA in major: A- Overall GPA: B+
	Coursework highlights: Advanced application development (SDLC, RUP), Services Operations Management, Technology Management, Project Management, Business Systems Analysis, Fundamentals of Computer Networking

Employment History	**Technical Support Analyst (Intern)**	Cool Fuel Inc., Paramount, CA	2006–Present
	▪ Assisted in the upgrading of five servers from Windows NT to Windows 2003		
	▪ Perform system administration for 150 users, including user creation, systems backups, security administration, and network printer configuration		
	▪ Provide networking technical support		
	▪ Developed reports in Excel, Visual Basic, and Crystal Reports		
	Computer Lab Technician	CSU Fullerton	2004–06
	▪ Part-time position managing the business school's computer lab facilities, consisting of 50 PCs, 10 MACs, and 5 mainframe terminals		
	▪ Provide technical support to faculty, administrators, and students on MS Office Suite and course-specific software		
	Clerk	Trader Joe's	2002–04

FIGURE 6-2 Pulling it all together

But, be careful not to go too far. Don't exaggerate or stretch the importance and degree of responsibility of your past jobs. Depending on the breadth of your background, a one-page résumé may be long enough. This is the rule especially if you have never held a full-time position.

You strike a bargain when applying for your first post-college job. You offer your talent, knowledge, and hard work in exchange for a salary and benefits on the assumption that the value you'll create for your employer will be worth at least as much as the income you'll receive. You can offer an extra measure of enthusiasm, energy, and dedication in exchange for the opportunity to learn and grow on the job. You must be willing to "pay your dues." You are starting at the bottom and are going to work your way up. Always remember, this is your first job and it will be an extension of your learning experience. Keep your expectations in check and you will be successful.

Paper Certifications

Paper certifications are a hot issue with IT professionals—those who have certification but no experience, and those who don't have certification but have years of on-the-job experience.

In the beginning, certifications were a sure-fire way of getting your foot in the door. Companies desperately needed knowledgeable professionals to get the job done. But, as the number of certifications granted has increased dramatically over the years, the value of a certification has decreased—and so has the cost involved in earning it.

IT professionals who are *paper-certified*, or who have earned a certification without previous work experience, face the same issues as recent college graduates. Without hands-on credentials, employers look at these candidates as entry-level professionals whom they will have to train.

Of course, certifications are valuable. Formal technology education provides crucial knowledge, something employers value greatly. If you do not have the experience to back up your certification, your résumé must stress your foundation knowledge and skill set *and* how trainable you are. Certainly, you will have an edge over other candidates applying for entry-level positions.

Figure 6-3 provides an example of how to turn a run-of-the-mill résumé into an effective résumé for candidates without much work experience. Nothing is wrong with admitting you just earned your certifications, especially if you don't have relevant job experience. Admit this up front and focus on your strengths. Here's what we did to alter the original résumé, shown in Figure 6-3, to make it much more effective.

▶ Strengthened the "Summary of Qualifications" section by combining technical and soft skills under one section.

▶ Used a skills-based résumé format.

▶ Focused on technology, job tasks, and processes learned as part of earning the certifications.

▶ Trimmed down the jobs listed outside of IT, to focus more on Tracy's technical skills rather than non IT experience.

▶ Substantiated certification and college experience with actual dates and course hours.

The key is to demonstrate what you learned and can do.

Tracy Johnson
13840 Riviera Street / Los Alamos, CA 88787
(555) 555-1098 / tjohnson@gmail.com

COMPUTER SKILLS

- Windows 95
- Windows 98
- Windows 2003
- DOS
- Internet
- HTML
- MS Office
- FrontPage

SUMMARY OF QUALIFICATIONS

MCSA for Server 2003 – Microsoft Certified Systems Administrator
A+ Computer Technician
Training and supervisory skills
Excellent presentation, oral, and written communication skills

PROFESSIONAL EXPERIENCE

FADZ Inc., Fullerton, CA   2003–05
Manager
- Analyzed and provided production reports to the management team
- Increased efficiencies through in-depth operational analysis
- Forecasted and planned financial position
- Interview and selected sales staff
- Advised and supported senior management on financial operations and performance

Flynn Signs & Graphics, Long Beach, CA   2000–03
Sales

- Generated sales of $200,000 of $2M annually
- Implemented and integrated revenue generating programs
- Increased revenue through market research and promotion
- Established customer requirements, schedules, and ground rules for numerous projects

Insight Design, Cerritos, CA   1998–00
Account Representative

- Performed pricing and bid analysis for sales team
- Utilized information technology to meet company and customer requirements
- Generated new customer base and achieved production standards
- Investigated and provided timely solutions to customer problems
- Sold and demonstrated products

EDUCATION

Learning Tree International, Irvine, CA
    MCSA for Server 2003
    A+ Computer Technician

Cypress College, Cypress, CA
    Completed two years of a four-year degree

FIGURE 6-3   The original paper certification example

Career Changer

Just a couple of decades ago, job-hopping was practically unheard of. People almost always stayed in the same careers and rarely even left the company that first hired them, potentially working for one company for at least 30 years! Today, pension plans have given way to 401(k) plans, which transfer from company-to-company, and there's a reason: job-hopping is a reality. And, career changing isn't at all uncommon today.

The IT industry has opened opportunities over the last 20 years that were unavailable to previous generations. With the gamut of jobs available in this industry, it continues to be a popular alternative to military careers, bartending, and construction work. The IT industry is also an upgrade path from traditional office work, marketing, and sales. The many different areas of specialization mean something is available for everyone—from programming and systems analysis to sales, support, project management, and even recruiting.

The perks are great—potential for six-figure salaries with a few years under your belt, flexible working hours, exciting travel—but, as technology becomes more complex, it gets harder to make the transition. The learning curve is longer than it was 20 years ago when networking was in its infancy, the de facto programming language was COBOL, and you only had one real database system to learn. There is simply more to learn to be qualified for entry-level positions. But, the prognosis is good for career changers, as tens of thousands of IT positions will still go unfilled in the United States alone over the next few years because of the lack of IT professionals to fill them.

Setting Realistic Expectations

Making a dramatic career change, such as moving from a blue-collar job to becoming a programmer, takes a long time. In many ways, career changers are in the same position as recent college graduates—facing a résumé with a recently granted certification, but not much in the area of practical experience. Unfortunately, this will be magnified by the need for immediate returns on putting that certification or two-year degree to work. Career changers are typically older individuals who have families to support and loans for their training to repay. This intensifies the need to find a good paying job as quickly as possible.

You may also come face-to-face with some harsh realities when looking for your first IT job. Because career changers are typically older workers, they may face age discrimination. How well will you fit in with a team of considerably younger recent college graduates? Do you have the energy to go the extra mile? Will your family obligations allow you to put in the longer hours? How much more will your benefits cost the organization? These questions are not here to discourage you, but rather to heighten your awareness. You need to address these issues in your résumé to increase potential employers' comfort with hiring you over someone younger.

You also have to face your own expectations of what jobs are available to career changers. What probably sold you to change your career was the opportunity of earning a high paying salary, job security, and the availability of many jobs. This is all true within the IT industry, but the common disclaimer applies: your results may vary. A career changer who recently earned their certification could have some difficulties in landing a job that meets all the previous expectations without practical, hands-on experience.

Even doctors need to go through a residency period before they are allowed to go out on their own. The same is true with IT professionals. Your first job will be tough. The money may not all be there, and the hours will be grueling, but you're going to learn what you need for your next job. Don't be fooled by the thousands of job openings. Take a look at your local paper to see what's *really* available in your area. Most likely, the job openings are for mid-level IT positions for workers with at least two or three years of experience. These are the realities most people face once they enter the job market. If you are aware of these realities and have planned for them, you won't be disillusioned and you're going to have a more successful time with your job hunt.

Your first job may not be your dream job, but with two to three years of experience, you'll be on your way to greater opportunities.

What You Have to Offer: Transitioning Your Skill Set

Career changers often have plenty of job experience—in the wrong kind of jobs. IT is specialized. Hiring managers are looking for candidates with specific technical skills. Much of your hard-earned experience is completely irrelevant. But, every cloud has a silver lining. Careful presentation of your past experience can set you ahead of college grads who have never been in the workforce before.

Unlike people seeking new positions in their current fields who want to present specific experience, career changers need to present a generic background—that is, emphasize skills rather than the specific responsibilities of current or former positions. Feel free to drastically simplify the job listings from your former life.

In addition, depending on how dramatic your career change is, you may want to deemphasize your previous employers. Force people to pay more attention to the skills you have to offer than to the names of your former employers. You can accomplish this in different ways.

Skills over Function

Experts say the average adult changes careers at least three times in their lifetime. Does this mean they start all over again each time? Probably not. Much experience can carry over from one job to the next and from one career to the next. A career change is an opportunity to apply lessons learned in working in one environment to the next. Career changers have a leg up on recent graduates. The trick is to write your résumé so it focuses on the skills, rather than on the job titles you've had.

To do so, we recommend you create a skills-based résumé rather than a chronological résumé. A skills-based résumé draws out your knowledge and skills, and it makes them more prominent on paper. Job history is downplayed by simply listing your employment history at the end of the résumé, with little information about the actual company and job. For an example of how to do this, see Figure 6-4.

We provided an example of someone who would like to make a career change from property management to IT sales. Jan has lots of experience, but none of it is directly supporting a position in IT. The goal is to demonstrate how he can be a valuable asset to any organization. In Figure 6-5, the skills-based résumé we created eliminates the outdated and irrelevant history, and now highlights Jan's ability to apply his general business knowledge to an IT position and

---

Tracy Johnson
13840 Riviera Street / Los Alamos, CA 88787
(555) 555-1098 / tjohnson@gmail.com

SUMMARY OF QUALIFICATIONS:

- Recent A+ / MCSA certified professional with hands-on experience in computer hardware troubleshooting and installation, and Windows Server 2003 administration
- Customer-focus driven, highly motivated, fast learner with excellent verbal communication skills and professional etiquette
- Six years business operations, management, and sales experience outside of IT

KEY KNOWLEDGE AREAS

PC Hardware/Operating Systems

- Install/configure PC/MACs desktop & laptops and peripherals (external storage, PDA, WAP, UPS)
- Preventive PC maintenance (defragging, scan disk, CHKDSK)
- Troubleshooting Windows (OS recovery, bluescreen, system lock-up, device conflicts)
- Troubleshoot HW/SW problems by working with users
- Install/config/upgrade Windows 95/98/XP
- Optimizing Windows configs (device drivers, virtual memory, temp files)
- Application install and configure

Networking

- Install/configure NICs, Internet access, and troubleshoot network connectivity problems
- Configure wireless connectivity (802.11, 802.11x, infrared, Bluetooth)
- Manage/maintain/optimizing server hardware (RAID, defragging volumes and partitions)
- Troubleshooting server hardware-device settings and drivers
- Monitor/analyze events, software update infrastructure, software site licensing, and remote server management
- Backup/recovery of files and systems
- Manage/test disaster recovery procedures (ASR, restoring data from shadow copy volumes, back up files and system state data to media, and configuring security for backup operations)
- Configure IPX/SPX, TCP/IP, IPv6, FTP, SMTP, HTTP, HTTPS, POP3/IMAP4, DHCP, DNS, and WINS
- Monitor/analyze events, software update infrastructure, software site licensing, and remote server management
- Manage user profiles and groups
- Create and manage accounts using Active Directory
- Troubleshooting user accounts, including resolving account lockouts and authentication issues
- Provide access to shared folders, troubleshoot terminal services, and configure files system permissions

FIGURE 6-4   From paper certification to professional résumé

```
EDUCATION & TRAINING
Learning Tree International – Irvine, CA                              2006
MCSA Certification
A+ Certification
    ▪ Nine-month intensive-training program, which included internships at the school.
Cypress College                                                    2003–05
    Sixty credit hours in general education and business management courses.
EMPLOYMENT HISTORY
FADZ Inc. / Sales Manager                                          2003–05
Flynn Signs / Account Executive                                   2000–03
Insight Design / Account Representative                           1998–00
```

FIGURE 6-4 *Continued*

his entrepreneurial experience, management, and sales skills. The possible positions Jane can immediately pursue include technical sales and technical customer service positions.

For IT professionals, the most important skills to present first are your technical skills. These should appear at the beginning of your skills section. Next, list all your other skills, whether they are management, project management, or sales. Chapter 4 provides detailed information on how to discover your hidden talents and skills to feature in a skills-based résumé.

Masking Your Previous Employers

If you are making dramatic career changes, deemphasize the names of your previous employers. As hiring managers sift through the pile of potential candidates, don't leave it up to them to have to make the connection between how your previous work experience relates to the job you are applying for. If a potential employer sees the name of an employer that is clearly in a different industry, they are likely to have preconceived notions of what your responsibilities were.

To avoid this dilemma, you can do several things. Keep to a functional, rather than chronological, format that enables you to present work history as the last part of your résumé. There, list employer names and employment dates only.

The next thing is to find alternative ways of listing the employers' names. Consider listing only the name of the company or parent organization without references to departments or divisions. You might also abbreviate the name of the company.

Many career changers are making the transition from military careers to the private sector. Private employers without military experience often have a hard time transferring military skills to the private sector. Unfamiliar with leadership and technology skills acquired in a

Jan Holmes
1654 234th St.
Laguna Hills, CA 90734
jholmes@aol.com
home: (555) 345-5555

February 19, 2002

Dear Hiring Manager,

I am submitting my résumé for consideration for the channel sales position listed in the Sunday *Los Angeles Times* on February 3, 2002. After 24 years in sales and management as an independent business owner, I believe that I bring a well-rounded set of skills that meet the requirements advertised for this position. I'd like to highlight some in particular that fit well with the position advertised.

- Entrepreneurial spirit from having owned and managed my own business for over 12 years
- Experienced in solution selling
- Technically knowledgeable
- Broad software knowledge
- Customer service focus

I have been involved with computers for over 15 years and have experience with building and upgrading computer systems for standalone as well as LAN systems. I am A+ certified and am currently pursuing NT and CCNA certificates. I have been attending Cerritos College on weeknights and Saturdays. To date, I've completed Network Fundamentals, LAN, WAN, and Cisco TCP/IP courses. As testament to my diverse capabilities, I was instrumental in helping the Cerritos Computer Lab move to a different location during the past year. This involved OS installs, mostly Windows NT 4.0, setting up of routers, hubs, and switches, and manufacturing RJ45 cables. I have also had hands-on experience with Cisco routers. I am very familiar with Windows 95, 98, NT 4.0, ME, 2000 Pro, MS-Office 97–2000 Pro, and have working knowledge of Linux/Mandrake 7.4. Due to my continual usage of upgrades and trial version software, I am well versed in a broad platform of software being used with cutting-edge companies.

I would like to meet with you to discuss your opportunity in more detail. I am available for a personal interview at your earliest convenience

Sincerely,

Jan Holmes

Jan Holmes

Enclosures: Résumé

FIGURE 6-5   Skills-based résumé for career changers and the accompanying cover letter

Jan Holmes
1654 234th St.
Laguna Hills, CA 90734
jholmes@aol.com
home: (555) 345-5555

Objective

I am seeking to apply my 24 years of sales and management experience to a position selling technical solutions.

Summary of Qualifications

- Seasoned sales and management professional experienced in solution selling
- Entrepreneurial spirit with over 12 years experience in running own businesses
- Technically knowledgeable with over 15 years computer experience and broad software knowledge

Technical Skills

Networking: LAN/WAN, Windows NT 4.0, Novell NetWare, Linux, Cisco, TCP/IP
Software: DOS, Windows 95/98, Windows 2000 Professional, Internet Explorer 5, Netscape 4/6, Access, PowerPoint, Photoshop, Norton Utilities, and various anti-virus software
Certifications: A+ certified, pursuing MCSE and CCNA

- Set up a network in our main office
- Made several databases using Access for direct marketing

Experience

PC/Networking

- Hands-on experience in the installation of the Cerritos College computer lab, including installation of Windows NT servers, configuration of Cisco routers, hubs, and switches, and cabling installation
- Management of Windows NT, including setting up and configuring user accounts, printing environment, and security
- PC software installation and upgrades

Small Business Sales and Operations

- Independent organic coffee distributor servicing grocery food chain stores working directly with store managers
- Established and built up custom shower wall business
- Four years experience in managing all business operations
- Proven ability to drive sales (40% increase in the first year of operation)
- Personnel management, including hiring and training installation team
- Effective inventory control and production

FIGURE 6-5   *Continued*

Property Management

- Managed eight apartment buildings totaling 850 units.
- Trained and supervised 26 employees ranging from managers to leasing agents and maintenance personnel.
- Prepared budgets and stayed within budgets while improving properties and clientele.
- Managed property advertisements in newspapers and magazines.
- Oversaw all outsourced bids and contracts for work needed.
- Provided weekly revenue and operations reports to executive management.

Work History

1999–Present	Branch Office Manager, Shower Walls, San Gabriel, CA
1998–1999	Owner, Holmes Showers, Modesto, CA
1998–1998	Property Manager, IRM Corporation, Concord, CA
1987–1998	Self-employed, Coffee Distributorship, Modesto, CA

Education

A.S. Network Administration, Cerritos College, Cerritos, CA

FIGURE 6-5 *Continued*

military environment, they don't understand the similarities in the use of technology, project management, and leadership. This is unfortunate, because military candidates often possess a highly developed set of skills that lend themselves well to a corporate environment. Here are some of the key things to remember:

▶ Don't assume that potential employers will understand military technical terms. Whenever possible, provide nonmilitary descriptions of networks, systems, and technologies.

▶ Consider using a functional résumé to provide a more comprehensive description of your abilities. By breaking out your technology, management, and leadership skills, your potential employer can get a broader perspective of your abilities and accomplishments.

▶ Be sure to spell out ambiguous job titles. Nonmilitary potential employers (particularly recruiters) may be put off by oversimplified, nondescriptive job titles or ranks.

Transition to Management

Making the transition from technician to technical management is the next step for some IT professionals. Again, beware the double-edged sword: management moves you beyond the helpdesk and earning additional certifications, but this may mean an end to the hands-on work that brought you to IT in the first place.

When you make the move to management, you may lose the "cool factor"—the opportunity to apply your creativity by maximizing the potential of software and hardware for new product releases. But, new doors may open. As chief information officer (CIO) or chief technology officer (CTO), you may help determine what the next big thing will be.

If you're ready to make the switch, you may wonder how you get from here to there. Demonstrating you have acquired the skill set to effectively lead a department and manage a business is critical. Downplay your technical background; emphasize your managerial potential. The skill sets you want to demonstrate are:

▶ How to hold effective meetings

▶ How to conduct performance evaluations

▶ How to write a proposal or report

▶ How to put together a project plan

▶ How to deliver a presentation to various audiences

▶ How to deal with difficult employees

▶ How to effectively plan your resources

▶ How to build and motivate a team of technical professionals

Samples of management résumés are included in Chapter 11.

Problem History

How nice it would be to graduate from college, find a great entry-level position, and then move up the corporate ladder from one wonderful job to the next, without a glitch along the way. Unfortunately, life doesn't quite work this way. We all have to face challenges in our careers and personal lives that affect our professional history. Some face these challenges voluntarily, such as the personal choice to start a family, while some are a circumstance of health or family issues. Even if you are able to cope with these issues, they may still come back to haunt you and your résumé. Perspective employers may see disruptions in work history as potential problems and may eliminate you from consideration.

The types of issues we address in this section include:

▶ Missing years of work

▶ Too many jobs

▶ Too few jobs

▶ Lack of formal education

▶ Being laid off, fired, or having been involved in a scandal

Missing Years of Work

Many people have, for one reason or another, unemployment gaps in their work history. Whether it is six months or six years, an employment gap may raise questions from the hiring manager. Depending on the length of time you were out of work, you may want or need to camouflage these gaps, so they are not prominent on your résumé.

Looking for Work

Taking a few months off in between jobs is common. The easiest way to prevent any questions from being raised regarding any time off is to represent the number of years of employment with each company, rather than being specific about months and years. For example:

Implementation Consultant, KPMG, New York, NY	*December 1995–April 1999*
Software Engineer, AMA, New York, NY	*January 1992–April 1995*

You can change them to read:

Implementation Consultant, KPMG, New York, NY	*1995–1999*
Software Engineer, AMA, New York, NY	*1992–1995*

As you can see, the eight-month gap simply disappears.

Returning to School or Raising a Family

If you returned to college for a graduate degree or took time off to raise a family, you may have a gap of a year or more. A simple solution is to include the reason for such gaps within the job descriptions themselves. For example:

Implementation Consultant, KPMG, New York, NY	*1992–1994*
Left to pursue M.B.A., NYU, August 1994	

or

Software Engineer, AMA, New York, NY	*1995–1999*
Left after birth of first child, July 1999	

So often, hiring managers are simply looking to cover all the dates. Amazing as it may seem, they don't always care what's written there, as long as the dates make sense.

Too Many Jobs

Another potential problem area may be having too many jobs in a relatively short time. Job-hopping no longer carries the stigma it once did. The average person is estimated to have seven to ten jobs in the course of a 40-year career. Having four different jobs in the course of five years is not a big deal. But, there is a point at which "several" jobs become "a lot of" jobs, and prospective employers start questioning your commitment, discipline, and loyalty.

IT professionals who do a lot of contract work may be faced with this dilemma. The best approach is to be as brief as possible about the job responsibilities *and* to focus on describing the projects you worked on. This helps focus employers on what you accomplished in each of these positions.

Handling Contract Positions

For those of you in the contracting world, your résumé may read as a long list of projects. That's OK as long as you bring those projects to life and help employers see how your experience may be valuable to them. For more tips on how to present your experience, see Chapter 11.

The Dream Job Turned Bad

We have all had these experiences—the dream job turned nightmare. The job you probably should have researched a bit more and asked more questions during the interview process turns bad and you leave. So what do you do? Generally, the rule of thumb is, if you held a job for less than three months, don't list it. Keep that one experience between you and the ex-employer rather than risk opening questions that draw you in defensively trying to explain why it wasn't your fault. If no one has let you in on this secret yet, it might be time for us to do so. There is no employment "permanent record." Only you, the ex-employer, and the Social Security Administration have any records of your previous employment.

If omitting a job leaves a gap in your employment history, you may want to consider camouflaging it, using the method previously described—only referencing dates of employment by their years.

Several Jobs, Same Company

When you work for the same company for more than five years, you may end up having held five different positions within that timeframe. Although this demonstrates great mobility and recognition of your talents, it may also be misconstrued by hiring managers as job-hopping. An easy way to paint this situation in a different light is how you group your positions within your résumé.

For example, here is an IT professional who spent six years working for a systems integration company. During those years, she held progressively higher positions.

Sr. Consultant, Methodologies and Best Practices   *2006–2008*

  SBA Integration / Consulting Services Division

Sr. Systems Engineer, Major Accounts   *2004–2006*

  SBA Integration / Sales Division

Sr. Technical Instructor   *2002–2004*

  SBA Integration / Education Division

One way to represent the same experience without listing each branch of the company separately is to use the following format.

SBA Integration, Springfield, IL

▶ Sr. Consultant, Methodologies and Best Practices — 2006–2008

▶ Sr. Systems Engineer, Major Accounts — 2004–2006

▶ Sr. Technical Instructor — 2002–2004

Too Few Jobs

While having too many jobs on your résumé is a bigger problem, sometimes having too few jobs can also been seen as a problem by hiring managers. Of course, you might have a perfectly good reason to have held a small number of positions, especially if you are new to the workforce.

One Job Too Long

Too much job-hopping is bad, but sometimes staying in the same position for too long (more than three years) may not be a good thing either. Staying in the same position raises questions of ability to learn and take on new responsibilities, enthusiasm for one's job, and general issues of whether you are someone worth promoting. As is often the case, the longer you stay, the more responsibilities you take on, so talk about those.

New to the Workforce

If you are new to the workforce, you have an easy answer to why you have only held limited positions. Refer to the previous section in this chapter on recent college graduates for examples of how to address this situation using a qualifications section.

Lack of Formal Education

Another potential problem, depending on the position you are applying for, is the lack of formal education. Typically, this means a two-year or four-year college degree. Even though IT certifications can get you into the entry-level positions, managerial positions, including development manager and director positions, require a formal degree. CIO positions may also even require an M.B.A.. The higher your ambitions, the more likely a degree is necessary.

In IT, one way to compensate for the lack of a degree is through certifications and significant on-the-job experience. If you are applying for a job that lists a degree as a requirement, don't lose heart. By emphasizing your experience in a qualifications section at the beginning of your résumé, you can draw the hiring manager in with your skills and knowledge, and divert him from the educational section. You can then downplay the educational section. The result of all this is, on reading your résumé, the reader may not even notice you don't have a college degree.

Layoffs and Firings

Two final scenarios may be red flags to hiring managers: layoffs and firings. Luckily, résumés don't have a "Layoffs and Firings" section, so it is neither necessary nor appropriate to bring these up on your résumé. Be assured, though, these issues come up when you go on an interview. For this reason, it's important you prepare what you will say about them in advance of any such discussion. See Chapter 10 on acing the interview for more help planning your strategy.

Layoffs

If you have recently been laid off from your job, it is important for you to realize that layoffs are incredibly common these days. Mergers, downsizing, and reorganizations have made pink slips a way of life. The hiring manager himself may have been laid off from one of his previous positions. So, instead of feeling as if you did something wrong to bring about the layoff and that it will brand you for life, stop right now. Going into an interview with a defensive attitude about this situation is unnecessary.

Be open and honest, and don't blame your previous employer. "My entire department was eliminated when we lost second-round funding" is a perfectly acceptable description. If you can add something like, "Overall, it was worth the risk—it was exciting to work in such a cutting-edge field," so much the better. You come across as a big person.

Firings

It's not easy to be fired. Whether the firing is performance-based or not, it hurts your confidence and self-esteem. But, remember, even if you did lose your job for performance reasons, your life is not meaningless. The job may not have played to your strengths.

Instead of beating yourself up, consider this an opportunity to find a job or career better suited to your aptitudes and strengths. As with layoffs, it is best if you do not make reference to having been fired on your résumé.

Swallow hard, shoulder some of the blame, and make a point of stressing what you learned from the situation, "Unfortunately, my manager and I disagreed on some of my job responsibilities. I've had to take a long look at my immediate and overall career goals. If I found myself in that situation again, here's how I'd handle it differently."

Again, Chapter 10 offers more examples on how to handle this situation in an interview.

Summing It Up

Don't get hung up on one "bad" part of your résumé. You can still create a résumé that will catch a hiring manager's eye and land you the job you want. Never forget, presentation is everything—present yourself professionally and that's how you'll be treated.

Remember your goal: to get a hiring manager to single out your résumé for attention. Bear this in mind as you address the problem areas of your résumé, and the solutions will come easily.

Chapter 7

Creative Ways to Get Hands-On Experience

How many times have you run into this situation? You open the paper to find ten ads for the system administrator position you have been seeking, but the ad calls for one to two years of experience. You just earned your MCSE. It's the IT professional's "chicken and the egg" dilemma: how do you get that first job without having the hands-on experience it requires? In Chapter 6, we focused on how to address this issue creatively on your résumé. In this chapter, we take a sidestep and provide you with examples of creative ways to get that experience.

In this chapter, we cover:

▶ Using your training center as a resource

▶ Volunteer work

▶ Building your own lab

▶ Simulations and paid labs

▶ Differentiating yourself from the other applicants

Getting Experience at Your Training Center

Many career changers begin their IT careers at their local training center. Training centers offer a full suite of training options for you. The good ones provide you with a career counselor who can work with you throughout your training and certification process. They map out your course work, lab work, and, possibly, work with you on placement. Throughout the country, niche training centers are popping up that specialize in providing intensive training programs that result in placement with local employers. In return for free or virtually free training, they take a cut of your first year's salary to repay the training costs. This is a great alternative to financing your education on your own.

A more traditional alternative is an unpaid internship through your training center. Internships typically are one-to-three months of placement with a local company, where you can get hands-on experience doing PC support, helpdesk duty, or general end user support. This is a great way of setting your expectations and getting an idea of what areas you want to work in once you are ready to join the full-time workforce. And, the experience looks great on your résumé.

Another way to maximize your experience while you're still earning your certification is to get hands-on experience at your training center. Here are some ideas that go a long way toward getting you the experience you need and creating a network of professionals who might help you land a job after your training is finished:

▶ Volunteer to help set up your next class or lab.

▶ Stay after class to complete or redo labs you didn't get to do in class.

▶ Redo the labs by trying out other configuration options, especially manual configurations, rather than using the product wizards.

▶ Ask to shadow a more experienced classmate on a typical workday to get an idea how their time and skills are used.

▶ Volunteer to help the instructor on one of their consulting projects to get real-world experience (and networking opportunities).

The instructor will be grateful for the assistance, and the training center will appreciate the extra free help.

On the (Unpaid) Job Training

It's not glamorous. It's unpaid and many times unappreciated. It's called volunteer work. In the end, *volunteer work* is hands-on experience you can use on your résumé. Schools, churches, non-profit associations, friends, and family businesses all need extra help maintaining their PCs and managing their networks. This may mean upgrading their systems, installing new versions of software and operating systems (OSs), or customizing their environment so it's more streamlined and easy-to-use. At other times, your help can be in the form of providing training services. There is no better way of testing what you know than having to teach it to someone else. Skills transfer can help you make friends, get referrals for paying jobs, and secure excellent references.

To find these opportunities, let people know about your career change. Keep them current on where you are and what skills you have mastered. I still get phone calls from family members who want me to troubleshoot their systems, upgrade their hard drives or modems, and help them get connected to the Internet. Unfortunately, my technical skills are now limited to plugging my network cable in to the right jack, but I still get these calls occasionally.

Blogging and RSS Feeds

Where do you turn when you have a technical question? The most common places to look are *message boards* and *blogs*, which provide the most timely information on incompatibilities and bugs. You probably have your own collection of your favorite message boards and blogs. If you don't, it's time to start making your list and setting up your Really Simple Syndication (RSS) feeds to keep you in the know. This lets you monitor the message forums for your particular area of training or certification. When someone posts a technical question, try to solve it yourself. Wait a few days for a support person to answer the question and compare the results to your findings. You can learn a lot doing this, including building your research skills and understanding real-world problems with the technologies you are learning about.

Hands-On Experience at Home

No true IT professional is without their own home lab. Building your home lab is going to require hardware, software, and some creativity, so you don't break the bank. The benefits of having a home network are it lets you try out what you've learned, evaluate new software releases, try new technologies, and become more productive.

Hardware

Whether it is two PCs and an XBOX, you should invest in creating your own home network. This doesn't have to cost a fortune. Part of the fun of building your network is, literally, in building all the components from scratch. The typical hardware components you should include are:

▶ Multiple PCs, each configured with a different OS, ranging from older models to high-end machines

▶ Hub

▶ Router

▶ Networkable printer

▶ Cable or DSL modem

Major hardware vendors also sell their refurbished units at a considerable discount. Dell Computers offers great values on refurbished laptops and desktop systems. If a vendor doesn't advertise its refurbished equipment, give them a call anyway. Online auctions can sometimes yield good deals, as well. eBay.com is an excellent place to look for the components to round out your network. PC fairs and swap meets are also opportunities to pick up low-cost equipment.

TIP *Be creative in finding the equipment you seek for your home network. You can use the experience you gain when you land your new job. You can even list this procurement experience on your résumé to help you get that first job.*

Software

Getting the right software is also key for building your home lab and getting the right experience. The trouble here is affording to stay on top of the latest software. Vendors have made it easier, though, if you are tied in to the right places. Evaluation versions, beta versions, and certification versions can all be used to help you get on your way. In the following section, you see how to get your hands on these types of software.

What software should you be looking for to round out your network?

Major operating systems

▶ Microsoft Windows Server

▶ Linux

▶ UNIX

Application packages

▶ Microsoft Office

▶ Internet Explorer

Utilities

▶ VMWare

▶ Symantec Antivirus

Evaluation Versions

Most vendors now have two-week to 90-day evaluation (eval) copies of their software available to preview before you buy. Most of the software is downloadable from the Web. If the vendor doesn't provide an eval from its web site, don't hesitate to call them directly.

The downside of evaluation software is you might have to give it back. Most evaluation copies time out. You might also have to deal with a limited feature set. If you need access to the full version, call the software manufacturer and ask for an unlimited version. It doesn't hurt to ask.

Beta Versions

Trying out beta versions of the latest OSs and software packages is always fun. A certain cool factor is associated with being in with software vendors and on their beta distribution lists. Your home lab is the ideal place to test these new products, because you are, most likely, not playing with live, mission-critical business data. When beta software messes up your existing installation, this can be frustrating, though. Remember, you're taking your system into your own hands when you install beta software on it. Be sure to back up your system, just in case those bugs haven't been worked out yet.

Certification Benefits

Are you maximizing your certification benefits from Microsoft and Cisco? These software vendors offer tens of thousands of dollars worth of software free, or almost free, as part of the benefits they provide to the professionals they have certified.

Magic Software: VMWare

Want to maximize your hardware investment? How do experienced IT professionals do it? They use a product called *VMWare*, which lets you split up your machine into virtual machines, each capable of running different OSs. For more information on this magic product, visit the VMWare web site at http://www.vmware.com/.

Online Labs

Like simulations, *hands-on labs* on rented material (usually accessible over the Internet) let you work on high-end equipment without breaking your wallet. The way these labs typically run is that you rent time on the vendors' systems. Prices range from $60 on up, depending on how much time you need to complete the lab.

The advantages of this method of getting hands-on experience is you can work on real equipment, much like the equipment you will eventually work on at your job. Another advantage is these labs are often structured with real-work scenarios for you to try. An added advantage is they allow the flexibility to deviate from the prescribed lab, just in case you want to try out different configuration options. The disadvantage is the cost of the experience.

Beyond Hands-On Experience

No matter how much hands-on experience post-training you get, IT managers are always looking for professionals with the most extensive experience for the job. If you want top dollar, the truth is you have to work up to it by demonstrating your capabilities on the job. Most likely, you must start in an entry-level position. Why not get that over with as quickly as possible? This means paying your dues early on and demonstrating your capabilities, so you can progress with your career. Here are some tips on getting the experience you need to build a successful IT career in an entry-level position:

▶ Become an expert in one particular application product. Access and Excel are excellent choices because they are more and more in demand within organizations. Most entry-level professionals settle on learning OSs, but those who are noticed most quickly are those who can work "magic" for executives using the applications they need to do their jobs.

▶ Take on difficult users and brush up your soft skills. Today's successful IT professional relies not only on technical skills, but also on people skills. Knowing how to survive in a corporate

HECTOR LOPEZ
121 Lions Avenue
Garden Grove, CA 92843
Home: (555) 554-5554 Email: hlopez@hotmail.com

Objective

Hard-working, recently certified IT professional seeking an entry-level position providing helpdesk support and network maintenance.

Summary of Qualifications

- Self-directed, results-oriented MCSE professional
- Highly motivated and eager to learn and apply new skills
- Strong interpersonal communication skills
- Work well independently and as part of a larger team

Technical Skills

- Windows NT, Windows 95/98
- MS Internet Information Server, MS Office 2000/97, QuickBooks, Outlook

Work Experience

Network Administrator, YMCA, Los Angeles, CA   2001 – Present

- Volunteer ten hours per week performing network administration and PC support services at the local YMCA
- Set up a 15-user Windows NT network with DSL Internet connectivity
- Configured MS Outlook email system and Internet Explorer
- Perform troubleshooting for hardware and software problems
- Install applications, upgrade PCs, and provide overall general maintenance of a Windows NT network

PC Support, Our Lady of the Nativity Church, Los Angeles, CA   2001 – Present

- Volunteer about five hours per month in general PC maintenance and provide technical support when needed
- Installed QuickBooks for managing church finances

Teacher Mentor, L.A. Public School System, Los Angeles, CA   2000 – Present

- Work one on one with four grade 8-12 teachers within the L.A. public school system providing mentoring and instruction on the use of Microsoft Office products
- Part of a city-wide program to increase teacher proficiency with office automation products and to help them increase the usage of IT technology in their classrooms

Ralphs Grocery Co., Anaheim, CA   1990 – 2000

Education and Professional Certifications

- MCSE (Microsoft Certified Systems Engineer)   2000

FIGURE 7-1 Pulling it all together

culture is a key part. The soft skills you should invest in developing include customer service and presentation skills.

► Continue your professional development by attending local conferences and users groups. Although users groups are decreasing in popularity, they are still critical for networking and discovering new opportunities to help build your career.

How to List this Experience

The experience you get from volunteer work contributes to your overall skills and qualifications. It enables you to list additional OSs, software packages, and technologies in the qualifications section at the beginning of your résumé. Figure 7-1 shows how one entry-level candidate used the experience he got from helping friends and setting up his own home network as legitimate experience, and helped build a stronger résumé for himself.

Summing It Up

As you can see, where there's a will, there's a way to get that hands-on experience you need to make you a better IT professional. Never underestimate the power of being resourceful. Determination and resourcefulness are qualities that can take you a long way. Plenty of resources are out there to help you get wherever you want to go.

Chapter 8

. . . .

How to Network When You Don't Know Anyone

Sure, it is easy to network in the IT industry . . . if you have been working in the field for ten years, and you are well known in the local IT community or even around the country. Unfortunately—and realistically—most entry-level candidates do not have those years or connections under their belts. So, how do you network when you don't know anyone?

In this chapter, we cover:

▶ Telling everyone you're looking for a job

▶ The networking interview

▶ IT professional groups and associations

▶ Online networking

Tell Everyone You're Looking for a Job

The first thing you have to do is get the word out that you are looking. Some people are too proud and don't want anyone to know they are looking for a job. If this is how you are going to be, you'll be looking even longer.

Of course, many people are unable to tell their employer and, maybe, not even coworkers, but everyone else needs to know. Even if you *think* you don't know anyone who could help you out, you don't know who everyone else knows.

Some employers might understand your leaving to advance your career, especially if you just received a new certification or are a career changer looking to move in the IT industry. Evaluate your personal situation and, if possible, use your boss as a reference. They may even be a great source for leads.

You've heard the phrase before, "It's not what you know, but who you know." Well, it didn't become a well-known saying for no reason—so get out there and meet people. Your best friend may have an uncle or a neighbor in a position to help.

So How Do You Bring It Up?

Whom you are talking to determines how you approach them for help. With your friends, you can be blunt—just ask them if they know of anyone who is hiring or who can help you get a job. When you speak to someone you do not know as well, you have to ask the right questions to get the assistance you need. The following are some key questions you can ask to uncover opportunities.

Talking to Your Friends

Your friends are your best place to start:

I am looking for a job in _____. Do you know anyone I could talk to about this?

Do you know anyone who is hiring?

Do you know anyone who works in IT? Would you mind introducing me or can I have their phone number?

Talking to Acquaintances

If you are talking to an acquaintance, such as a neighbor or a friend of a friend, you can take a slightly different approach. Try to compliment them and see if they can help you out:

I value your opinion and I was hoping to talk to you about my job search.

I know you have worked in the _____ field for a while and I admire what you have done with your career. I was hoping to get some advice from you as I begin to look for a new position.

I have seen what you have done at _____ and would love to get some advice from you as I enter the IT field.

The Networking Interview

Now that you have the word out that you are looking, we hope you have come across someone in the IT industry. What is your next step?

Request a Meeting, Not an Interview

Request a time to meet. You are not requesting an *interview*. Do not use that word. You are not going to tell them you want to meet to discuss a job opportunity—you are requesting time to get more information about what they do. Here are some examples of what you are requesting:

Hello, my name is _____. I was talking to _____ and they suggested I call you to ask if we could get together for about 15 minutes. I am entering the IT field and I was hoping to get your opinion on the industry and the workforce in our area. I would also like to find out what you did to become so successful in your field.

I am interested in getting into the industry. I know you are successful and I was hoping we could meet for a few minutes, so you could tell me a little more about what you do.

I am preparing to begin my IT career and I wanted to get a better idea about what the industry is like. I know you are doing well and I would like to get a little of your time to find out more about what you do.

I am hoping I could get a few minutes to talk to you about the IT industry and find out how you became so successful in your field. Maybe you could provide me with a little insight into what I could do to get into IT.

Not everyone will say yes, so you need to be prepared for those responses, as well. The best way to handle them is simply to say, "Thank you anyway. I appreciate your time," and then move on to the next person. The good thing about the previous approach is it can work when you're requesting meetings over the phone, as well as over e-mail. If you're particularly sensitive to rejection, get your confidence up by sending an e-mail.

What Do You Want to Get out of this Interview?

Once you get the time to speak with someone in the industry, what are you going to say and what do you want to get out of the interview?

First, what do you want to accomplish?

To get a job   Even though you are not saying you are there to find a job, this is your ultimate goal. This contact may have a position for you, either at their company or elsewhere.

Advice about what to do next   They can provide insight into companies that are hiring and what positions might best suit you.

References   People in the industry know other people in the industry. You want to leverage them to get to speak to others. Ask them for three to five other people you could speak to.

Tips for building experience   Find out what hiring managers in the industry are looking for and discuss ways to get that initial experience.

What Are You Going to Say?

When you are in the networking interview, begin by talking about the person you are interviewing. Do not waste this valuable time bragging about yourself. If you do, the interviewer will most likely cut the meeting short. Play off their ego.

Begin the conversation with the following topics:

Can you tell me a little bit more about what you do?

How did you become so successful in the industry?

What did you do to get into this position?

What steps did you take; where did you work?

Then, explain your interests and what you would like to do:

If you were in my position what would you do?

What advice could you give me to accomplish my goals?

What steps can I take to achieve the success that you have?

What educational requirements would you look for when filling a similar position?

It is imperative you get *them* to talk about what you should do and solicit their advice. Because of this conversation, you will stand out in their mind later. If they hear of an opening in their company or another company, they could recommend you as a good match for this position.

Ending the Interview and Getting More Names

You should not end the interview. Stay as long as possible. If this person is taking the time to talk to you, take full advantage of their time and do not leave until they kick you out! Keep the interviewer engaged in conversation by asking as many questions about them as possible.

When you feel they are ending the interview, ask for the names of three to five people in the industry that they think would be beneficial for you to meet. Do not feel uncomfortable asking for these references. They might have a friend who could use someone with your skill set and qualifications.

Now, you have the names of more industry contacts and you can contact them to set up networking interviews.

Think this Sounds Like Too Much Work?

Well, it does take work to network in the industry! But, once you make this extra effort, who do you think will be the most likely to get a job? Someone who e-mail-blasts their résumé, or you, who puts the time and creativity into your job hunt and makes contacts?

After you accept a position, contact and thank everyone who helped you out along the way—anyone who gave you a networking interview or a referral, or who took the time to give you some information. You want to keep these people as contacts as you are establishing yourself in the industry.

IT Professional Groups

Professional associations are great resources for networking. Most national or global IT professional associations also have local chapters that may provide opportunities to meet professionals in your area. If you are particularly into a specific technology search out their user group in your area. A lot of the times these groups are just a couple of dozen of people that get together for the same purpose—networking.

If you're looking for nonvendor-related associations, try some of these:

IIBA   International Institute of Business Analysis (http://www.iiba.com)

IEEE   Institute of Electrical and Electronics Engineers, Inc. (http:/www.ieee.org)

IET   Institution of Engineering and Technology (http://www. theiet.org)

PMI   Project Management Institute (http://www.pmi.org)

itSMF   The Service Management Forum (http://www.itsmf.org)

Online Networking

Look on the Internet for more information about local groups in your area and online networking opportunities. Make some contacts and, maybe, even some friends. And, remember, not everyone in IT is a computer geek—you aren't, right?

Summing It Up

Companies know that internal referrals make the best long-term employees. Reaching out to your friends and family as well as making new connections is a critical strategy for finding the job you want. Consider sharpening not just your technical networking skills but your people networking skills using the techniques in this chapter.

Chapter 9

Résumé Faux Pas: Why You Are Not
Getting Any Phone Calls

You wrote your résumé and sent it out to countless employers, but you are not getting any calls. So what's the problem?

You might think your résumé is great, but you may be surprised to find out how many rules you are breaking. Analyze your résumé against some of the most common résumé faux pas and change that lack of response. Remember, a simple faux pas can cost you an interview, even if you have outstanding information on your résumé. In this chapter, we analyze your résumé by using the Résumé Faux Pas Checklist, which includes:

▶ Generic objective statements

▶ Burying top qualifications

▶ Sending the same résumé to all employers

▶ Unrelated experience or job titles

▶ Missing keywords

▶ Unfriendly formatting of electronic résumés

And many more!

The Résumé Faux Pas Checklist

Get out your résumé and a pen, and see if your résumé contains any of these blunders.

Generic Objective Statements

Out with the traditional objective statement, including the generic comments about the type of position you are pursuing. Instead, use this opening space to write something powerful about yourself, highlighting your strong points and key qualifications. Avoid such statements as:

> *I want to work in an environment where I not only learn from the company, but the company learns from me as well.*

> *Position as a computer technician in a challenging and growing company with possibility for promotion.*

> *I am looking for a position in IT where I can apply my skills and knowledge while working in a fast-paced environment.*

> *I plan on furthering my technology education as needed.*

Now that you know what *not* to include in your objective statement, review Chapter 2 for tips on how to write a winning statement.

Burying Your Top Qualifications

Lead with your strong points as they relate to that job. We have seen many examples where people stuck to the traditional résumé format of listing an objective statement followed by education, experience, achievements, and additional information. This layout does not work best for everyone. Here is a scenario where that is evident:

> A branch manager working in retail is changing careers. In his experience section, he lists all the daily responsibilities of his current position first, such as increasing sales, hiring employees, managing finances, and scheduling. His last point is that he set up a network in the store. This is a prime example of burying his top qualifications.

If he were applying for another retail management position, this résumé would be fine. But, because he is trying to get into IT, he should leverage his networking experience.

Here is another example of hiding key qualifications:

> A candidate has a technical background, but in his experience section, he only listed his daily duties. He waited to quantify his accomplishments in his final section of "Additional Information," which included: "Decreased CPU downtime by 80 percent, achieved 15 percent reduction in CPU maintenance costs, and increased stability in classroom CPU production by reducing downtime, enabling students and staff to produce efficiently and on time."

These points are key. They should be at the beginning of his résumé, not buried at the end on the second page.

Sending the Same Résumé to All Potential Employers

You need to customize your résumé for each job or you will miss your opportunity to show an employer exactly how you can help them. You need to use the details of each job description when creating a résumé, as well as adding in some points about the company you discovered through research. Do not just blast a generic résumé to every job opening you find. Take the additional time and it will pay off.

Unrelated Experience or Education

Those things not related to IT should be left off your résumé or at least de-emphasized. For example:

▶ Courses taken in psychology, stress management, and physical education

▶ Degree in ministry of spirituality or cellular biology

▶ Designer of Class of 2000 yearbook from cover-to-cover

▶ Internship as a middle-school English tutor

Job Titles Not Related to IT

You may need to camouflage some of your experience by leaving out titles and descriptions of unrelated jobs, especially if you are a career changer. Instead, just list the company and the years of employment. We have received actual résumés that included job descriptions of a press operator, a Burger King cashier, and a sanitation dispatcher. If you have anything like this on your résumé, get rid of it. Review more about common résumé dilemmas, including those for career changers and recent graduates, in Chapter 6.

Weak Job Titles

If your job title does not accurately depict what you did, get creative. If you have multiple job roles, do not try to represent them all through your title, such as computer technologist/helpdesk/telecommunications. Think of a more powerful title, rather than listing all three. For some insider tips about powerful job titles, refer to Chapter 1, where you also can find a chart of interchangeable job titles to use to project a stronger image.

Missing Keywords

Use keywords to get your résumé noticed. Be sure to include all the buzzwords for qualifications you possess, as related to the position. Also, use what the employer wants and include those key phrases in your résumé. If you are unsure of what keywords relate to the position you seek, analyze several job descriptions and try to incorporate the keywords used. Refer to Chapter 3 for more specifics about the use of keywords.

Mismatched with the Job Description

Be sure what you say in your résumé and your cover letter is appropriate to the position you are applying for. Use the key points of the job description to match yourself to it.

For example, a candidate was applying for director of IT. She stated that she wants a project-oriented position. This put her out of the running right away because a management position is inappropriate for someone with such a request.

Similarly, if you are applying for a management position, do not highlight all of your project experience. You need to demonstrate your management abilities, not your ability to handle tasks.

Excluding Studies in Progress

If you don't have a formal degree or certification, but have studies in progress, include them in your résumé. For example:

▶ If you are attending college, but haven't graduated, list the number of credit hours you have toward your degree (if you have at least one year under your belt), such as "Orange Coast College, 24 credit hours toward Computer Science degree."

▶ If you have taken relevant courses, list those. Include a section entitled "Related Courses" and include the course titles, such as Data Communications, Network Administration, or Network Administration and Installation. It is unnecessary to include descriptions of each class. Remember to exclude irrelevant courses.

▶ If you are currently taking a class or studying for a certification exam, include that certification with the expected date of achievement.

Emphasizing Your Age

If your age could hurt your odds of being considered for the position—either too young or too old—deemphasize whenever possible. As a career changer, you do not want to highlight that you have 24 years in the workforce. If you were seeking a position in the same industry where those years were accrued, it would be valuable. Conversely, this is the same as announcing that you are over 40 with no experience in the industry. For tips on how to hide youth or experience, refer to Chapter 6.

Unfriendly Formatting of Electronic Résumés

When sending your résumé electronically, you need to format it differently than you would for paper. You can find out more about formatting your résumé for the eWorld in Chapter 3. The following are some key points:

▶ Use carriage returns or hard breaks to guarantee consistency and easier reading. If your text all runs together, nothing will catch the reader's eye.

▶ Highlight areas of your résumé by using capitalization and special characters, such as asterisks, hyphens, and lines.

▶ Remember, the formatting you do in word processing, such as bold and italics, is often lost through e-mail. Create your electronic résumé in a text editor, such as Notepad, and make sure it is easy to identify the key points of your résumé.

▶ Use a descriptive subject line (not just "Résumé"), because that gets lost in the sea of résumés in the Human Resource (HR) manager's inbox. Instead, include the position you're responding to and something about your skill set. For example, "Job #142, Network Engineer, Certified MCSE, Available Immediately" will get noticed.

Using the Wrong Layout for You

Make sure you put your best foot forward. If you don't have experience in the industry, begin your résumé with your skill set and your education. On the other hand, if your experience is your strong point, lead with it.

Don't think you have to stick to the traditional résumé layout. Modify it to whatever best serves you. Review the Résumé Encyclopedia in Chapter 11 for examples of different ways to present your experience and background.

Simply Listing Your Job Responsibilities

Do more than just list your daily tasks under each job title. Quantify your accomplishments whenever possible. Demonstrate how you solved problems and what the results were. Chapter 4 walks you through the process of uncovering your hidden talents and tailoring your résumé for any job posting.

Highlighting Trivial Skills

You need to highlight your top computer skills, especially as a recent graduate or someone without experience in the industry. Even if you do not have the highest level of experience or the strongest skill set, do not highlight outdated or basic skills, such as:

▶ Passed Microsoft Networking Essentials exam

▶ Proficient in Windows 3.1

▶ Extensive experience with Web surfing using Internet Explorer 4.0

You can also build your skill set even if you don't have any professional work experience. Find out about creative ways to get hands-on experience in Chapter 7.

Including Why You Left Each Position

Including why you left each position is unnecessary. Save this for the interview, especially if the reasons were negative. Phrases such as "company-wide layoffs," "my boss doesn't know what he is doing," and "wanted to make more money" do not belong on your résumé.

Exaggerations that Backfire

Be careful to present yourself honestly. If you try to exaggerate your qualifications, you may be setting yourself up for failure. Here is an example of a candidate who got caught in a tall tale before even making it to the interview:

> Becky made an opening statement about her "20 years of professional experience." Most would think that is referring to post-college experience. But, when you drill down into her experience, her total work history only added up to about six years. She must have been including her lawn-mowing jobs starting at age ten, as well as her part-time college positions. This exaggeration cost Becky her credibility and threw her out of the running.

Typos or Spelling Mistakes

Proofread, proofread, proofread. And then have at least five other people proofread for you. Even a small spelling or grammatical error can cost you. Here are some classic examples:

> Certifications: CompuTIA, Aplus, Cisco Networking 1
>
> Disposed of $15 million in assets.
>
> Temporary labtop computer support technician
>
> Director of IT from 1896–2000
>
> Explicit attention to to detail
>
> Ability to meet deadlines while maintaining composer
>
> Competed 14 years of college (and only received a B.S.!)
>
> Accomplishments: Oversight entire IT department

Too Long or Too Wordy

Be concise in the words you use and don't be long-winded. You want the employer to be able to read your résumé quickly and catch all the key points. Readers should have a summary of your experience and skills, with just enough detail to show them the depth of your abilities. Save the rest for the interview. Remember to keep your résumé to one or two pages unless it's truly warranted. Find out more about the technical requirements for a winning résumé in Chapter 2.

Unprofessional Appearance

Remember, appearance counts, so don't try to save money by using cheap paper. Use high-quality paper with a matching cover letter. When mailing your résumé, use a large envelope, so you don't have to fold it. This keeps your résumé crisp, which is important if it needs to be scanned or faxed.

Salary History

Do not include your salary history or salary requirements anywhere on your résumé. If your request is too high, you could eliminate yourself from the running before an employer even meets you. Once they want to hire you, you can negotiate the salary. An employer is more flexible after they have made up their mind that they want you. By revealing this information too soon, you may not even be considered.

You may also be selling yourself short if you state lower salary requirements than the position usually pays. You may need to disclose your salary requirements in the interview or in a cover letter, but do not place it anywhere on your actual résumé. If you don't list your salary requirements, you won't necessarily get tossed aside. Just make sure you're applying for positions that match your experience. If your résumé is interesting enough, someone will call you back.

Outdated Extracurricular Activities

First, extracurricular activities are only appropriate if they are related to the position you are applying for. Second, realize when they are outdated and need to be removed. Here are some prime examples of what not to include (note how outdated or irrelevant these activities are):

Secretary of the debate team, 1991

Graduated 1983, GPA 3.4, Dean's List

Math Club member, 1998

Use of Personal Pronouns

Your résumé is a business communication, so it needs to be professional and concise. Do not use any personal pronouns, such as "I" or "me." Here is an example of how you can get rid of personal pronouns:

I implemented a tracking system for the technical helpdesk, and when I did this, productivity was increased and reporting was enabled.

This statement should be changed to:

Implemented a tracking system for the technical helpdesk, which increased productivity and enabled reporting.

Personal Interests or Information

There is no place in your résumé for personal interests. Even if you are using a résumé tool that prompts you to include such information, disregard it. Far too many résumés we receive include hobbies, such as reading books, surfing the Web, or water skiing. No hiring manager wants to hear any of this.

Along those same lines, do not include personal information such as your age, sex, religion, race, or marital status.

High School Graduation Date

There is never a time when you would want to include that you graduated from high school in 1978. Even if you are in college and have not yet graduated, it is more impressive to state you have studies in progress than to default to your high-school diploma.

Unprofessional E-Mail Addresses

This should go without saying, but make sure the e-mail address you are listing on your résumé is professional. You do not want an employer to try to contact you at gobaltimoreravens@beer.com.

Sending Additional Materials with Your Résumé

Do not enclose letters of recommendation or other papers with your résumé unless they are specifically requested. You can bring these items to your interview and present them, if appropriate.

Including References on Your Résumé

References do not belong on your résumé. Because you are sending your résumé to many people and you do not know where it may end up, you don't want just anyone calling your references. This information should be shared during the interview process, separate from your résumé.

Likewise, the statement "References available upon request" should be removed. Obviously, you will have references when required, and this only wastes space. To view a sample reference sheet, refer to Chapter 2.

Humor

Your résumé is not the place to demonstrate your cheesy sense of humor. Do not try to be cute, clever, or funny when preparing your résumé. Here are some examples of humor gone bad:

You have seen the rest, now meet the best.

You will only need to keep this résumé and can use the rest to heat your house.

Let's meet so I can astound you with my excellence.

Also known as . . . Mr. Right, Mr. Perfect-for-this-Job, or Mr. Productive.

I am enclosing a few bucks to guarantee my interview.

How Did You Do?

This was not like one of those quizzes in *Maxim* or *Cosmopolitan*, where a less-than-perfect score means you're still in the game. After analyzing your résumé against these classic résumé faux pas, if you scored less than 100 percent, you need help. Now is the time to reevaluate and rewrite.

Summing It Up

If you've followed all the advices in this book and still aren't getting calls from employers and recruiters, consider rereading this chapter. Even simple résumé faux-pas can cause a potential employer to immediate toss your resume in the "no" pile—or worse yet, never find your résumé amongst the hundreds they receive each week.

The earlier chapters can offer you solid advice on how to improve all aspects of your résumé. After pinpointing those areas that need improvement, find the chapter or chapters that outline your weaknesses. Make some enhancements and review this checklist again to see how much you have improved.

Chapter 10

. . . .

The Interview

Remember, the real purpose of your résumé is to get you the interview. Once you land the all-important interview, you're halfway to a new job. At this point, whether you get the offer or not, it is mostly up to you and how you handle the interview. Your role at the interview is that of a salesperson—you're selling yourself. Your goal is simple: to walk away with a job offer. In this chapter, we cover how to handle the interview. Here's what's in store:

▶ What really happens in the interview process?

▶ Skills to demonstrate

▶ How to prepare

▶ Common questions for different areas of IT

▶ Questions to ask the interviewer

▶ Following up after the interview

What Really Happens in the Interview Process?

Interviews intimidate many professionals in all fields. In the IT world, where so much is done by e-mail, phone, and fax, an in-person meeting can be especially difficult. But getting past your fear and fine-tuning your interviewing skills can give your career a real boost.

A crucial first step is to understand that, at an interview, you play a specific role. With practice, you can play your role to perfection. To give a command performance, it's important to think of the interviewer as an ally, not as the enemy. Avoid a smug and overconfident attitude. Instead, approach the interview as a chance to help solve a problem. The interviewer wants to be able to hire you. You can help them make that decision by showing them why you're right for the job—and the company.

Along these same lines, avoid appearing too eager to land the job. Overeagerness hurts your credibility and may be a turn-off to the interviewer, who may question your reasons for wanting the position so badly.

These days, your first interview is likely to be with an internal recruiter. Typically, this is not a technical person but, rather, someone who has found your résumé in their database of applicants and has picked out enough key words to feel it might be a good fit for one of their positions. As a rule, they work from a set of questions used with all candidates for that position. Their job is to make sure you're not a homicidal maniac and to check out whether you know the basics of the job you applied for. They're also looking for any discrepancies in your work history that may tip them off to a poor work ethic or unreliable patterns of behavior.

Taking these interviews seriously is important. If you want to advance to the next round, don't come across too picky, odd, or high maintenance. Be truthful and build a relationship with this person. They are the gatekeepers who will recommend whether you ever get to speak to the hiring manager.

Once you make it past the recruiter, your next interview may be with the hiring manager. Their job is to establish you're a normal, functioning member of society. Once that's done, you're more likely to be handed off to a more technical person, probably the person who will be your immediate supervisor when you start work. Other members of the technical team may also be present.

Your interviewer wants to get a sense of who you are, certainly, but they also want to gauge your technical ability. Expect to be asked fairly specific questions (we cover these in detail in the section, "Common Questions for Different Areas of IT"), which tests your technical knowledge, your ability to think on your feet, and your response to common crisis situations in your particular field. Don't be surprised if you're asked many of the same questions the hiring manager previously asked you.

If you've been sitting with one person answering questions for some time and she suggests meeting the rest of the team, take it as a good sign, but don't start pouring the champagne just yet. Never assume the second, third, or even the seventh interview is "just a formality," even if the person who first interviewed you says it is. Smile and shake hands with everyone you're introduced to. Always be your best, keep track of everyone you meet, and never get irritated at answering the same questions again.

So, just how do you put your best foot forward? Read on.

TIP *If possible, arrange your interview for a Tuesday, Wednesday, or Thursday morning. You want your interviewer to be fresh, not pressed to get their week started or daydreaming about the weekend. Avoid after-lunch interviews when your interviewer is likely to be sleepy. Most people are at their least productive in the early afternoon.*

Skills to Demonstrate

One of the first things your interviewer will notice is your communications skills. Do you speak clearly and coherently? How's your grammar? What kind of an impression will you make on the company's clients? Make an audio or video recording of yourself speaking and analyze it. Brush up on your writing skills if they're an important part of the job you want.

 TIP *Ahead of time, listen carefully to yourself speaking. Is your speech peppered with "like," "you know," "stuff," and other unprofessional filler words? Instead of these words, pause. Take a breath. Try to eliminate these words completely—or at least, you know, get rid of most of them.*

Of course, an interview isn't only about the questions posed and the answers given. A lot of reading between the lines goes on. By anticipating what hidden clues the interviewer is looking for, you can make them easy to spot.

Here's a rundown of some of the most crucial skills you should make an effort to display.

 TIP *Be specific. It's great if you're good at many different things, but don't talk about them in general terms. Be ready to share examples of how you used specific tools to solve problems and get results.*

Technical Capability

Your interviewer needs to know you possess the necessary skills to do the job, especially if you don't have extensive hands-on experience in the specific technology you'll be working in.

What to say: *My [class projects/internships/previous work] gave me a chance to put theory into practice. I don't have years of hands-on experience, but I'm confident I can handle the work here. I was trained for this position; I'm ready for the responsibility.*

Flexibility and Passion for Technology

Can you keep up with the rapid pace of change in the IT world? Technology quickly becomes obsolete—if you're not interested in learning, so will your job.

What to say: *I love being in a field that requires me to stay on top of cutting-edge developments. It's exciting to watch technology evolve and work with the latest tools.*

Team Orientation and Enthusiasm

The ability to work well with others is an important skill in any organization. In IT, it's often necessary for architects, developers, and sales engineers to work together to satisfy clients.

What to say: *I'd like to have the chance to work with people from different parts of the company and to be involved in the whole life cycle of a project—from conception through completion. This is a great way to gain a better understanding of the company's role in the industry, and it's always rewarding to be part of a team that brings an idea to fruition.*

Responsibility

Do you pass the buck? If you say you can finish a job, do you? A potential employer needs to know you're responsible, and that you can set goals for yourself and for the good of the company.

What to say: *I'm realistic and honest about what I can and can't do in a given period of time. I not only want to constantly improve my skills as a developer, but also the company's position in the industry. I won't promise a rush job just to make you happy, but if I tell you you'll have something by deadline, then you'll have it.*

How to Prepare

Invest a little extra time at the beginning of the interview process. This pays off richly in the end. If you're offered a last-minute chance to interview for the job of your dreams, you can accept without hesitation. Also, by properly preparing yourself, you'll exude confidence, appear more organized, and be better able to concentrate on the task at hand: getting that job offer.

Make sure you have a stack of printed copies of your résumé, as well as matching paper and envelopes for printing cover letters, thank you notes, and other important correspondence. Keep the templates for your letters in an easily accessible folder on your computer. Stamp the envelopes ahead of time and put your return address on them. Set up a form to keep track of when and where you sent your résumé and when you need to follow up. Include a column for notes you can enter after the interview.

You should have a nice portfolio to take on your interviews. Make sure it's not cluttered with loose old papers. Take with you several clean copies of your résumé, pen and paper for notes, and copies of your references. Also, include a copy of the job description with key areas highlighted and any questions you might have thought up written neatly in the margins.

TIP *Don't let your portfolio become a catch-all for clutter. Clean it out every night. You don't want to realize that you are on your last sheet of portfolio paper, while you tell a potential employer about how proactive you are.*

Research the Company

As soon as you're offered an interview with a particular company, spend some time at its web site. (If a recruiter arranged the interview, they should be able to provide you with some basic information, but always double-check it.) Read the company's mission statement. How do they present themselves? Use your favorite search engine to find any recent press coverage of the company. If you have time, call the corporate office and request a copy of its last annual report. Take notes. If you have questions about a large, public company, call its corporate communications department and pretend you're interested in buying some stock. They should answer your inquiries. Also check out www.vault.com for "insider information" posted anonymously by actual employees. Of course, be sure to verify all information. If you can't verify it, don't even think about bringing this up at your interview.

The day before the interview, make sure you know where you're going and how to get there, the name and phone number of the person you'll meet, and what time your meeting is. Always allow at least 20 minutes extra travel time. You should arrive about ten minutes early.

Psych Yourself Up

Convince yourself first. Read over the accomplishments you list on your résumé. Read them out loud—hearing them spoken is a powerful ego-booster. Envision yourself on the job, solving problems, participating in staff meetings, accepting an award from the company president. If you believe you're the best person for the job, it'll be that much easier to convince the interviewer.

TIP Carry a small index card with some of your greatest life achievements recorded on it. Review it immediately before an interview for an instant kick in the seat of the pants.

Dress Up

Always err on the side of caution when it comes to how you dress. Choose clothes that are a bit conservative. Never show up at an interview in jeans, even if they tell you the company is casual. Business casual means nice slacks and a pressed, button-down shirt, at the least. You can't go wrong in a suit and tie (or a nice dress)—they may tease you a little, but it's better than being underdressed.

Choose two or three outfits that can work for interviews—clothes that look professional and make you feel good about yourself. Make sure they are clean, pressed, and in good shape. Shine your shoes. Trim your nails, get a haircut, and make sure your mother wouldn't be embarrassed to see you.

TIP Call ahead to verify the correct spelling and pronunciation of the interviewer's name. See if you can get any other information about the interviewer from her assistant, but don't be pushy. Honesty is much more effective. A simple, "I'd really like to get this job. Any 'inside information' you can give me?" asked in a lighthearted way could yield gold.

Common Questions for Different Areas of IT

Your interviewer has five major concerns. Every question they ask you helps her answer one or more of those concerns. Yes, the questions—and your answers—are important at face value, but understanding the underlying concerns is critical because they're the ones who determine whether you get the offer or the boot. During an interview, the interviewer has to determine:

▶ If you can do the job

▶ If you will do the job

▶ If you get along with others

▶ If you're manageable

▶ If the company can afford you

As you go over the questions and answers provided in the following sections, bear in mind that your answers should serve both the asked and unasked questions.

TIP If you don't understand a question, don't try to answer it. Instead, be honest. Say, "I'm not sure I understand what you're asking." The interviewer will rephrase the question. Once you know what they're asking, you can give a clear answer.

Common Questions

The questions that follow are sure to pop up in nearly every interview you have. Make sure you can answer each one. Write out your answers, if need be, and practice saying them until they sound natural.

TIP If you're being interviewed by more than one person at once, try to position your chair somewhere that lets you keep all the interviewers in your line of sight. Direct most of the answer to the person who posed the question, including the others with occasional glances. This is generally more effective than swiveling back and forth frantically while you speak.

Tell me a little bit about yourself.   Keep your answer short and professional. A 20-minute description of the yoga class you teach is not going to win you any points. Review your résumé ahead of time and come up with a one-minute capsule description of who you are. Try a catchy introduction, along the lines of: "I'm a California native, and I've been interested in technology ever since I took my Speak 'n' Spell apart." Give your pitch, which should touch briefly on your strongest skills, and then stop talking.

What do you know about our company?   Use the research you did earlier to your advantage. Talk about what you learned, and invite the interviewer to share more information. "I've read about the self-driving cars you're developing. It must be fascinating to work with that kind of cutting-edge technology. How long do you think it will be before they're on the road?"

TIP Look at the language the company uses in the job ad and in other company literature. Try to use their words when describing yourself and your work. It's a subtle way to make yourself fit in to their culture.

Why do you want to work here? Why do you want this position?   The key here is to focus on the company's needs, rather than on what you want. "I understand from my reading that the problem you're trying to solve now is keeping your cars from crashing into walls. I've solved similar problems in my current job, and I can also help you." Give specific examples of how your skills can help.

What is your greatest weakness?   This is a classic interview question. The typical advice is to make your "weakness" perfectionism, one of the oldest tricks in the book. Try for a slightly more original response, but never share your personal weaknesses. Aim for an industry-specific response: "I get frustrated when technology doesn't keep pace with what I want to do. I'm constantly trying to develop new solutions." Or "I have a hard time working on just a single part of the development process. I prefer to be involved in the whole life cycle of a project."

TIP Say what you need to say, and then stop. Don't fear silence. "Um . . ." at the end of a strong answer weakens it. If you've said your piece, sit back and wait for the next question.

Where do you see yourself five years from now?   The interviewer wants to know if you have ambition. Do you see this position as a stepping stone? Do you plan to leave the company after they invest time and money in training you? Try to tailor your answer to the company's products and services, and aim at a position one or two levels above where you currently are: "In five years, I'd like to be managing your wireless device team—but I'd still like to be involved in the hands-on technical work occasionally."

Why are you leaving your job?   The interviewer needs to know if you had problems with your previous employer, and what those problems might mean for you now. If your reason for leaving is simple and clear, say so. "I'm moving and the commute will be too difficult" or "There's no more room for me to grow" are perfectly acceptable reasons. If you've been fired, see the next section.

TIP If you're offered a drink during the interview, take one. Most interviewees are quick to decline when offered coffee, juice, or water. Accepting indicates a certain amount of confidence. You can take sips to buy a few seconds while you think about your answers.

The Tough Questions

These questions aren't designed to trip you up. The interviewer needs the answers. Remember, the unasked questions are at the heart of the interview. Can you get the job done? Can the company afford you? Remind yourself that they want to hire you or they wouldn't have invited you to interview. Your job is to show the interviewer that they can, in fact, bring you on board.

TIP *If the interview isn't going the way you want it to, don't be afraid to stop and start over. If you've fumbled an answer, simply stop speaking, take a deep breath, and say, "I'm sorry. I really want this job, and I'm a bit nervous. Let me try that again." What's the interviewer going to do, stab you with a letter opener? On the contrary, admitting you're human goes a long way toward establishing rapport.*

Salary History

Too often, that awkward moment occurs when the interviewer asks what you're currently making. Whether you're grossly underpaid (and, therefore, looking for a new job) or simply ready to make the jump to the next level, you probably don't want to toss those numbers around lightly. You can't just ignore the question, and it's not always easy (or wise) to turn it around, à la "Well, how much are you offering?" So what can you do?

First, give the big picture answer. "Most people at my level earn in the mid-50s. I chose to work at my last job for less than my market value because I needed the experience. But, now that I have it, I need to be sure I'm adequately compensated for my skills."

If the interviewer persists, "But how much are they paying you?" try to avoid a specific number. "The high 40s" should suffice. But you must know exactly how much you want to be making, so if they ask, you're ready to answer. Give a $3,000 to $5,000 range, because the company will undoubtedly come back with something lower than what you said. By giving yourself some wiggle room, you improve your chances of getting what you want.

Salary Negotiations

If the interviewer puts a figure on the table and it's less than you want, you have to negotiate. Believe it or not, you're in the best position now, before you have the job. The company wants to hire you, and you can convince them you're worth the extra money.

If you've researched salary information ahead of time (and you wouldn't be negotiating unless you had, right?), you know what your range is. So, when the interviewer says, "We're prepared to offer you $50,000 a year," you can respond with confidence, "The typical range for people at my level is $65,000 to $70,000 a year." Then shut up. Do not speak. As the silence stretches out, repeat silently, "This is not their final offer." Be careful not to move your lips. Let the interviewer fill the awkward silence with explanations.

 TIP *Make sure you know what the market will bear for someone with your experience. Never underestimate your worth—it's hard to make a significant salary jump after you start working. But, don't delude yourself into thinking you'll make $100,000 a year in an entry-level position, either.*

If the company can't afford you, decide how badly you need this particular job. The oldest rule of negotiating is he who cares the least wins. If you're absolutely not willing to work for what they're offering, walk away. They may surprise you and come back with a new offer.

If, on the other hand, the electricity was shut off last week, your rent is due, and nothing else is on the horizon, you may have a problem. Try for a compromise: can you take extra vacation days or pick up your commuting costs in lieu of more money? Will the company give you a salary review after three months? Or, can you work a four-day work week and pick up some extra money on the side by doing freelance projects?

Getting Laid Off or Fired

Getting laid off no longer has the stigma it once carried. Especially in the IT world, job turnover has suffered with the economy's downturn. If your company went bankrupt, lost an important round of funding, or had to downsize to stay afloat, that's not your fault. Give a straightforward answer: "Unfortunately, the company was forced to cut costs and many people were let go."

If you're not sure why you were let go, find out. Talk to your old employer, and listen to the reason. Determine what you need to do better this time. Try to put a positive spin on your firing. Use it to show you can accept responsibility and that you've learned from your past mistakes. "My boss and I weren't able to see eye-to-eye on many issues, but I've had time to think, and here's how I would have handled the situation differently." In other words, explain any problems you had (or still have) with an employer, but don't describe that employer in negative terms.

 TIP *Here's a phrase that works like magic to put an interviewer on your side: "I agree." If you can find a way to use this phrase once or twice—any more than that and you'll sound like a yes-man—you'll score big points. People like to hear they're right. Tell them they are, and they'll like you. Simple, but true.*

Leaves of Absence

Be prepared to explain your leave of absence in matter-of-fact terms: "I have two children and took time off to be with them. Now they're in day care, and I'm eager to return to work." Or, "I had the opportunity to travel around the world for several months. It was a chance to broaden my world perspective."

If your "leave of absence" was simply the result of not finding a job quickly, explain you are being selective. Try something like, "I'm more interested in finding the right fit than in taking a quick fix. It's easy to find a job. Finding the right position is more difficult."

Changing Careers

If you are new to the IT world, you may have to explain why you've chosen to change careers. Turn your past experience into benefits for your potential employer. Don't be afraid to get a bit passionate—in fact, that's a good thing. For example, you might say, "I worked in customer relations for many years, but I became fascinated by technology when I first discovered the Internet. I've taken several programming courses, and now I'm ready to make the switch to full-time developer. My CR background is a real plus for this position because I'm familiar with client needs and the usability of the databases you develop here."

 TIP *Never say, "I can't." If the interviewer asks, "Can you use this technology?" the correct answer is always yes or a variation of it. Try, "My exposure to X is limited, but I'm happy to put in the time necessary to become more familiar with it."*

Questions to Ask the Interviewer

At the end of the interview, you have a chance to ask the interviewer your own questions. Always take advantage of this opportunity. First, you should be genuinely interested in some of the company specifics. Merely asking the questions displays that interest to the interviewer, and it also gets you the answers you need to make your final decision. These are just a few of the possible questions you can ask:

▶ What's a typical working day like?

▶ How much contact is there with management?

▶ Will I have opportunities to take seminars or attend conferences?

▶ Is this position more analytical or more people-oriented?

▶ How much travel is normally expected?

▶ What is the best thing about working here? The worst thing?

▶ Why did you decide to work here?

▶ Do you have any reservations about hiring me that I can address?

For your final question, bolster your confidence and ask for the job. Say something like, "I'm interested in this position. What's the next step?" Granted, not every company will make you an offer on the spot. But, you'd be surprised at how many are willing to do so if you "ask for the sale" at the end of the interview.

TIP *If your interviewer is frequently interrupted by office goings-on, acknowledge it. Say something like, "I appreciate the time you're taking to speak with me. I can see people depend on you a lot here—your time must really be at a premium."*

Other Situations

While you can't prepare for every single possibility at a job interview, a bit of research can cover most eventualities. Take some time to review these special situations.

Getting Past the Gatekeeper (Recruiter) Interview

A *gatekeeper* is anyone who stands between you and the hiring manager you want to approach. In the past, secretaries and administrative assistants were the first line of defense. Today, you may have to get past two assistants just to get to the recruiter, who can still decide not to send your résumé on to the company. How can you improve your chances?

▶ Always be professional and courteous in your correspondence and phone calls. Don't regard the gatekeeper as an obstacle but, instead, as a partner. Recognize their importance to your career. Be genuinely interested in what they have to say. Always start off with, "Hi, my name is . . . and I'm calling about. . . . Can you tell me the best person to speak with?" When you have the person's ear, your first question should be, "Do you have a few minutes to speak with me now?"

► Get a bit personal. A simple, "You must be swamped" can work wonders.

► Make every contact count. Even if you're not speaking to the decision-maker, get at least one piece of useful information. "What's the best time of day to speak to him?" Or, "Does he prefer to be addressed as Mr. Smith or John?"

► Be honest, and try to get the recruiter on your side. "From the description I read, this job sounds perfect for me. How can I get an interview with that company?"

 TIP *If you get an answering machine when you call, don't be afraid to leave a message. State your name, ask for confirmation that information you sent was received or for a callback with more information about an advertised position, and leave your number.*

Phone Interviews

A phone interview can be intimidating for many people. You don't have the opportunity to make eye contact or size up the person you're speaking with. But a phone interview can be a great way to make a first impression if you know what you're doing.

Ahead of time, type and print the major points you want to make, such as your strengths and how you've put them to use for your current employer. Be sure to include some questions for the interviewer in your notes, too. As long as the person isn't sitting opposite you, you can refer to your written sheet. Just make sure you don't read long, prepared statements verbatim.

Use a phone that works well and is comfortable for you. Don't do a phone interview on a cell phone! The connection is too unreliable. And try not to use a cordless phone, either. Sit in one place—preferably, a quiet, closed room—for the duration of the interview. Have a glass of water nearby.

It goes without saying that you should disable your call-waiting feature while you're on the interview. If the connection is terrible and you're afraid you won't be able to hear everything, ask to call back. Do a trial run with a friend the day before. Test your equipment, presentation, and preparation. Then, relax and wait for the call!

 TIP *Smile when you speak on the phone. People can hear it in your voice. A genuine smile tells the interviewer you're friendly, easygoing, and relaxed.*

Dining Interviews

The dining interview can be awkward for many people. But, if you make a good impression at this one, it goes a long way. If you must face the dining interview, follow these simple rules for success:

► Place your napkin in your lap as early as possible.

► Wait for your host to open his menu before you open yours. Ask your host if they have any recommendations. Don't choose the most expensive item, but don't go for the cheapest, either.

▶ Eat to the left, drink to the right. The bread plate to your left is yours, as is the glass on your right. Utensils go from the outside in. Skip a course, skip a fork.

▶ Unless you are adventurous, don't order something you've never heard of. Stick with what you know—and don't order spaghetti!

▶ Don't order alcohol, even if your host does.

▶ Don't speak with your mouth full. If your host asks you a question just as you take a bite, chew, swallow, and then speak. Your host will understand, and you can use the extra time to form your response.

 TIP *Take small bites. They're a lot easier to swallow in a hurry.*

▶ Eat at a normal pace. Don't rush or drag out the meal.

▶ At the end of the meal, fold your napkin and place it on the table.

▶ Don't offer to pay.

▶ Send a thank you note after the interview. Specifically thank your host for the meal.

Illegal Questions to Watch For

Certain questions are illegal for a prospective employer to ask, but some do it anyway. This puts you in an awkward position. Do you answer the question and possibly risk the job? Or, do you refuse to answer and mark yourself as uncooperative?

A third option exists: look at what the employer really wants to know, and answer that question. If the interviewer asks if you have children, you can say, "If you're worried about my availability, you don't need to be. When I commit to a job, I give it everything I have." Always smile and speak confidently when you give your answer. The interviewer should be well aware of what they can and cannot legally ask. Here are several other examples of illegal questions and answers you can offer.

Question	Answer
Are you a U.S. citizen? Where were you born? What's your first language?	The interviewer needs to know if you are authorized to work in the United States. **What to say:** I'm authorized to work in the United States.
How old are you? When did you graduate? When were you born?	The interviewer needs to know if you are over 18 or how close you are to retirement. **What to say:** I have been in IT for more than *xx* years.

Question	Answer
Are you married?	The interviewer is allowed to ask you about your willingness and ability to relocate, travel, and/or work overtime—if every applicant is asked the same questions.
Do you plan to have children?	
How many children do you have?	
What kind of child care arrangements do you have?	
	What to say: I can travel and work overtime as necessary for the job. I'm willing to relocate if needed.
Do you have any disabilities?	The interviewer needs to determine whether you can perform the essential functions of this job with or without reasonable accommodations.
How is your health?	
Have you had any recent or past illnesses or operations?	
	What to say: I am physically able to perform this job without any problem.

TIP Not every question is asked to try to elicit illegal information. The interviewer may simply be intrigued by your accent. Use your best judgment—if a question doesn't offend you and you don't think your position is in jeopardy, go ahead and answer.

Following Up after the Interview

So few people bother to send a written note of thanks after an interview. Set yourself apart from the crowd. A simple handwritten or typed note thanking the interviewer for their time and consideration is a great way to get your name in front of them again, plus it's truly a nice thing to do. To make a stellar impression, send an actual piece of mail. In the age of electronic communications, people appreciate letters.

Your note doesn't have to be fancy. Try something like this:

Thank you for taking the time to meet with me today. I was delighted to share my vision with you for how I would fit into your team, and I enjoyed your explanation of [insert specific technical detail answered by the interviewer here].

Please don't hesitate to call me if you have any more questions about my qualifications. As we agreed, I plan to follow up with you at the end of next week. I look forward to speaking with you then.

Summing It Up

Dozens of candidates apply for IT positions every day. Only a few are chosen to interview. If you've made it to that level, the company wants to hire you. Whether they choose you depends almost entirely on the interview. Set yourself apart from the crowd by following these steps:

▶ Research the company and prepare answers to common questions ahead of time.

▶ Arrive at your interview a few minutes early.

▶ Dress the part, and err on the side of conservatism.

▶ Take your time when you answer questions. Don't let tough questions trip you up.

▶ Ask the interviewer intelligent questions that indicate your interest in the company and the position.

▶ Determine your worth and hold your ground in salary negotiations.

▶ Send a thank you note immediately after the interview. Mention specific information you were grateful to receive.

Careful preparation on your part indicates to the company that you care about the job. Companies need reliable people who are passionate about their work. If you can't put a little effort into your appearance or you aren't interested enough in what the company does to ask questions, why should they hire you? Go the extra mile now to take your career to new heights.

In our next and final chapter, you will find all the examples you need to create a winning résumé for any position in IT.

Be sure to check out the companion to this book, *Ace the IT Interview*, for more interview questions tailored to the jobs in this book.

Part II

Résumé Encyclopedia

In This Part

CHAPTER 11 A Résumé Encyclopedia

Chapter 11

A Résumé Encyclopedia

Getting started is the hardest part of any writing task. The *Résumé Encyclopedia* is just what you need to turn your experience, or lack thereof, into a masterpiece that gets noticed and can get you the job.

This chapter provides you with examples of résumés for the top jobs in the industry today, along with key areas to highlight as a part of your résumé. These valuable tips should help you in tailoring your résumé for those key qualifications hiring managers are seeking.

Application Developer

Key Areas to Highlight

Profile Section

▶ You want to convey your technical expertise and awareness of existing and emerging IT technologies and methodologies.

▶ You also want to include personal qualities, such as attention to detail, efficiency, thoroughness, and project lead experience. Highlight communication skills, such as your ability to communicate effectively with team members and clients, particularly nontechnical colleagues.

▶ Employers look for people with the necessary programming skills who can think logically and pay close attention to detail. They also look for developers who use ingenuity and creativity in designing solutions. They want to see that you can work with abstract concepts and do technical analysis.

▶ Remember to include relevant industries you may have worked in.

Experience Section

▶ Focus not only on the description of the projects you worked on, but also on the business benefits that resulted.

▶ Include benefits you personally brought to the projects, such as team leadership.

▶ Include understanding business practices and approaches, such as ERP, financial services, accounting, and Human Resources (HR).

▶ Give specific details on projects or contracts successfully completed or extended, whether you were the lead or a team member.

▶ Highlight any planning, analysis, design, implementation, and testing responsibilities.

▶ Provide examples of having design-effective technical architectures.

▶ Include knowledge of development methodologies. (See Figures 11-1 and 11-2.)

Mehal Upahyaha   mupahyaha@gmail.com

124 Elm Street ▪ San Meteo, CA 88767 ▪ 889-909-9878

Java ▪ J2EE ▪ EJB ▪ Weblogic ▪ Websphere ▪ Hibernate ▪ Struts ▪ UML

SUMMARY

- Sr. Developer with nine years experience in full life-cycle development, including analysis, design, development, deployment, testing, documentation, implementation, and maintenance of application software in web-based environment, distributed N-tier architecture, and client/server architecture.

- Experience in designing and developing object-oriented software applications, ranging from e-business, B2B applications, service delivery, asset management, and Internet and intranet applications.
- Sound knowledge of developing applications based on architectures such as Apache Struts Framework, Spring Framework, and MVC architecture.
- Experience in implementing core Java & J2EE design patterns, such as Singleton, Factory Pattern, Service Locator, Business Delegate, DOA, Session Façade, and Value Object.
- Solid understanding of business needs and requirements. Expertise in creating software requirements specification (SRS), preparing functional design documents (FDD), detailed technical design document (TDD), UML diagrams, and exhaustive test plans.
- Strong management, planning, architecting, analyzing, designing, and programming capabilities.
- Excellent analytical, problem solving, communication, and team skills.

TECHNICAL PROFILE

Languages:	Java, C++, HTML, SQL, PL/SQL
Technologies:	J2EE, Servlets, JSP, JDBC, EJB, Hibernate, RMI, JavaBeans, Spring, JSF, MQ Series
Script Languages:	JavaScript
Java IDE'S:	RAD (Rational Application Developer), WebSphere Studio Application Developer (WSAD), NetBean, MyEclipse, and BEA Workshop
Methodologies:	OOAD, UML, Rational Rose 98/2000, Rational RequisitePro, RUP
Application Server:	IBM Websphere, Weblogic Server, Tomcat
Other Tools:	Rational ClearCase, ClearQuest, Microsoft Visio, Visual Source Safe, Borland StarTeam, StarTrack
Software Testing:	Test Plan/Test Cases/Test Suite, Unit Test, Component Test, Regression Test, Junit
Framework:	Struts Framework, Spring Framework, and MVC Framework
Database:	Oracle, DB2, MYSQL
Operating System:	AIX-UNIX, Windows NT

EXPERIENCE

Sr. Developer	Hewlett Packard, Cupertino, CA	July 2005 to Present

Develop and maintain the backend application supporting consumer order directly off the HP web site. This application sits between the consumer web site and the HP ERP system.

- Responsible for gathering system requirements, analysis, design, prototyping, development, and UAT of this system. Also manage an offshore development team.

FIGURE 11-1 Application developer sample résumé

Mehal Upahyaha Page 2

- Additional responsibilities include converting business test cases into technical use cases, ensuring that the quality process is followed and implemented in each SDLC stage, monitoring the development activities by conducting reviews of each development, and configuration management.
- Provided application support during the initial deployment of the application in production environment.

Environment: Java 1.4, JavaScript, JSP/Servlets, EJB 2.0, JMS, JNDI, JDBC, Struts, Spring 1.1, Hibernate, JAXP 1.1, BEA Weblogic 9.1 Workshop, Ant, Log4j, Junit, Oracle 9i, TOAD, Rational XDE, ClearCase, ClearQuest.

Sr. Developer SBC, NY March 2004 to July 2005

This application is used for integrating financial systems and applications for multichannel banking. It consists of a front-end portal framework and an integration (BEA Web Logic Integration) layer between SBC's legacy system and the channel infrastructure.

- Worked with the business analyst in gathering requirements, analysis, and design, and then documenting functional and technical requirements, including software architecture documentation, HLDs and LLDs and technical design using UML diagrams.
- Validated design patterns and implemented design patterns, including Service Locator, Front Controller, Session Façade, Value Object, Singleton, and Façade.
- Implemented STRUTS (MVC) web frameworks.
- Wrote the test plan, test cases, and test scenario units.

Environment: J2EE, Servlet/JSP, EJB 2.0, Struts, Web Sphere 5.1, Quartz Scheduler, XML, DB2, IBM WSAD 5.1, Rational ClearCase, ClearQuest.

Consulting Developer Strategem Technologies Pte Ltd, Singapore October 2002 to March 2004

Customer, MANSION, is a worldwide gaming service provider. Reengineered existing portal from C++, PHP, and ASP.NET to J2EE platform. New architecture included N-tier architecture implemented through SOA to provide business services to different applications, Tangosol for in-memory entity caching, and Model 2X for multilingual and multichannel support.

- Served as the module lead involved in application and architecture design.
- Responsible for gathering the system requirements, conducting the feasibility study, prototyping, analysis, design, system architecture, development, unit testing, and user acceptance testing.
- Wrote detailed functional and technical design documentation for the requirements, owning and controlling the documents.
- Used RAD for development and deploying the code. Monitored the development activities and conducted project reviews at each stage.

Environment: Java, J2EE, JSP, EJB, JNDI, JDBC, Servlets, BEA Workshop, WebLogic 7.0, Oracle 8i, Struts framework, Borland Star Team, Borland Star Track.

EDUCATION

MBA, University Of Pune, India
BS Software Engineering, University of Bombay, India

FIGURE 11-1 *Continued*

119 N. 12th Street, Guelph, MI 58447 ▪ (701) 522-8591 ▪ jeffsmith@hotmail.com

Jeff Smith

Summary of Skills	▪ Ten-year career in commercial and enterprise web software development with team lead experience. ▪ Collaborative, solutions driven senior software engineer with experience in all phases of the software development lifecycle, including client management. ▪ Extensive experience with developing e-commerce systems, custom shopping carts, and integration with third-party payment gateways. ▪ Dedicated to keeping up with new technologies and applying them to solve business needs. ▪ Well-regarded communication skills, resourcefulness, and personal presentation.
Technical Skills	**Languages** — Java, J2EE (JSP, Servlets, JDBC, EJBs, JMS, Struts, Java Swings, AWT, JFC), PHP, Perl, XML, PLSQL, C/C++, Visual Basic, Visual C++
	RDBMS/DBMS — MYSQL, PostGRE SQL, Oracle, MS SQL Server, Sybase, MS Access, FoxPro
	Server/Client Script — UNIX/Linux, ANT, PERL, Python, Shell Script, Active Server Pages (ASP), VBScript, AJAX, XML, JavaScript
	User Interface — HTML, DHTML, CSS, JSP, XSL, and Swing as application and Applets
	Server — Apache HTTP Server, Weblogic, JRUN, Jakarta-Tomcat, IIS
	Operating Systems — Debian GNU/Linux, CentOS, Red Hat Linux, UNIX, Windows NT/9X/2000/XP/Vista
	Multimedia — Photoshop, Flash, ImageReady
	Hardware — Dell, Intel-based PCs, IBM Server Station
	Other tools — TRAC 0.9.6, Eclipse SDK 3.2, TOAD 2.0 for MYSQL, ER-Studio, Dreamweaver, FrontPage, Crystal Reports, PageMaker, COM/DCOM, Visual Source Safe, MFC, ATL, ADO
Employment History	**Sr. Software Engineer** Be Josie, Inc., Santa Ana, CA 9/2004- Present ▪ Developed www.bejosie.com web portal using PHP5/MYSQL5, Drupal 7.2. ▪ Developed migration application for data transfer using PHP/XML. ▪ Worked closely with development team to automate nightly builds of their product using Subversion/ANT/Perl/bash and other scripting languages. Used Eclipse/DBG debugger for debugging and Subversion as CVS.

FIGURE 11-2 Web application developer sample résumé

Jeff Smith

Page 2

- Created, maintained, and supported the build environments using ANT/PERL scripting for development, integration, and staging.
- Identified, set up, and supported key infrastructure requirements for the development and testing teams.
- Installed update source control systems on different platforms.
- Provided support for production systems.

Sr. Systems Engineer,
Twinn Software, Aliso Viejo, CA   6/2002–9/2004

- Developed front-end applets that could be used in a web browser and could generate charts of real-time quotes by reading the values from the corresponding database.
- Middleware development with servlets and JSPs that performed custom analytics on the data reading from the database or from the real-time updated stream. Middle tier development followed J2EE standards.
- Developed and customized a content management system using Drupal. The system supported an e-commerce-based web site using OSCommerce with LAMP extension.
- Developed an HSBC Payment Gateway for e-commerce using servlets.
- Developed applications for concurrency, XML parsing, XML validation, and report generation.

Sr. Software Architect,
SystemsPro Corp., Mission Viejo, CA   2/2000–6/2002

- Developed new web software applications and dynamic web sites.
- Had high-phased interaction with the client, translating needs into technical requirements, selecting the best implementation method and hands on development that included coding, GUI, database development, implementation, and integration with existing systems.
- Developed coding standards using Java, J2EE, EJB, Swing, XML, JSP, and MYSQL.
- Developed object-oriented C++ components and displays using JavaScript and HTML.
- Developed e-commerce systems using OSCommerce, developed custom shopping carts, developed custom extensions to existing e-commerce shopping cart systems, and integrated with third-party payment gateways
- Served as project coordinator leading several projects, defining project proposals, and setting and managing project budgets.

Education | **B.S. Information Technology**,
California State Polytechnic University, Pomona, CA   1999

FIGURE 11-2 *Continued*

Architect

Key Areas to Highlight

Profile Section

▶ Highlight your experience in scoping, architecting, and leading technical teams in the delivery of challenging technical solutions.

▶ Introduce your ability to think strategically and systematically, as well as your abilities to come up with innovative solutions, to manage large projects, to define and implement processes, and to work collaboratively with those across the organization.

▶ Discuss your broad understanding of business processes and industry knowledge, change management, configuration management, consultancy skills, leadership qualities, and credibility.

▶ Assure the reader you have experience with full software development life cycle (SDLC) from design to build, rollout, and support. In addition, mention your broad knowledge of the latest application development and integration architectures and platforms (J2EE, .NET, EAI, SOA, and so forth) with deep understanding in at least one of them.

Experience Section

▶ Provide details of projects you worked on, with particular emphasis on innovative solutions to solve business problems.

▶ Give examples of having taken the senior technical role in influencing the technical direction of a project or program.

▶ Describe your ability with good communication skills in dealing with developers, project managers, clients, and vendors, including the ability to communicate persuasively to explain or support technology design decisions.

▶ Highlight these competencies: information gathering, production of architectural documentation, presentation skills, ability to explain technical concepts to nontechnical people, stakeholder management, time management, prioritization, and providing architectural governance.

▶ Provide examples of continuous improvement, maintenance of a technology framework, and architecture best practice repository

▶ Explain your experience with large complex projects involving distributed components, multiple products, technologies, vendors, and/or platforms.

▶ Give examples of how you mentored and provided support to peers, less-technical consultants, and software developers regarding project activities and technology decisions.

▶ Provide examples of any IT governance boards/committees you participated on. (See Figure 11-3.)

John Peterson

1522 Bernardo Center Dr. ▪ *San Diego, CA 89998* ▪ *(858) 666-3333* ▪ *John.Peterson@yahoo.com*

SUMMARY

- **Enterprise Architect** with five-plus years in the Financial Services industry
- Demonstrated business leadership, and strong technical and functional knowledge of Financial Services, including business process modeling and SOA
- Experienced in developing talented teams focused on exceeding objectives

WORK EXPERIENCE

Enterprise Architect, *Home Lending Center, San Diego, CA*   Dec '04-Present

Chief Architect and member of the IT Steering Committee of a premier subprime mortgage bank based in San Diego, CA.

Responsibilities include the creation of an **Enterprise Architecture** for the organization based on the **Zachman Framework**, creating **position papers** for elements of the IT Strategy and a Business IT Alignment plan, **procuring software solutions** from IT vendors, evaluating current and future **project roadmaps**, leading onsite IT development projects in a **Project Architect** role, and evaluating IT **project proposals**.

Analyzed the subprime mortgage banking business and did a **comparative study** of employer and a competitor, and then presented findings to the Director of Enterprise Architecture.

Provide **standards and guidelines** for technology platforms, business process automation, enterprise SOA, and business IT alignment.

Assumed the dual role of Project Architect and IT owner to lead a major project to facilitate securitization of loans using a Real Estate Mortgage Investment Conduit. Activities included making presentations of the Solution Architecture to business stakeholders and IT Leadership to get the project funded, providing the detailed technical design and leading a team of developers, business analysts, QA and system administrators to implement the project.

Solution Architect, *Blue Ribbon Insurance, San Diego, CA*   Feb '02–Dec '04

Technical Lead and **Architect** for a team of seven J2EE developers and a business analyst in the Internet Policy Self Service group. Responsible for the Coverage Calculator, Policy Updates, Billing Information, and Reports. Supported addition of new Financial Products and new markets. Supported Auto, Home, and Life Insurance products from a **WebSphere**-based custom solution.

Created and implemented reusable SOAP-based Business Services for internal and external customers based on the **ACORD standards**. Assumed responsibility for maintenance and support of the **Enterprise Business Rules Engine**.

Tasks included evaluating business requirements, creating the architecture based on nonfunctional and functional requirements, presenting the architecture to IT and business leadership, negotiating issues with business leaders, troubleshooting, and code reviews.

FIGURE 11-3 Architect sample résumé

John Peterson   Page 2

Sr. Software Engineer, *Janus, Inc., Woodland Hills, CA*   Jan '99–Feb '02

Senior Developer in a team of 15 members that designed and implemented the workflow module of an **enterprise ordering and services platform** that integrated legacy hardware and software provisioning, trouble ticket, ERP, shipping and billing systems with a web-based order entry interface. Interacted closely with a business process reengineering consultant to design the software. The workflow was constructed using **Java Message Driven beans, stateless session EJBs**, and a replicated **ORACLE** database to save runtime state.

Architected and implemented the change order module as a custom **ORACLE-based rules engine** to route any combination of valid changes to the ordered products. Designed message structures using XML schema, and implemented messaging using **MQ Series** and **JMS**. Designed and implemented a daemon process to route orders that had timed out due to error conditions to a manual queue.

Independent Contractor, *Third Wave Contracting, San Francisco, CA*   Feb '95–Jan '99

Responsibilities included business development, object-oriented analysis, design and construction of enterprise information systems. Led groups of developers and provided technical support to marketing. Primarily served as an onsite consultant to client organizations.

Supported application design and development services to multiple clients with emphasis on **Java and J2EE technologies**. Specific tasks involved Architecture related work, messaging with MQSeries, transaction processing, session and entity bean development, container managed persistence, bean managed persistence, declarative and programmatic security, XSLT transformations, implementing filters and servlets, development of custom tags to be used in JSP pages, development of JSP pages using Struts, development of helper classes, JavaBeans and patterns in Java, administration of application servers, java simulations, presentation of designs, and UML models.

Applications Programmer, *ABC Systems Inc., San Diego, CA*   Aug '90–Jan '95

Implemented the Message Center GUI and client code for the Customer Care OnLine application. The client was implemented using Visual C++ and MFC with a third-party Proto View Data Table control. The module is MDI with an ORACLE back end that is abstracted with a middle tier data layer.

Implemented the application wide disclosures management module for the Customer Care application in Visual C++ and MFC. This module ensures that the Customer Care operators inform customers about mandatory information without fail.

EDUCATION

M.S., Computer Science, University of California, San Diego, CA   1990

FIGURE 11-3 *Continued*

Business Analyst

Key Areas to Highlight

Profile Section

▶ The business analyst role is the most mission-critical role in IT today, in fact, it is the vital link between business needs and IT. Make sure you don't come across as just a techie, but highlight your success with meeting business goals. Your opening statement should be business-related.

▶ Have a strong statement about your general experience by providing an overview of your experience, including the number of years' experience as a BA/BSA, breadth of your experience, industries, types of systems supported (client/server, Windows, web-based systems), and development methodologies (waterfall, Agile, RUP).

▶ Describe the types of teams you've worked on, highlighting their size, geographic span, and the strategic importance of the system.

▶ Identify your strengths, including consulting skills, working through the people issues with project management, risk assessment and mitigation, identification of faulty architecture, managing relationships with stakeholders, ability to acquire a good understanding of the problem domain quickly, reengineering business processes, defining continuous improvement processes, building consensus of requirements, strong business acumen, user-interface prototyping, team building, and recognizing and accelerating peer's strengths by delegating the "right task to the right person."

Experience Section

▶ When providing details of the projects you've worked on, first describe the business application, including its strategic importance, the business goals, the users, and how it fits in with the overall business. List the technical environment separately.

▶ Provide details for which parts of the SDLC you were responsible and techniques for how you went about accomplishing these (that is, running workshops for developing use cases, storyboarding design, and user interface prototyping).

▶ Discuss innovation solutions that helped solve business problems.

▶ Describe your ability with good communication skills in dealing with developers, project managers, clients, and vendors, including your ability to communicate persuasively to explain or support technology design decisions.

▶ Step back and provide a broader perspective on your experience. Make sure you include examples of all aspects of project management and business analysis, including requirements gathering, analysis, business process modeling, architecture, prototyping, use case development, test cases, user acceptance testing, and training.

▶ Include your technical expertise, as well as software development, software development tools, and database design. (See Figure 11-4.)

Ted Franks
1001 Park Avenue, New York, NY 10023

212-666-0989 (cell)
tedfranks@gmail.com

Professional Summary

- Seven years of experience as a **Business Analyst** and **Client Relationship Manager** in the **financial industry**.
- Good understanding of basic principles of **financial markets and instruments, Basel risk management, portfolio risk, trading and settlements** concepts.
- Excellent **client relationship management**, communication and presentation skills.
- Worked on multiple projects in a **fast-paced environment**. Good team player.
- Pursuing a certificate in **Financial Risk Management**.

Technical Skills

Business Analysis

- Rational Unified Process (RUP)
- Unified Modeling Language (UML)
- Software Development Life Cycle (SDLC)
- Object Oriented Analysis and Design Concepts (OOAD)
- Business Process Reengineering (BPR)
- Test Lifecycle
- Multitier Web Applications
- Data Warehousing
- Business Intelligence (BI)
- Data Modeling (ORDBMS)
- Service Oriented Architecture (SOA)
- Prototyping
- Agile and eXtreme programming methodologies

Business Documentation

- Documented Business Requirement
- Use Case Specification
- Functional and Nonfunctional Specification
- System Requirement Specification
- UML diagrams (Use Case, Class, and Sequence)
- Traceability Matrix
- Project Estimate
- Change-Version Control
- Training and User Manuals
- Master Test Plan Review (Integration, System, and Acceptance)

Methodologies	RUP, SDLC, OOAD, UML, Data Modeling, SOA, Agile, eXtreme
Modeling Tools	Rational Rose, MS Visio
Project Management	MS Project, Rational RequisitePro
Testing Tools	Mercury and Rational- Quality Center (Test Director), QuickTest Professional, LoadRunner, VrGen, Rational ClearQuest, Manual Testing
Databases	Oracle, Sybase, SQL Server, Informix
Reporting Tools	Crystal Reports, Rational SoDA
Source Code Control	CVS, PVCS, Rational ClearCase
Operating Systems	Windows, UNIX (Solaris), Linux
GUI	Visual Basic

FIGURE 11-4   Business systems analyst sample résumé

Ted Franks   Page 2

Career Experience

Business Analyst	Reuters, NY	Jan. 06–Present

Major Project: Time series analytics implementation. Time Series Analytics provides the capability to extract desired time series across financial instruments for any period, frequency, and tenor, and to provide analytical metrics. Created as a Microsoft Windows application interoperating with Reuters networks and historical market databases hosted in different global locations. Developed according to Reuter's standards for usability, performance, and reliability.

Responsibilities:

- Helped the technical team with the business proposal documentation and presentation.
- Met with client groups to determine user requirements and goals.
- Analyzed business requirements and segregated them into high-level use cases and class diagrams.
- Developed documentation (requirements document, functional specification, and testing plans).
- Conducted weekly meetings to facilitate discussion among the different users to resolve issues.
- Set up definitions and process for test phases, including product test, integration test, and system test.
- Maintained requirements traceability matrix throughout the project.
- Performed system testing to ensure that the compiled software components of the applications adhered to project standards, performance criteria, and functional specifications.

Environment: RUP, Rational Requisite Pro, Rational ClearCase, Rational ClearQuest, MS Visio, UML, SQL, C++, CORBA, and object databases.

Business Analyst	HSBC, NJ	Nov. 04–Dec. 05

Major Project: Consumer-lending web site. Designed and developed consumer-lending web site for HFC (HSBC Finance Corporation), a member of the HSBC Group. Web site enables customers to apply online for personal, real-estate, and auto loans, and to get an instant response.

Responsibilities:

- Worked with business requirements document and user centered design (UCD) to create UML use case, class, and sequence diagrams for developers.
- Assisted with data conversion activities and all levels of testing.
- Participated in the logical and physical design sessions and developed design documents.
- Designed new process flows for the existing system, as well as for the enhanced system.

FIGURE 11-4 *Continued*

Ted Franks   Page 3

- Conducted and led status report meetings with the business and IT teams on a weekly basis.
- Conducted technical review sessions and facilitated other project meetings as required.
- Worked with project management to schedule, manage, scope, and analyze change requests.
- Documented test cases during requirements gathering, analysis, and design phases.
- Responsible for addressing, diagnosing and resolving issues that arise on a daily basis for the team. Also responsible for documenting the causes, analysis, and final resolution to the issues/errors.

Environment: Rational RequisitePro, MS Project 2002, MS Visio, Test Director, Java, Windows NT/2000.

Education

New York University, NY—**Pursuing a Certificate in Financial Risk Management**
Coursework in securities and investment management, measurement and management of financial risk, as well as the nature and operation of markets in futures, options, swaps, and other derivative instruments. Anticipated completion: June 2007.

Rutgers University, NJ—Masters in **International Relations**

Seton Hall University, NJ—BA in **Management Information Systems**

FIGURE 11-4 *Continued*

Consultant

Key Areas to Highlight

Profile Section

▶ Highlight your proven track record in meeting customer needs. Elaborate by mentioning your customer satisfaction record for bringing projects in on time and on budget.

▶ Include a list of the industries and business areas you've worked in.

▶ Identify the range of technologies in which you're proficient. Remember, too much breadth may be considered a negative because customers typically look to hire contractors who are specialists.

▶ Remember to list your interpersonal skills: effective communication, strong project management, adaptability, flexibility, and a solid understanding of business practices.

Experience Section

▶ Highlight projects you lead through the entire life cycle and provide a good description of what was involved in each phase.

▶ Provide details on the project: objective and business challenge addressed, number of man hours, size of team, your exact role, technology solutions, and if the project came in on time/budget.

▶ If you were the project lead on any of your projects, make sure you identify that and the various departments you worked with, along with the number of people you've managed and their roles.

▶ Describe your customer management responsibilities, including helping clients with project management and change management activities.

▶ List other services you may have provided, including documentation and training. (See Figure 11-5.)

CIO

Key Areas to Highlight

Profile Section

▶ Chief information officers (CIOs) aren't just technology leaders, they are business leaders. Open with a powerful statement about the business contributions you've made to the organizations you've been with.

Jennifer Hoffman   jenniferhoffman@gmail.com
65 Granny Avenue, Santa Ana, CA   (cell) 787-999-0897

**Project Management, IT Strategy, Infrastructure, ITIL, IT Governance & Controls,
Team Development, Portfolio Management**

Dynamic leader with strong problem solving, planning, team-building, and project management skills. Hands-on, collaborative management style. Skilled in forming internal strategic alliances, driving cultural change and managing the vendor community. Strong communications and presentation skills effective at all levels of the organization. Cost-conscious and results-oriented.

Recent Engagements

Establishing a Process Methodology Office

> ***Client Need:*** *Client sought to standardize IT processes across the enterprise to achieve operating efficiencies, increase standard of delivery, and reduce IT costs.*
>
> ***Solution Implemented:*** *Established a process methodology office.*

- Identified business process improvement needs, established methods to optimize or reengineer existing business processes.
- Led a number of cross-functional teams through a coauthoring process to develop and deploy a process mapping methodology resulting in significant, measurable improvements across all operating units.
- Initiated a corporate "Best Practice IS Our Standard" campaign to reinforce and invigorate the cultural change necessary to support a more disciplined approach to process management.
- Developed planning methodology to support scalable growth. Increased gross margin and reduced program attrition across key programs by standardizing processes across all locations.

Establishing a Program Management Office

> ***Client Need:*** *Client sought to create alignment of IT project to strategic business initiatives, provide greater measurable business value to its clients, and provide transparency between IT and business users.*
>
> ***Solution Implemented:*** *Established a program management office.*

- Responsible for driving new portfolio management initiatives, project management methodologies, and systems development lifecycles to accommodate an extremely complex global technology architecture.
- Worked to implement a quarterly review process for business and IT users, resulting in an immediate cost reduction of over $20 million by closing nonperforming projects, duplicated efforts, and initiatives that were not strategically aligned or providing measurable business value.

FIGURE 11-5 Consultant sample résumé

- Successfully implemented a portfolio management application, allowing users to have access to timely project and portfolio statistics and reporting, providing an unprecedented level of transparency between the IT and Business users.

- In partnership with the finance and internal audit departments, created the documentation publishing, sign-off requirements, and governance framework to support Sarbanes-Oxley compliance.

- Championed the development of a IT leadership development and technical training program to support building business skills in IT, information gathering, business analysis, and to help users working on "sunset" systems to develop the skill sets necessary to enable their transitions into other technical areas, resulting in increased employee engagement and lower-than-expected attrition.

Client References

CGC, Anaheim, CA
Mays Company, Indianapolis, IN

Credentials

MBA, Wharton School of Business, University of Pennsylvania
BS Computer Science, Rutgers University

FIGURE 11-5 *Continued*

▶ Be sure to mention how you've successfully driven a compelling technology agenda and helped develop the next generation of technology leaders.

▶ Provide an overview of the industries you've work in, your functional knowledge, the scope and scale of your largest IT group, and your geographic management responsibilities.

Experience Section

▶ For a CIO, you want to tell the business story. Business stories are results-oriented. All the examples you provide should discuss cost savings, increased revenue and profitability, increased customer retention, reduced cycle times, or increased productivity.

▶ You can break out your résumé into other sections that focus on key competencies and provide examples of these under each section. These competencies can include: strategy, team leadership, execution, and influence. Under these sections, include details on strategic visioning and direction setting, shifting organizational cultures to be performance/results-oriented, and running IT as a business.

▶ Emphasize strong leadership and business management capabilities. Technical skills should not be the highlight of your résumé. (See Figure 11-6.)

JASON PREWITT

434 Thoreau Lane ▪ Forrest City, AK 92676
949-388-7876 Res ▪ 949-235-4656 Cell ▪ jprewitt@gmail.com

Vice President of Technology/Chief Information Officer

Senior executive, most recently a Chief Information Officer in direct marketing, retail distribution industry. Results driven performance in environments where functional responsibilities have been aligned to business and profit strategies. Ability to structure and empower high-performance IT organizations around the needs of a business. Successful experiences in procuring, installing, and managing state of the art technology systems that were reliable management information tools specific to a company's business and its markets. Demonstrated skills in delivering revenue-generating IT platforms utilized in e-commerce sales and distribution.

▪ IT Strategy	▪ Business Planning	▪ Infrastructure Design
▪ IT Architecture	▪ Process Improvement	▪ Operations Optimization
▪ Strategic Planning	▪ Project Management	▪ Operational Streamlining
▪ Team Leadership	▪ Software design	▪ Technical Architecture
▪ Strategic Relationships	▪ Contract Negotiation	▪ Change Management
▪ Systems Integration	▪ Large Scale Deployments	▪ Cost Containment

PROFESSIONAL EXPERIENCE

Vice President of Information Technology/Chief Information Officer   2003 to Present
Autozone, Forrest City, AK

Responsible for all aspects of information technology at Autozone, including IT strategy, staff development, system development, IT operations, Internet, and e-commerce system development and marketing program support.

- Developed and implemented an IT strategic plan to support revenue growth from $90MM to $200MM in response to investor expectations. Led negotiations and purchase of new technology platforms, development of new staff competencies, and ownership of project as well as corporate change management for all development and implementation projects. Total cost was $3.5 million.

- Replaced all outdated technologies in a three-year time period, including all major IT hardware, software, and application platforms to better position the revenue-generating functions in the organization to achieve its long-term growth commitments to her parent company. Typical contract savings averaged 45 percent discount off list prices.

- Upgraded leadership and development competencies of the IT team. Created a high-performing team through a reorganization and upgrade of its leadership and development competencies, resulting in new abilities to implement the strategic plan.

- Negotiated, purchased, and integrated a $2MM e-commerce platform. Fully operational, this new retail e-commerce environment supports 1.2MM weekly site visits and is the channel for 65 percent of the corporate sales revenue, representing a 25 percent annual sales revenue growth rate.

FIGURE 11-6 CIO sample résumé

JASON PREWITT

- Drove the initiative to significantly reduce IT development and data management costs, resulting in the negotiation of an off-shore contract with an Indian firm that shifted development and data maintenance to an off-shore facility. This resulted in the creation of a 30-person team producing a cost savings of nearly 50 percent of internal IT and data-management labor expense.

- Contributed to corporate profit goals through a reduction of overall IT annual expense by 23 percent. This operating result was accomplished through implementation of modern technologies requiring fewer support technicians and providing the business with an end user capability to maintain its environment and reduce its dependency on IT resources.

Director, Information Technology   2000 to 2003
Chicago Stock Exchange, Chicago, IL

Responsible for managing all aspects of system development projects, as well as the production support of the trading floor commodity futures trade system. Managed a 35-person staff through four direct reports.

Provided management direction to technology and business teams in their coordinated initiative to improve system performance of the trading floor. Redesigned transaction databases that improved reliability and increased transaction volume throughput by over 150 percent.

Responded to the needs of the executive business team with comprehensive planning, technology, and resources required to achieve their financial and operating goals.

Director, Information Technology   1999 to 2000
State Farm Insurance, Chicago, IL

Responsible for managing all aspects of system development in the Commercial Lines business. Managed a 120-person staff through 6 direct reports. Accountable for annual $12 million budget.

Introduced project planning approach to key business executives that prioritized 60,000 hours of system projects into a functional implementation plan that prioritized the backlog of existing system initiatives and integrated new user interface technologies.

Implemented software engineering project methodologies and processes that streamlined software development, and delivered higher quality products on-time and within budget.

Implemented formal project management practices required to effectively plan, monitor, and assess the true status of large development projects.

Additional Experience

Senior Software Product Development Manager   1995 to 1999
Telelogic, Lake Forest, IL

Consultant   1999 to 1994
EDS, Chicago, IL

Senior Development Manager   1988 to 1993
Charles Schwab, Riverwoods, IL

EDUCATION

M.S., Computer Science/Telecommunications Systems, Rutgers University
B.S., Business Administration and Information Systems, University of Maryland

FIGURE 11-6 *Continued*

Database Administrator (DBA)

Key Areas to Highlight

Profile Section

▶ Employers no longer look only for database skills. Be sure to highlight a well-rounded mix of skills in Database Administrator (DBA) duties and development or project management.

▶ Give details of the number of years' experience, the industries you've worked in, and the types of projects you've worked on.

▶ Differentiate yourself by broadening your skill set to include business-facing skills, industry knowledge, and interpersonal skills.

Experience

▶ Provide examples of how you understand the way companies use data and why, including data-modeling techniques, database theory, data warehousing, and data mining.

▶ Provide examples of the types of projects you've worked on and the development environments. Java, Windows, J2EE, and portals provide a competitive advantage.

▶ Read through the job description and be sure to tailor your résumé to include technologies the company is looking for.

▶ Companies value DBAs who have an understanding of finance or accounting, the business processes DBAs support. Be sure to list your experience in the application of the technology, not only the technical stuff. (See Figure 11-7.)

Helpdesk/Desktop Support Specialist

Key Areas to Highlight

Profile Section

▶ Emphasize your proven customer service, flexibility, communication skills, initiative, ability to solve and prevent problems, successful team player, assertiveness, tactful manner, consistency in maintaining service levels to the highest standards, and comfort in resolving problems in a short timeframe and under stressful circumstances.

▶ Provide a brief description of the technologies you've supported and the industries you've worked in.

Penn Jackson   852-666-0989 *(cell)*
89 Appleton Lane, Kansas City, Missouri 77854   pjackson@gmail.com

Professional Summary

IT professional with over 20 years experience in **software engineering** and **database design** with a specialty in **data architecture** and **data integration**. Excel in translating business requirements into a solid data architecture that serves as the foundation for IT design. Bring wealth of practical knowledge and understanding of software development best practices, with proven experience as a team leader and mentor.

- **Data analysis, data modeling, data integration**
- **Database design**
- **Object-oriented analysis and design**
- **Java and C++ development**

- Strong written and oral communication skills.
- Project management of full lifecycle software development projects.
- Persistence, personal integrity, resourcefulness, and exceptional problem-solving skills.

Technical Skills

Databases:	SQL Server, Oracle, Sybase, ODBC, JDBC
Languages:	Java, C++, C, Lisp, Fortran, APL, SQL, XML
Platforms and Tools:	Windows, UNIX, ERwin, Cognos, Crystal Reports

Career Experience

Senior Data Integration Analyst   Sprint Nextel, Overland Park, Kansas   2006–Present

Data integration analyst for a conversion project that replaced two existing Sprint sales compensation systems with an instance of Callidus TrueComp. Served as liaison between business and IT, gathering business requirements and advising IT during design and development phases. Constructed logical data models of existing systems and built database procedures to import legacy data into TrueComp.

Environment: Callidus TrueComp, ETL, SAP

Software Development Team Lead   Euronet, Leawood, Kansas   2000–2006

Team lead and data architect for development of a proprietary billing system and web site. Gathered and documented business requirements, constructed logical and physical data models, built ERwin entity relationship diagrams, led software design sessions, and instituted coding standards. Managed the project from design to production in less than six months.

Managed the data integration of billing systems from five separate companies acquired by Euronet. Reverse-engineered data models of the originating systems, defined the data mapping into the billing system, constructed database procedures and DTS packages to import the data, and managed parallel testing processes to confirm data validity. Data integration tasks were completed in eight months, saving the company millions of dollars in overhead and payroll.

FIGURE 11-7 DBA sample résumé

Penn Jackson   Page 2

Installed and maintained the database and transaction processing software for the PaySpot data center, which sells prepaid telephone minutes to retail stores. Served as SQL Server database administrator and team lead/senior software engineer for all maintenance and new development of the transaction processing system.

Environment: SQL Server, C#, .NET, Java, Struts, JDBC, DB2, AS/400

Sr. Software Engineer	Digital Archaeology, Lenexa, Kansas	1998–2000

Designed and implemented new functionality for the Discovery Suite data mining utility. Developed a task scheduler and a common framework in C++ for importing data through ODBC database connections. Assisted in the development and testing of a Java-based web interface to the system.

Environment: C++, ODBC, Java

Independent Consultant	Fortis Benefits, Kansas City, Missouri	1997–1998

Developed Windows applications for data entry and maintenance of insurance policy information. Responsible for creating C++ objects used in Windows and UNIX applications to retrieve and update insurance information from an Oracle database. Designed and implemented SmartEdit, a Windows application that performs data validation tasks using rules stored on an SQL database.

DBA	Capital Mortgage, Richmond, Virginia	1992–1995

Team lead and data architect for the development of a portfolio management system for mortgage-backed securities. The system was implemented with C++, Powerbuilder, SQL Server, and ERwin SQL. Responsible for its object-oriented design, C++ coding, database design and maintenance, and for the algorithms that comprise the system's analytical engine.

Education

Master of Business Administration,
University of Arkansas, Fayetteville, AR

Bachelor of Science, Physics
University of Arkansas, Fayetteville, AR

FIGURE 11-7   *Continued*

Experience Section

▶ Describe your working knowledge of different workstation hardware, peripheral devices, networks, and system software. Technical skills should include working a knowledge of Microsoft Server, Windows XP, and 2003; MS Office; Outlook; as well as a general understanding of local area network/wide area network (LAN/WAN) networking, virus protection products, and communication protocols.

▶ Provide examples that substantiate proven customer-service skills and knowledge areas. Include examples of identifying and implementing process improvements.

▶ Continue to highlight teamwork, flexibility, attention to detail, taking initiative, follow-through, effective listening, and organizational skills.

▶ Provide examples of technologies and processes you're familiar with. Don't generalize your responsibilities. Breakdown generic job titles, such as. Helpdesk Analyst, by providing as much detail as you can without being redundant.

▶ Provide both the acronyms and the complete spelling of technologies. (See Figure 11-8 and Figure 11-9.)

IT Manager

Key Areas to Highlight

Profile Section

▶ Provide a summary of your business, technology, people, and process skills. Hiring managers want to know you have experience ensuring availability and security of information systems, including corporate applications, databases, and telecommunications, as well as networks (LAN and WAN). They are also looking for your ability to manage internal IT staff and manage multiple projects simultaneously on time and within budget.

▶ Other areas worth mentioning are your ability to lead network support staff, develop relationships with functional groups, and manage and source vendors and consulting groups. They also look for your ability to stay abreast of advances in technology to help business operations use information systems to improve efficiency, productivity, and a competitive edge.

▶ Highlight understanding of business topics: budgeting, project management, developing teams, cutting costs, increasing efficiency, speaking with the business using its language, prioritizing business requirements, using effective communication, and developing strategies (infrastructure, outsourcing, people, business applications, and portfolio management).

▶ Résumé should be about business results achieved with the technology, not only technical details. This means including your experience with developing and maintaining an IT budget.

Joseph Mathews   jmathews@yahoo.com
675 Highlands Avenue ▪ Kansas City, Kansas 56445   (876) 555-1212

PROFILE

- Extensive experience with LAN installation, network reconfiguration, connectivity, network security, Internet, and software/hardware configuration
- Track record for implementing, optimizing, and maintaining high-performance and high-availability network systems
- Proven ability to lead and motivate teams to maximize levels of productivity
- Excellent communicator, with experience working at client sites to facilitate project implementations, support, and training
- Exposed to diverse internal and external technical environments, recognized for ability to manage multiple tasks simultaneously
- Creative, analytical thinker with demonstrated ability to troubleshoot problems, determine strategies to resolve issues, and consistently implement effective solutions
- Microsoft Certified Desktop Support Technician (MCDST)

TECHNICAL SKILLS

Hardware: IBM, Dell, Gateway, Toshiba Notebooks, Compaq Printers HP, Epson, Okidata, Toshiba Peripherals Tape Backups, Memory, Modems, Motherboards, Network Cards, PCMCIA, I/O devices Networks Hubs, Routers, Cabling, 10/l00Base-T

Platforms: Windows 95, 98, NT, 2000, XP, Macintosh, Citrix, Terminal Server, RedHat Linux

Software: Microsoft Office (Access, Excel, FrontPage, Outlook, Outlook Express, PowerPoint, Project, Publisher, Visio, Word), Netscape, Adobe Illustrator, Lotus Notes

Databases: SQL Server, Lotus Notes, MS Access

Tools: Remedy Call Tracking Application, Asset Insight (Inventory Management), DameWare Utilities

FIGURE 11-8   Helpdesk specialist sample résumé

Joseph Mathews Page 2

PROFESSIONAL EXPERIENCE

Help Desk Support Team Leader

GE Capital ITS, Kansas City, Kansas 4/2004–Present

- Managed 18 agents supporting 20,000 employees. Responsible for ensuring the team provided first-level support for Nortel Networks' employees worldwide. Created a graduated perk system for rewarding helpdesk staff for outstanding performance as monitored by spot checks and silent monitoring, creating plans to help poor performing agents achieve their objectives, and, if needed, recommending them for termination.
- Prepared, analyzed, and acted on the team's daily performance in relation to customers SLA's (Service Level Agreement). Improved average calls per hour 22 percent, to the highest in the organization.
- Conducted coaching/training for the team to achieve team goals and organized team-building events and methods of motivating the team.
- Managed escalation issues in PC and customer service environment.
- Prepared reports and presentations for upper management.
- Decreased talk time through effective use of call-handling techniques.
- Created a project tracking system to insure all projects started were successfully completed.

Help Desk Analyst

GE Capital ITS, Kansas City, Kansas 8/2000–4/2004

- Provided first-level PC support for Nortel employees worldwide; maintaining 80 percent first-level resolution. Coordinated with second- and third-level support groups to ensure the appropriate support group was informed of the issue, and then monitored it to ensure the issue was resolved to the customer's satisfaction.
- Skilled in diagnosing and repairing server/workstation network connectivity issues (Win9x, WinNT, Win2000, OS/2).
- Supported Office 2000, Palm Pilots, Netscape, IE, RAS, cable modems, DSL modems, VPDN, Exchange and Notes environment.
- Worked as a field technician troubleshooting PC, Laptop, and hardware issues.
- Used Remedy support tool.

Senior Desktop Support Technician

ABC Computer Group, Kansas City, Kansas 9/1995–2/2000

- Supervised four junior technicians.
- Created a database for tracking repairs and replacements.
- Developed new processes for handling incoming stock for tracking.
- Set up and directed trade shows.
- Trained customer employees in several PC-related topics.
- Tracked stock and maintained records of inventory.
- Handled escalations and irate customers.

EDUCATION

DeVRY Institute of Technology, Kansas City, Kansas 6/1999

B.S. in Computer Science

FIGURE 11-8 *Continued*

Jason Brass   jasonbrass@gmail.com
24 Elm Street • Farsville, NC 88767 • 889-909-9878

Desktop Support • Help Desk • IT Support • CHDP • CompTIA A+

SUMMARY

- Certified Help Desk Professional and A+ certified senior member of the desktop support team providing support for 2,000 users across a five-building campus. Experienced in maintaining 24/7 presence in a mission-critical production environment.
- Interact positively with a diverse range of end users and groups. Communicate well with customers via the phone and e-mail. Provide hands-on support as needed.
- Successful resolution of hardware/software issues. Meet or exceed established SLAs by positively establishing customer expectations, and communicating processes and procedures.
- Motivated self-starter and team builder with an aptitude for learning new skills quickly.

TECHNICAL PROFILE

Operating Systems: Windows 98/2000/XP, Windows 2003 Server, RedHat Linux

Networking: Active Directory, TCP/IP, DNS, DHCP, TELNET, SSH, TFTP, FTP, firewalls, Sonic VPN, Cisco VPN, Citrix Secure Access Gateway, RSA Administration

Databases: MS SQL Server, Microsoft Access, ACT CRM

Applications: Lotus Notes, MS Outlook, MS Office 2003, SAP, Siebel, Dreamweaver, Macromedia Studio, Adobe Acrobat Professional and Reader

Support Tools: Heat, Remedy, GoToAssist, Network Streaming Remote Support, Intuit Track-IT, Ghost, Norton Anti-Virus, Magic, Dameware Remote Control, Trend Office Scan, Symantec AV Corporate Edition, CA ARCServeIT, Veritas Backup, Symantec Enterprise Products

Hardware: Dell desktops, laptops, and servers, IBM desktops and laptops, HP desktops and notebooks, Sony Vaio laptops, network cabling, NetGear routers and hubs, Cisco routers, Sonic firewall, HP routers and hubs, 3Com routers and hubs, Linksys routers and hubs, 802.11g wireless routers, HP, Toshiba, and Lexmark printers

SKILLS

Desktop Support

- Install, configure, and troubleshoot desktop equipment for new users and deploy desktop applications as needed.
- Assign user accounts on both LAN and web servers, and granted permissions to shared resources.

FIGURE 11-9   Desktop support specialist sample résumé

Jason Brass Page 2

- Create and edit documentation for installation and training manuals for employees.
- Install and configure antivirus software on user desktops.
- Analyze frequent problems and consult with network manager, VP of Information Systems, and Software Developers to design and offer training sessions to address end user problems.
- Collect frequently asked questions and wrote formal answers to ensure accuracy of responses and consistency with other helpdesk personnel.
- Monitor available network and desktop disk space to ensure sufficient space for regular and backup operations.
- Maintain server and desktop event logs, and respond to critical system events and failures.
- Perform nightly network backup and data recovery functions.

Help Desk

- Provide telephone and remote technical support.
- Provide first-level support for end users using Citrix Presentation Server-based applications.
- Assign and troubleshoot Citrix Metaframe application permissions and sessions for end –users.
- RSA Secure ID Administration.
- Create and maintain Vantive user accounts.
- Maintain SAP R3, Enterprise Portal, and Business Warehouse accounts.
- Evaluate various application errors for user and escalating problems based on the experienced errors. Perform root/cause analysis.
- Document support issues and resolutions in Help Desk Software. Follow up with end users on resolution satisfaction.

EMPLOYMENT HISTORY

Help Desk Analyst 2006 to Present
Simms Inc., Atlanta, GA

Senior Computer Technician 2002 to 2006
Kyocera Wireless Corporation, San Diego, California

Help Desk Technician 2001 to 2002
PDSHeart, Conyers, GA / West Palm Beach, FL

CERTIFICATIONS

Certified Help Desk Professional, STI Knowledge 2005
CompTIA A+, New Horizons, Atlanta, GA 2004

FIGURE 11-9 *Continued*

Experience Section

▶ Provide the size and location of your teams. Include specific IT functions you've been responsible for. Provide examples of achievements in each of these areas.

▶ Employers want to see progressive experience in IT and actual experience as a manager over your own team.

▶ Provide examples of having increased customer service, improved workforce productivity, helped the company grow revenues through new services, reduced overall costs, come up with innovative services/products to help create a competitive advantage, facilitated better decision making, provided a more secure and stable environment, adhered to regulatory compliance (Sarbanes-Oxley Act of 2002) (SOX), and improved overall service quality. (See Figure 11-10.)

Infrastructure Specialist/Network Engineer

Key Areas to Highlight

Profile Section

▶ Provide a summary of your experience, including the number of years you've been a network engineer, a description of the IT infrastructure you've been responsible for supporting, and the types of systems (WANs, LANs, directory services, perimeter security, data management, telecommunications, computing platforms, and messaging) you've worked on.

▶ Emphasize that your work maintains the highest possible standards and maximizes employee productivity.

▶ Highlight technical expertise in the design, implementation, and support of IT services, as well as systems including the coordination of changes to global IT infrastructure. In addition, include what role you played in reviewing, identifying, and implementing new technologies that improved IT systems and services, and reduced costs.

▶ You want to demonstrate how you maintain a broad knowledge of current and emerging state-of-the-art computer/network systems technologies, architectures, and products. You can mention how you keep abreast of new technology developments and industry trends through active participation in user groups or professional associations.

Thomas Banks
2343 High Road · Catonsville, MD 23433

(410) 455-5678
thomasbanks@gmail.com

Technical Direction · Infrastructure Planning · IT Director · Team Management · Budgeting · Strategic Planning · Vendor Selection · Project Management · Business Analysis · IT Security/Strategy · Network Management · Process Improvement

Seasoned technical specialist and leader with more than 20 years of combined experience impacting corporate performance through skillful alignment of technical resources with enterprise objectives. Experience in orchestrating the design, development, and deployment of IT strategies within diverse business platforms. Proven leadership in identifying and eliminating operational discrepancies with the upgrade of existing systems and implementation of customized solutions. Experienced in developing talented teams focused on exceeding objectives.

PROFESSIONAL EXPERIENCE

Information Technology Director

EASY PRINTS INC.   *Raleigh, North Carolina*   *2003–Present*
Provider of commercial printing services with annual revenues of $100M.

- Led IT strategy including solutions development, budgeting, network design, helpdesk, and computing functions. IT department comprised of 11 team members servicing 5 multistate locations. Managed $2.1M budget and assisted in monthly P&L reviews. Supported 350+ user environment.

- Improved overall IT project management success by establishing an IT Steering Committee and IT Policies/Standard Operating Procedures. These efforts were estimated to have saved the department $210K annually.

- Saved $96K in telecommunications' costs annually by renegotiating existing contracts and further reduced nonlabor expenditures by 40 percent in two years through IT vendor standardization.

- Consolidated technical platforms, including migration of 42-server Windows NT environment to 18 MS Windows 2003 server environment, and CheckPoint Firewall to Cisco PIXs Firewall environment.

- Enhanced technical operations within a 120,000 square-foot warehouse facility by implementing wireless network environment. Improved warehouse management operations by implementing a new barcode scanner system.

- Reduced data entry and manual processes with the implementation of interfaces in .NET environment that connected two main corporate systems.

Information Technology Director/Service Bureau IT Manager

KIMBERLY CLARK   *Greensboro, North Carolina*   *1999–2003*
Garment label printing company servicing markets in Hong Kong, China, and Mexico. Annual revenues totaled over $60M.

FIGURE 11-10 IT manager sample résumé

Thomas Banks   Page 2

- Successfully consolidated three IT departments into a single unit that reported directly to the executive vice president. Served as primary leader of the organization's global IT department with locations in the U.S., Hong Kong, and Mexico. Managed networking, prepress support, global development, helpdesk, business community relations, workflow design, and business process improvements. Served as member of the Board of Directors for the Mexico facility.
- Facilitated annual revenue growth from $24M to $60M by eliminating a 24-hour delay in the transfer of production specifications to overseas locations, and standardized workflow order management to a single process for all product types by initiating the implementation of an in-house ERP system.
- Produced over $800K in new revenue within the first year of introducing a graphic/variable data-management application for a new business unit that facilitated rapid turnaround of order delivery.
- Generated more than $153K savings annually through expert realignment and cross training of technical staff.
- Enabled consolidation of financial data from local/overseas locations with the introduction of ACCPAC Professional Series 6.5 accounting package (GL, AP, AR, and multicurrency).

Senior Systems Analyst

PIXAR GARMENTS   *Cleveland, Ohio*   *1996–1999*

Apparel identification company with locations in Asia, Latin America, Europe, and North America. Annual revenues totaled over $350M. Recruited to direct the implementation of a new MRPII system within the organization's Ohio and Hong Kong locations. Identified and collected user requirements, defined business process for system configuration, and programmed modifications.

- Enhanced performance of MRPII system through modification, introducing ordering, quoting for printing products, and consolidation of shipments.
- Eliminated lost paperwork with the design and development of a Job Tracking System.
- Achieved successful completion of this complex project (with a history of failures), implementing the system within both locations in 11 months.

Additional Experience

IT Manager, Development Services, Outsourced Solutions Inc., Baltimore, MD   1994–1996
Development Manager, Biomed, Inc., Cleveland, OH   1992–1994
Network Operations Manager, American Red Cross, Cincinnati, OH   1990–1992

EDUCATION/PROFESSIONAL DEVELOPMENT

Master of Business Administration in Operations Management
Wake Forest University, Raleigh, NC

Bachelor of Science in Information Processing Systems
University of Cleveland, Cleveland, OH

FIGURE 11-10 *Continued*

Experience Section

▶ Provide examples of having lead or assisted on large technical efforts in the deployment of new technologies. For each project, describe not only the technology, but also the business benefits that resulted. Include benefits that you, personally, brought to the projects, such as team leadership.

▶ Provide a range of projects in which you have experience to demonstrate your breadth and to get the most possible hits. Don't only focus on the exciting projects—also include the roll out of standard platforms and solutions throughout the business.

▶ Highlight any planning, analysis, design, implementation, and support responsibilities. These can include documentation of configuration details, standard operating procedures, and training materials.

▶ Are you looking for more details to include? What responsibilities did you hold that involved recommending, implementing, maintaining, developing, planning, evaluating, installing, configuring, and supporting?

▶ Don't forget the soft skills: strong troubleshooting, analysis, and incident resolution skills, as well as team work and mentoring.

▶ These days, it's not only about the technology; it's also about the business processes of running an IT department. If you're trained in IT service management, that is, Information Technology Infrastructure Library (ITIL), make sure you include that experience! (See Figure 11-11 and Figure 11-12.)

119 N. 12th Street, Guelph, MI 58447 ▪ (701) 522-8591 ▪ sgerman@hotmail.com

Scott German

Summary of Skills	<ul><li>Certified system engineer with broad experience in IT systems management and infrastructure planning.</li><li>Ten years experience administering, maintaining, and supporting secure networks.</li><li>Solid track record for the implementation of technology solutions for optimizing operational efficiency.</li><li>Experienced team leader focused on meeting business needs by delivering excellent service, effectively prioritizing multiple mission-critical tasks and working well under pressure.</li><li>Great work ethic, interpersonal skills, and solid critical thinking and problem-solving skills.</li></ul>	
Technical Skills	**Systems**	Windows NT/2000/2003 Server, Solaris 8, Red Hat Linux 7.*x*, Cisco IOS
	Networking	IPX/SPX, TCP/IP, IPv6, IPSec, FTP, SMTP, HTTP, HTTPS, POP3/IMAP4, DHCP, DNS, WINS
	Server Applications	Exchange 5.5/2000/2003, SQL 7.0/2000 Server, BIND 8.*x* (DNS), IIS 5.0/6.0, Oracle 8*i*/9*i*/10g, Active Directory, MS ISA Server 2002/2004, RightFax Server 8.7, McAfee Groupshield for Exchange, Veritas Backup Exec, PowerQuest Deploy Center, Veritas NetBackup, SMS 2003, Citrix Metaframe XP, Live Communication Server 2003, WebLogic 8, ColdFusion, HP OpenView, Microsoft Cluster Services, Veritas Storage Foundations, Veritas Cluster Services, F5 BigIP Load Balancer
	Network Hardware	HP ProLiant Servers, Dell PowerEdge Servers, Dell Power Connect Switches, Lucent Pipeline router, EMC CX700, Brocade SAN Switches, 3Com switchers/hubs, HP SureStore Backup drives, Cisco VPN Concentrator, Cisco Catalyst, APS UPS
	Desktop Applications	MS Office 2003, MS Project 2003, MS Visio 2003, Norton Antivirus, McAfee Virus Scan, Symantec Ghost, Clearcase
Employment History	**Infrastructure Engineering Supervisor** First American Title Co., Santa Ana, CA 9/2006–Present <ul><li>Manage a team of five systems engineers who were responsible for the daily implementation and maintenance of Microsoft Exchange, Active Directory, SQL Server, and BEA Weblogic. Team served as tier II & III escalation support.</li></ul>	

FIGURE 11-11 Web application developer sample résumé

Scott German Page 2

- Streamlined operations, and optimized environment through automation and standardization, including:
  - Automated application deployments for testing, production, and disaster recovery environments, resulting in the reduction of deployment time from 1 hour to under 15 minutes.
  - Automated server operating system builds, and postbuild software installation and configuration, reducing the amount of time spent performing manual operations.
  - Eliminated manual system administrative tasks with the use of scripting techniques and third-party applications.
  - Implemented a change management process for patch management across development, testing, staging, and production environments increasing environment consistency and reducing overall system deployment time. Deployed Microsoft SMS for server and desktop patch management.
  - Centralized all systems documentation in using Clearcase.
  - Implemented HP Systems Insight Manager to support monitoring of production environment.
  - Successfully implemented weekly maintenance windows via a change management process

Sr. Systems Engineer
Twinn Software, Aliso Viejo, CA 6/03–9/2006

- Successfully led the migration team responsible for upgrading the corporate network from Windows NT, Exchange 5.5, and SQL 7.0 to Windows 2000 (Active Directory), Exchange 2000, SQL 2000, ISA 2000, and IIS 5.0. This included the migration of 250 servers and 2,000 desktops. Team consisted of server administrators and desktop support specialists in five U.S. sites.
- Part of the business continuity/disaster recovery team. This effort included designing and building out the technical infrastructure for the corporate data center in CA. Responsible for the specification and procurement of network software/hardware for the project.
- Additionally, authored, and implemented the Network Operational Procedure Manual to meet business continuity needs.
- Responsible for hiring, mentoring, and training new engineering team members.
- Maintained VPN and security infrastructure, including:
  - Implemented and configured a remote VPN solution for developers using Microsoft RRAS
  - Implemented a firewall solution using Microsoft ISA 2000 Server
  - Maintained corporate web site and host web sites running on IIS 5.0
  - Maintained external DNS services (BIND and MS DNS Services)

Systems Administrator
SystemsPro Corp., Mission Viejo, CA 2/2000–5/2003

- Designed, implemented, and supported LAN, WAN, and wireless networks of more than 1,000 systems.
- Configured and maintained Cisco switches, routers, and CiscoWorks.

FIGURE 11-11 *Continued*

Scott German Page 3

- Installed and administered Active Directory and provided technical support services for servers (Win2K/2003/Solaris/Linux), clients (Win NT/2000/XP), and client/server applications, including backup and restoration of data, OS upgrades, and security patches, and user account creation and maintenance.
- Installed, configured, and maintained domain controller, SQL, Exchange, DNS, DHCP, WINS, and IIS.
- Created and managed user accounts and groups, and set up trusts among the domains.
- Provided support for corporate security initiatives, such as intrusion detection, virus protection, and firewall administration.
- Documented and tracked calls using Remedy and solved trouble tickets daily.
- Design and supported storage area network (SAN) and performed backups using Veritas NetBackup.

Education | **B.S. Information Technology,**
California State Polytechnic University, Pomona, CA   2000

Figure 11-11 *Continued*

GUY PATTERSON

89 Thoreau Drive ▪ Elizabeth, NJ 07202 ▪ 908-989-0099 ▪ guypatterson@gmail.com

Network Administrator ▪ Desktop Support ▪ Networking ▪ Windows 2000 ▪ Windows 2003 ▪ Cisco

PROFESSIONAL SUMMARY

- Seasoned network administrator and desktop support specialist with eight+ years experience in Windows LAN/WAN/VPN environments.
- Proficient at designing and implementing enterprise-wide networking, security, and connectivity solutions that substantially improve operating stability, efficiency, and profitability.
- Persistent in identifying and resolving problems. Peak performer under intense pressure and tight deadlines.
- Skilled technologist who thrives in a fast-paced, changing environment, and brings an uncompromising commitment to quality and customer satisfaction.
- Consistently deliver IT deployment projects on-time/budget, with minimal disruption to critical-business processes.

TECHNICAL SKILLS

PLATFORMS: MS Windows 2003/XP/2000/NT/98/95, Novell NetWare, Red Hat Linux

SOFTWARE: MS Exchange 2003/2000/5.5, Active Directory, Terminal Services, Sendmail, IIS 6.0/5.0, Veritas Backup Exec for NT, SolarWinds, Observer Suite, GFI Mail Essentials, Symantec Mail Security, Norton Antivirus Corp Edition, Norton Antivirus for Exchange, MS Office 2000/2003, SiteScope

NETWORK/SECURITY: VPN, certificate services, SSL, Terminal Services, FTP, DNS, DHCP, WINS, RAS

HARDWARE: Dell Servers/Workstations/Laptops, Xpro Servers, Compaq Workstations, Toshiba Laptops, Exabyte Tape Autoloaders, Sonicwall Firewalls, Cisco Routers/Switches, HP Pro Curve Switches, NICS, Hubs, RJ-45 Cabling, SCSI & IDE Hard Drives, Memory & Peripheral Devices

CERTIFICATIONS

MCSE - Microsoft Certified Systems Engineer
MCP+I - Microsoft Certified Professional + Internet
CNE - Certified Novell Engineer 5.0/4.11

FIGURE 11-12 Network engineer sample résumé

GUY PATTERSON   Page 2

PROFESSIONAL EXPERIENCE

SR. NETWORK ADMINISTRATOR   07/2005–Present
The Banus Group, Morristown, NJ

Oversee the overall operation of a 30-server network. Monitor-mixed Windows desktops/servers, WAN connectivity, Cisco routers, Sonic firewalls, and VPN access. Manage projects to increase productivity and performance. Supervise a team of three desktop technicians. Select, configure, install, maintain, and administer all hardware/software. Configure and manage network routers, managed switches, and firewalls. Document hardware configurations, "share" implementations, and account administration. Register and manage multiple domains used by the company.

Establish and maintain disaster recovery procedures and documentation, including backup/recovery, offsite storage of backup tapes, fault-tolerant disk arrays with hot swappable drives and duplicate OS installations.

Proactively monitor server and network, ensuring 99.9 percent uptime. Provide 24/7 support during outages and critical production runs.

Key Accomplishments

- Reorganized and recabled the network operations center for increased visual appeal, efficiency, and manageability.

- Seamlessly migrated a 30-server Windows NT 4.0 infrastructure to 2000 AD & MS Exchange from 5.5 to 2003, increasing security, stability, reliability, and productivity. Set up and managed a lab environment to effectively test out all major rollouts before move into production.

- Developed the disaster recovery plan, enterprise-wide security structure/policy, and comprehensive backup strategy.

- Implemented VPN access with two-factor authentication, supporting remote users while meeting clients' security requirements. Deployed FTP services using SSL/128-bit encryption to handle sensitive client file transfers.

- Led a major server consolidation and optimization project, requiring migration of servers to a unified Dell platform. Decreased overall downtime by 15 percent.

- Set up a training schedule for desktop technicians with measurable goals, promoting employee growth, and continued customer satisfaction.

- Took initiative to learn Cisco router management and took over role when engineer left the company, eliminating need to hire new staff.

FIGURE 11-12 *Continued*

GUY PATTERSON   Page 3

NETWORK ADMINISTRATOR   2000–2005
UBS, New York, NY

- Member of a 20-person network support team responsible for providing Level 1 and 2 support for 75 Windows 2003 servers.
- Daily responsibilities included installing, configuring, and troubleshooting MS Windows 2003 servers, MS Outlook Exchange 5.5, and SMS Server, and remote and onsite support for 5,000 network users. Installation of hardware and software as needed, including handheld devices, such as Palm and Blackberry.

Key Accomplishments

- Successful migration of 25 Windows NT servers to Windows 2003. Migration was completed in record time with minimal impact to the users.
- Installation and configuration of various software and application, including Novell Client 32, Visio Professional, Attachmate, PC Docs, MS Office 2003, and BackOffice 2000.
- Oversaw the move of all servers to a new location as part of a corporate move.
- Replaced an outdated Token Ring network with a new 10/100Mbs Ethernet network.

EDUCATION

The Chubb Institute   2000

Union County College, Union, NJ   1998
    A.A., Computer Science

FIGURE 11-12 *Continued*

Multimedia Specialist

Key Areas to Highlight

Profile Section

▶ Your goal is to demonstrate your creativity and flexibility so, first, make sure your résumés' presentation rocks and that it's available in multiple formats, including online!

▶ Key skills to include: solid grasp of graphic design, web design and usability principles, current on web technologies, creative thinker who can take an idea from conception to completion, strong design skills, good eye for typography, layout, color, screen layout, and information design.

▶ Provide an overview of what you're capable of producing—from corporate web sites to print-based materials to multimedia presentations on CD and DVD.

▶ Proficiency in the latest tools, including Adobe Photoshop, Adobe Illustrator, Macromedia Flash MX/Fireworks MX, Dreamweaver, and working knowledge of print production processes and software, such as QuarkXpress.

▶ An added bonus is the ability to work well with clients, such as sales and marketing departments, and the IT technical folks.

Experience

▶ To more effectively showcase your capabilities, you could separate your experience area into a work product section and a work history section. Consider grouping your work products into categories, and then provide examples of projects under each category, along with a brief description.

▶ Each project should include deliverable format, the business requirement, a short description of the end product, identification of the people with whom you collaborated to produce it, and how it met the business need. (See Figure 11-13.)

Project Manager

Key Areas to Highlight

Profile Section

▶ Specify how many years of project management experience you have, along with the industry and type of software or systems (that is, custom developed or off-the-shelf implementations).

▶ Emphasize your management experience and include the different aspects of project management you've been involved with (that is, scoping, budgeting, risk management, designing, and so forth)

▶ Describe the skills that have contributed to your success as a project manager: strong communication skills for communicating at all levels of the organization and project team, good interpersonal skills, goal-focused, ability to anticipate problems and recognize warning signals, ability to manage details and ambiguity, detailed knowledge and experience in project management methodologies and tools, and strong analysis and problem-solving skills.

▶ Overview the types of projects you've worked on, tailoring your résumé to the position you're applying for.

▶ Briefly mention the technology environment and the types of roles you've worked with.

Jackie Forbes

786 Treeline Drive, Somerset, NJ   07300 ▪ home (908) 676-6545 ▪ jackieforbes@hotmail.com

profile	Multimedia developer of interactive learning programs and presentations since 1986. Specializing in animation, sound, video, and database integration to create dynamic experiences. Strong design skills along with the ability to work well with clients.
	Windows (all versions) • NT Workstation • Mac Classic • Mac OSX • single or multiuser • English and bilingual • Internet • intranet • DVD • CD-ROM • kiosks
programming environments	Director Lingo • Flash Actionscript 2.0 • JavaScript • VBScript •ASP • PHP • SQL • Visual Basic • UNIX • OOP Structures/Design
development environments	Macromedia Captivate • Adobe Director • Adobe Flash •Roxio CD Creator/Toast • Magic Modules - BuddyApi / BuddyFile • DirectImage • GlobalSCAPE Inc. • CuteHTML • Bare Bones Software - • BBEdit • Apple Computer, Inc. - XCode • Adobe Acrobat • Mscape Iconographer • Microangelo Icon Utilities
net development	HTML 4.01 • XHTML • XML • CSS • JavaScript • VBScript • ASP • PHP
web environments	Adobe PhotoShop • Adobe ImageReady • Corel Painter • GifBuilder • Dreamweaver • Fireworks • Illustrator • Director MX • Freehand • Authorware • Visual Communicator • After Effects • Quark • InDesign • Internet Explorer • Netscape • Mozilla • FireFox • Opera • Safari
database	MySQL • ODBC • Filemaker • Microsoft Access • Custom Design - Director Lingo
sound/mucic development	Digital Performer • Audacity • LAME • GarageBand
technical writing	Adobe Acrobat • HTMLHelp • Flash Paper • Custom Bubbles • Windows Help
work highlights	Abbott Observatory Virtual Tour Apr. 2005–present **Programming/Technical Design/CD Mastering**
	Bilingual (English/Spanish) virtual tour of the observatory designed to run stand-alone or in a dedicated kiosk. CD-ROM is compatible with Windows 95/2000/2003/XP, Mac Classic, and OSX operating systems. CD-ROM includes a screensaver builder and a self- install/uninstall function. Kiosk tracks the frequency of section usage. Kiosks are used by 20,000 visitors each year.

FIGURE 11-13 Multimedia Specialist sample résumé

Jackie Forbes   Page 2

Toolbox: Adobe Director • Adobe Flash • Roxio CD Creator/Toast • Adobe PhotoShop • Authorware

Lick Observatory   University of California   Feb. 2005–Feb. 2006
Programming/Exhibit Installation

Interactive touch-screen exhibits found throughout the observatory covering topics such as the history of the observatory, in-depth presentations on special exhibits, and educational topics, such as a day-in-the-life of observatory workers. Extensive use of digitized video. Touch-screen exhibits are viewed by 50,000 visitors each year.

Toolbox: Adobe Director • Adobe Flash • Roxio CD Creator/Toast • Adobe PhotoShop • Authorware

General Electric   Huntsville, NC   Feb. 2000–Feb. 2005
Ecommerce development/Web development

Led web development team responsible for creating and maintaining the organization's intranet accessed by 2,000 employees. Created static and dynamic templates for easy maintenance.

Toolbox: Homesite, Perl, SourceSafe, TeamSite, HTML, Dreamweaver, Fireworks, Photoshop.

other projects
- CD-ROM English language preschool program to teach colors and shapes
- Conversion of repair manuals from paper to CD-ROM Jiffy Lube
- Four kiosks to teach water conservation for the State Of Nevada
- CBT on Object Oriented Programming for Microsoft University
- Sales presentations for Microsoft, Boeing, and Caterpillar
- Legal Animations for court exhibits

education   Bachelor of Arts, Multimedia Technology   Sep. 2000
George Mason University, Fairfax, VA

FIGURE 11-13 *Continued*

Experience Section

▶ As you describe each of the projects you've worked on, make sure you identify the object of the project, the business goal it met, the value of the project to the organization, the number of people involved on the project, the number of man hours to complete the project, and if it came in on time/budget. Identify any challenges you solved along the way (that is, motivating team members , managing scope, managing crises, and so forth)

Jack Frost   jackfrost@yahoo.com
654 Highlands Avenue ▪ Kansas City, Kansas 56445   (876) 555-1212

**Project management (including Agile) · Business Analysis · SDLC · Change
Management · Systems Integration · Web-Based System Design and Delivery
· Business Process Engineering · Client Relationship Management**

PROFILE

- PMP-certified IT Project Manager with MBA and over ten years experience in high tech, communications, and banking industries managing a broad range of IT projects, including business intelligence, data warehouse, web application development, and customer-relationship management projects.
- Full Project Lifecycle Management experience, including defining and implementing project management methodologies, analysis, and prioritization of projects, and staffing, training, and communicating to Senior/Executive Management. Excellent oral and written skills.
- A good communicator with excellent interpersonal and organizational skills, comfortable working with people at any level in the organization.

PROFESSIONAL EXPERIENCE

Sr. Project Manager

Countrywide Home Loan, Dallas, TX   4/2004–Present
Adjustable Rate Mortgage (ARM) Loan Servicing Re-engineering   *Budget: $4 million*

Project consisted of reengineering the current loan servicing system that ran in a RPG (AS/400) legacy green screen environment to using object-oriented technologies. This was an 18-month project. Managed team of seven geographically dispersed developers and business analysts.

- Member of the IT Methodology Advisory Board (MAB). Provided recommendations on technology and methodology standards. Recommendations included: Agile project management, MS Project, PMBOK, Websphere, UML, Java, Dimensions, FiTNesse, AS/400, IBM iSeries and pSeries servers, Visio, Spring, Hibernate, Oracle, DB2, MVC (Model-view-controller), and Dashboard (KPI). Standardization reduced cycle time and maintenance requirements across IT.
- Effectively worked with the client executive management team in helping to understand the benefits of transitioning from the current pure waterfall software development practice to the Agile practice. The implementation of this methodology reduced development time by 25 percent and provided a more positive working relationship between IT and a client group in comparison to past projects.
- Overall responsibilities included project planning, prioritization, scheduling, resource planning, tracking, and collaboration. Daily responsibilities included leading recurring daily project status (scrum) meetings and providing weekly/biweekly status reports/update to executive management.

Figure 11-14 Project manager sample résumé

Jack Frost Page 2

- Managed the team to four-week time-boxed iterations. This approach allowed for greater interaction with the client, increased communication, increased feedback, and provided a shorter time frame from learning to implementation.
- Collaborated with other IT teams, including architecture, compliance, and engineering.

Project Lead

State of California, Sacramento, CA	2/2002–4/2004
State of California Portal Web Sites	*Budget: $2 million*

Directed a team of ten developers in maintaining the California portal web sites spanning multiple application and Oracle servers running on Solaris. Coordinated the sharing of resources and services between government agencies. Provided 24/7 in-house and telephone support.

- Maintained 99 percent uptime of critical servers through proactive monitoring.
- Collaborated with development team to improve portal application.
- Aided in the training and development of the Verity search engine and its smooth integration with application servers.
- Identified numerous areas that lacked processes, and instituted procedures to ensure effective implementation.
- Streamlined processes for first-level operations and internal customer communication channels.

EDUCATION AND CREDENTIALS

PMP Certification (Project Management Professional),
PMI (Project Management Institute)

M.B.A., International Business
Our Lady of the Lake University, Dallas/San Antonio, TX

Customer Relationship Management Certified
Siebel CRM

FIGURE 11-14 Continued

▶ Provide evidence of having used standard software development life cycle and project management practices for requirements gathering, building work breakdown structures, estimating, risk management, and so forth.

▶ Reference your demonstrated ability to work cross-functionally, manage large teams, communicate openly with the team, manage expectations, adhere to standard practices, secure buy-in, and work across geographic regions. (See Figure 11-14.)

Quality Assurance Specialist

Key Areas to Highlight

Profile Section

▶ Highlight your total experience in quality assurance, including number of years, types of applications you have experience testing, and industries you've worked in.

▶ Demonstrate your range of experience in testing processes and methodology (manual to automated), along with solid understanding and experience in the software development lifecycle.

▶ You may benefit from detailing your QA experience in a separate section, in addition to listing your technical experience. This may include listing areas of expertise, including manual testing, automated testing (and respective tools used), GUI testing, functional/integration testing, reliability and recovery testing, system testing, performance/stress testing, UAT, regression testing, and so forth.

▶ Mention any experience beyond systems testing, for example, involvement in designing, building, and configuring test labs or helping to establish or mature a company's QA practices or team.

▶ Good personal qualities to draw out: good communication skills for communicating within IT and with clients; a strong desire for quality; attention to detail; analytical ability; and the ability to work collaboratively with business analysts, testers, developers, and other IT members in complex testing projects.

▶ Don't forget to mention any certifications you may have.

Experience Section

▶ Detail each role by including more details on the systems you tested, their application, and the testing processes and requirements (quality policies, procedures, test plans, and test case documents).

▶ Employers want to see your proficiency with testing processes and test strategy development, as well as detailed test planning. Include experience in documenting and packaging test suites, in addition to test data for other groups to use.

▶ Additional experience to highlight if you can:

   ▶ Having implemented new testing tools and methodologies

   ▶ Participating in issue resolution with different IT groups, as necessary

   ▶ Working with other IT groups to mitigate unresolved issues

▶ Remember, testing is like software development. It looks different, depending on the application and the technology. Be specific in identifying your technical experience. (See Figure 11-15.)

Jesse Barth   jessebarth@hotmail.com
1233 Elm Street, New York, NY   435-888-9090 (home)

Quality Assurance, Quality Control, Testing, Automation, Test Management, Project Management

Profile

- Over seven years experience in software quality management, project management, quality assurance, quality control, and testing of client/server and web-based applications.
- Experienced in implementing QA processes and tools, leading multiple projects, developing test strategies, setting up test environments, and metrics and measurement.
- A self-starter with a goal-oriented approach to problem solving, well organized, and excellent communication skills. Experienced working with customers, users, project teams, and senior management.
- Certified PMP (Project Management Institute) and CSQA (Quality Assurance Institute).

Technical Skills

Operating systems	MS Windows 95/98/NT/2000/XP, Linux, UNIX (HP, Sun)
Languages	VB.NET, Java, TSL, SQL, PL/SQL, C, C++, VB6.0
Internet Technologies	ASP, VB Script, JavaScript, Java, JSP, HTML, DHTML, XML, IIS
Databases	ORACLE 9i/8i, MS-SQL Server 2005/2000, DB2 and MS Access, FileNet
Tools	Rational Robot, Quick Test Pro, Quality Center/Test Director, WinRunner, LoadRunner, Rational Clear Quest, Rational Test Manager, PVCS Tracker, Silk Test

- Manual testing	- Automated testing	- GUI testing
- Functional/integration testing	- Reliability and recovery testing	- System testing
- Performance/stress testing	- Regression testing	- UAT
- Black box testing	- White box testing	- Usability testing
- Security testing	- Compatibility testing	- Beta testing

Professional Experience

QA Manager   All scripts, Chicago, IL   2005–Present

All scripts is the leading provider of clinical software, connectivity, and information solutions that physicians and other healthcare professionals use to improve patient care.

- Served as the QA Manager for various projects associated with the release of the Touchmate product.

FIGURE 11-15 Quality assurance specialist sample résumé

- Managed daily operational functions associated with quality assurance. Responsibility for over 14-member team of QA analysts, automated, and manual testers. Responsible for developing the test strategy/test plan for every project and release, estimating of work effort, prioritizing work, distributing work assignments, and resource planning. Provided status reports to upper management on a regular basis.
- Implemented development process improvements, including requirements sign off by QA, mandatory documentation by development, and new process around bug-tracking tool. Also, improved efficiency and traceability by implementing requirements entry, test case creation, and defect tracking in Quality Center.
- Worked with customers to understand and resolve issues and maintain a high level of customer satisfaction. Coordinated a partnership program with clients that helped perform testing by real users.

Environment: WinRunner, LoadRunner, LoadRunner Analysis, Quality Center, Window NT and UNIX, SQL, C for LoadRunner

QA Manager   Zurich North America, Chicago, IL   2003–2005

Zurich North America is a leading commercial property-casualty insurance provider serving the multinational, middle market, and small business sectors in the United States. Served as the QA Manager for different projects related to integrating claims processing systems across Zurich.

- Responsibilities included planning, implementing, and monitoring QA process; implementing process improvements; conducting training; facilitating peer reviews; and managing work assessments, work assignments, status reviews, and generation of reports.
- Managed different types of testing, including sanity, integration, functional, and performance testing.
- Developed performance test plan and performed root cause analysis of major problems. Implemented process changes so problems don't occur again.
- Built suites in Rational Test Manager with sync points, think times, and multiple user groups to simulate real users. Set up test agents, added to the suites, and created data stores for rational test manager to store logs. Led the performance testing efforts by coordinating activities and people from different groups. Analyzed the performance results and generated reports.

Environment: Test Director, WinRunner, TSL, SQL, PL/SQL, Oracle 9i, Windows NT/XP, PVCS Tracker, FileNet eProcess, XML

Quality Assurance Analyst II   International Decision Systems, MN   2001–2003

International Decision Systems delivers a range of services to ensure today's business thrives from system-selection forward. Today, more than 42 percent of the U.S. leases receivables and 20 percent of the world's lease receivables are entrusted to IDS solution suites.

- Worked with product development to develop test scenarios and test cases based on different methodologies, including use cases, supplementary specifications, and narratives.
- Planned, scheduled, coordinated, and implemented testing projects to meet project schedule.

Figure 11-15 *Continued*

- Maintained the testing environment for the entire functional testing group, including creating test environment set up from scratch, and maintaining preview and one-back environments for upcoming and patch releases.
- Stayed current on latest release of testing tools and maintain builds of testing tools used by the QA group.
- Maintained and updated test databases.
- Worked with distribution and version control mechanisms.

Environment: Test Director, Windows 2000/98, ASP, IIS

QA Testing Analyst   Digital River, Inc, Eden Prairie, Minnesota   1999–2001

Digital River is a global leader in e-commerce outsourcing.

- Performed functional, user interface, integration, regression, and acceptance testing.
- Developed test plans and cases, set up hardware/software environments, and recommended improvements for the development team.
- Wrote test plans and created test cases against functional requirements and other nonsource-code development artifacts.
- Performed white box test based on preset path and conditions for online store application.
- Used automation tool to automate test cases and verified results.
- Translated manual test cases into automated generalized test suites.
- Tested intranet applications running in a clustered environment consisting of NT and UNIX servers.
- Executed test cases, diagnosed and resolved problems, and generated problem reports.
- Successfully implemented test plans and produced summary reports.
- Executed test cases, diagnosed and resolved problems, and generated problem reports.

Environment: Test Director, Windows 2000/98, ASP

Education

B.S. in Computer Engineering, University of Memphis, Memphis, TN

FIGURE 11-15 *Continued*

Security Analyst

Key Areas to Highlight

Profile Section

▶ Organizations want security professionals with a broader mix of skills, with the emphasis shifting from in-depth technical expertise to good business and interpersonal skills. This means providing your experience in business terms, such as security evaluation, risk analysis, assessment, and mitigation.

▶ Begin with a strong statement about your network security/information assurance experience, including certifications and security clearances. List your specialties from server hardening and security vulnerability scanning to transport boundary configuration, including VPNs, firewalls, intrusion-detection system configuration, monitoring, and performance.

▶ Security analysts must have broad experience in networking technologies. Provide a summary of your experience, including the number of years in networking and the types of systems.

Experience Section

▶ Employers are looking for the following skills. Make sure you intersperse these throughout your résumé.

  ▶ **Technology** Broad knowledge of networking technologies and more specialized experience with identity management, strong authentication, biometrics, anti-virus, intrusion detection, antispyware, firewalls, encryption, and mobile and virtual environments.

  ▶ **Technical** Architecture skills that demonstrate big-picture thinking for aligning and integrating technologies.

  ▶ **People** Ability to speak the language of senior managers and communicating across the organization, interpersonal skills, and relationship management skills.

  ▶ **Business** Business acumen, understanding organizational cultures, and sound knowledge of general business concepts.

  ▶ **Process management** Service and operations management, vendor management skills, and ITIL experience is a plus.

▶ As you describe your role, separate it into describing the every day responsibilities and high-impact projects. You can also draw attention to business results.

▶ Highlight your risk-management capabilities, including different approaches, such as scenario planning for detailed, methodology-based assessment tools.

▶ Don't forget to include regulatory compliance experience with Sarbanes-Oxley and other regulatory agencies. (See Figure 11-16.)

Shawna Kvislen

1632 Prairie Drive, Sioux City, IA 67543 ▪ 550-787-9089 ▪ Shawna_kvislen@hotmail.com

KEY QUALIFICATIONS

- Security specialist with over nine years experience in **designing, implementing, and configuring secure networks,** with four years of experience in implementing, troubleshooting, and supporting advanced **IDS systems.**
- Well versed in current published attack methodologies. Experienced in the use of automated host-based intrusion detection and response systems, firewalls, proxy servers, strong certificate-based encryption, and router and switch access control lists.
- Skilled in developing effective relationships with management, coworkers, customers, and vendors. Team player with solid communication skills. Detail-oriented individual in time-sensitive situations.
- **CCSP** and **CISSP** certified.

TECHNICAL SKILLS

Operating systems: Windows NT/95/98/XP, NetWare, Linux, SunOS, Solaris, FreeBSD, OpenBSD, MacOS, OpenBSD, NetBSD, AIX, HP-UX

Security systems: Snort, Alert Logic, Enterasys Dragon, AirMagnet, ISS, Trend Micro Viruswall, Symantec Security Information Manager, ServGate Edge Force M Series, Blue Coat SG, AV, RA appliances, Check Point Firewall-1, Cisco PIX, Net Ranger, Black Ice

Tools: Encase, Symantec Forensic Utility, TCT Forensic Tool

Web servers: WebSphere, MS IIS, Netscape Enterprise Server, Netscape FastTrack Server, Apache Webserver

Devices: Cisco Routers, Juniper Net Screen, Nortel devices, Nbase Xyplex terminal servers, AlertLogic

Protocols: TCP/IP, IPX/SPX, ATM, OSPF, RIP, EIGRP, IGRP, BGP, MBGP, HSRP, IKE, IPSec, PPP, IGMP, DCP, L2TP

CERTIFICATIONS

MCSE, CCSP, CISSP

EXPERIENCE

Network Security Analyst, Tricon Manufacturing   6/2003–Present

- Consulted with and advised senior management of current and future security threats and appropriate security countermeasures to combat against unauthorized access to IT assets.
- Responsible for system administration of over 30 Cisco and Alert Logic IDS sensors, including the configuration, installation, and auditing of PIX and Netscreen firewalls.

FIGURE 11-16 Security specialist sample résumé

Shawna Kvislen

- Conducted evaluations of existing technical documents for accuracy and completeness, and developed a penetration testing and vulnerability analysis plan.
- Responsible for the importing and maintaining proxy logs for a 30,000+ enterprise user-wide reporting solution.
- Research, evaluate, test, recommend, and implement new security products and releases.
- Additional responsibilities include troubleshooting security-related problems, and interfaces with internal and external audit requirements in compliance with SOX.

Internet Security Analyst, Vistainfo   4/2000–6/2003

- Maintenance of the firewall rule-base, overall network security, development of VPN connections between company and customer locations, firewall monitoring and alert, and monitoring the corporate network for possible network intrusion.
- Extensive knowledge of firewall setup and administration using Checkpoint Firewall-1, Linux iptables, NATs, and VPNs.
- Experienced in bandwidth management, monitoring, and ensuring quality of service.
- Addition responsibilities included administering and creating secure UNIX (Solaris, Linux, OpenBSD, FreeBSD) and Windows NT environments.
- Project included centralizing 70+ company domain names hosted at different ISPs to the company's own name servers running Open BSD and BIND 8.x/BIND 9.x.
- Also migrated 20+ company nationwide locations to one namespace. Configured DNSSEC, multiple views, zone delegation, multiple name servers, DHCP, and host registration with DNS via dynamic updates and TSIG signed zone transfers. Tested interoperability with Microsoft DNS servers.

Network Administrator, Trinity College   10/1998–4/2000

- Managed and performed the statistical and tactical aspects of disaster recovery, auditing, and security policies, procedures, and guidelines.
- Performed security administration functions (maintaining users, groups, IDs, and passwords) for HP, UNIX, and FileNet systems at corporate and field locations.
- Implemented and oversaw the installation and configuration of Windows (95/98/NT), Novell, and UNIX operating systems.
- Worked with other network administrators in troubleshooting and maintaining the network with over 2,000 client computers while ensuring top security.

EDUCATION

BS in Computer Science, California Technical University, 1998

FIGURE 11-16 *Continued*

Technical Writer

Key Areas to Highlight

Profile Section

▶ The most important skill you can highlight as a technical writer is your ability to communicate effectively with and understand customers and internal teams, and to deliver documents necessary to make them successful.

▶ As a writer, you also want to ensure you demonstrate you have the ability to adapt your writing style to various industries and technical environments.

▶ A broad knowledgebase is important, especially one that spans different computer environments from software and hardware, in general, to specific systems. As a part of this include a general sense of the scope of the projects you have worked with and the deliverables you produced.

▶ Qualities to highlight about yourself: creative, self-directed, team-oriented, customer-focused, and productive.

Experience Section

▶ To more effectively showcase your capabilities, separate your experience area into a work product section and a work history section. Consider grouping your work products into categories, and then provide examples of projects under each, along with a brief description of each.

▶ Each project should include deliverable format, the business requirement, and a short description of the end product, along with the identification of whomever you collaborated with to produce it and how it met the business need. (See Figure 11-17.)

Telecommunications Specialist

Key Areas to Highlight

Profile Section

▶ The world of voice and data is converging and, in this role, you want to highlight your experience with designing and implementing next-generation data and voice solutions. Provide an overview of how long you've worked in this area, your experience with key technologies, such as telephony, data, video, and multimedia services and the role you planned—planning and designing, administering, or both.

Jamie Guthrie
233 Elm Street, New York, NY

jamieguthrie@hotmail.com
435-888-9090 (home)

Technical Writing/Documentation/Communications Specialist

Profile

Skilled professional with over **eight years** of **technical writing**, **systems analysis**, and **corporate communications** experience.

- Strong writing, editing, proofreading, and instructional design skills. Sensitive to deadlines and priorities. Ability to manage multiple tasks simultaneously and to manage cross-departmental relationships.
- Expert at learning new software both to use and to document. Skilled researcher, both independently and by interviewing subject matter experts (SMEs). Although not an engineer or programmer, adept at gleaning information from those experts and translating their inputs into documentation easily understandable by the end user.
- Applied knowledge of Rational Unified Process (RUP) and Microsoft Framework Development methodologies.
- Creative, focused, positive, and persistent problem solver. Enthusiastic team player as well as highly achieving independent contributor. Develop and maintain an excellent rapport with customers and coworkers.

▪ Online help	▪ Training	▪ Proposals	▪ User guides
▪ Manuals	▪ SDLC documentation	▪ Policies & procedures	▪ Quick references
▪ FAQs	▪ Release notes	▪ Business plans	▪ Statements of work
▪ Marketing materials	▪ Newsletters	▪ Presentations	▪ Brochures
▪ Internet web site	▪ Intranet web site		

Tools

MS Office Suite (Word, Excel, Powerpoint, Visio) ▪ MS SharePoint ▪ Outlook ▪ FrontPage
▪ RoboHelp ▪ HTML ▪ Doc-to-Help ▪ Adobe Acrobat ▪ Adobe Photoshop ▪ DreamWeaver
▪ FrameMaker ▪ Fireworks ▪ PageMaker ▪ ClearQuest/ClearCase ▪ Visual SourceSafe

Professional Experience

TECHNICAL WRITER/PROJECT LEAD   Library of Congress   2006–Present

- Serve as project lead on the Library of Congress Technical Documentation Team. As lead on this project, provide guidance to team of technical writers regarding documentation content, format, and overall presentation of their materials. Establish and implement standards for online help, user guides, release notes, and quick tips.
- Work hand-in-hand with management and the IT development team to consolidate and produce documentation in line with system enhancements and patch releases.

TECHNICAL WRITER/TEAM LEADER   US Postal Service, Washington, D.C.   2004–2006

- Led a project team of four technical writers and a web site developer on the deployment of context-sensitive online help (using RoboHelp) to support the job requirements and instructional needs of over 3,600 U.S. Postal Inspectors and employees nationwide.
- Developed user guides to introduce and ensure the seamless adaptation of automated business processes.

FIGURE 17 Technical writer sample résumé

Jamie Guthrie Page 2

- Reengineered and implemented revised format and content standards for online help, requirements specifications, use cases, functional specifications, release notes, and FAQs. Revised standards resulted in a 50 percent decrease in calls to the helpdesk.
- Developed Systems Development Life Cycle (SDLC) documentation based on meetings among USPS managers, inspectors, and developers.
- Collaborated with management on proposals, annual reports, and policies and procedures manuals.

TECHNICAL WRITER   FAA   2003–2004

- Developed user guides and quick start guides for the Federal Aviation Administration (FAA), incorporating specified instructional requirements and ensuring overall content accuracy.
- Acted as a liaison between clients and developers to both gather and manage system requirements.
- Developed presentation material and instructional guides to reinforce training and to assist in testing prior to the release of GUI software applications.
- Directly impacted business development by contributing to and providing content feedback for Technical Proposals, Whitepapers, Training Plans and Public Relations Material, including: Brochures, Product Summaries, and Department Overviews.

TECHNICAL WRITER   Fannie Mae, Inc.   2001–2003

- Provided technical writing and communications support to a team of business and technical experts on a critical Sarbanes-Oxley/compliance initiative.
- Consulted with policy stakeholders and the Office of the CIO to develop policies, standards, and procedures consistent with the organization's IT policy framework and consistent with the internal policy approval process.
- Provided input and feedback on the IT policy framework, templates, and the overall policy schedule.
- Collaborated with communications team to draft and publish policy and standard communications.

EDUCATION

Rutgers University, Camden, NJ, 1997
B.A. in English and Communications (Dual Degree). Served as editor-in-chief of the university's literary magazine and as a staff writer for the university's newspaper. Received two writing awards.

Temple University, Philadelphia, PA
Completed a web site Design and Development certificate program, including courses in HTML, Dreamweaver, and PhotoShop.

Moore College of Art & Design, Philadelphia, PA
Completed several desktop publishing, web site design, and HTML courses.

MEMBERSHIPS

Society for Technical Communication (STC)

Figure 11-17 *Continued*

Ralph Emerson   ralphemerson@hotmail.com
233 Elm Street, New York, NY   435-888-9090 (home)

IP Voice & Routing and Switching Network Engineer

Avaya, Nortel, Cisco/Routing and Switching Data Network Architecture/Voice
and Data Planner/Operations Enterprise Engineer

Professional Highlights

Expert in the design and implementation of cost-effective, high-performance, state-of-the-art IP voice and data networking solutions to address complex business requirements for small-to-large enterprises. Respected leader of diverse, cross-functional, data network operations groups and highly regarded as a key technical resource, critical thinker, and out-of-the-box problem solver. **ITIL certified** with a **master's degree** in telecommunications and **12 years experience** in the IT industry. Proactive, forward-thinking individual with high energy, motivating personality, strong mentorship abilities, and an eagerness to learn new technologies.

Technology

Telecom Platforms:	Avaya (S8700, G3R, G3Si, Prologix versions), Avaya BCMS & CMS (ACDs/PBXs)
Network Topologies:	ISDN, PRI/BRI, Frame Relay, T1, T3, DS3, DID, DOD.
IVR Platforms:	Avaya TM
Design Skills:	Call center and call routing design, PBX design, installation, administration & maintenance, IVR, voicemail, VoIP interfaces with PBXs.
Protocols:	TCP/IP, ICMP, UDP, SNMP, SMTP, BGP, and OSPF
Hardware:	Avaya Definity PBX, Intuity Voicemail System, Nortel Passport 7480, Cisco IGX 8430, Cisco MGX, Cisco 2600 series router, Cisco 2900 Switch, Avaya Cajun Switch. Nortel Baystack 470
Software:	Avaya S8700 programming, Cisco IOS, Cisco IGX 8430 programming, Nortel Passport 7480 programming, Microsoft Windows 95/98/2000/NT/2003, Windows NT Terminal Server
CRMs:	NICE CLS Server and loggers, Witness Systems

Experience

Principal Voice Engineer   Citigroup, New York, NY   June 2006–Present

Citigroup's operations encompass a premier global corporate and investment bank and a well-established consumer business under the Citibank and CitiFinancial brands.

- Responsible for the overall voice and data architecture of the Global Contact Center, which provides telecommunication products and services, such as voice, e-mail, Internet, data processing, and desktop support to Citigroup's business units.

FIGURE 11-18 Telecommunications specialist sample résumé

Ralph Emerson   Page 2

- Managed a team of 18 engineers from data (LAN), voice, telecom (WAN), and application support side, which achieved 99.975 percent of uptime consistently for a period of six months.

- Planned, proposed, and implemented changes in existing network infrastructure during expansion and reduced expenses for additional equipment (multiplexer).

- Established and documented procedures for Technology Risk Assessment Manuals (TRAMs) on voice, LAN, and WAN side.

- Proposed and conducted training sessions for helpdesk to support MIS, operations and sales departments. Initiatives increased technical skills of users (call center agents) and eliminated overtime for technical staff.

Principal Technical Engineer   Level 4, Broomfield, CO   May 2002–June 2006

Level 4 is an international communications company. The company operates one of the largest communications and Internet backbones in the world.

- Doubled network performance by installing a state-of-the-art clustered gigabit backbone. Project was completed three months ahead of schedule and $120K under budget.

- Improved customer satisfaction, increased department-wide productivity, and reduced expenses by establishing the organization's first NOC. The system reduced the need for second and third shifts.

- Reduced network vulnerabilities by redesigning and implementing consistent security throughout the enterprise using a layered approach and the latest technologies. Helped prepare the network for successful IT-compliance auditing.

- Developed disaster recovery procedure that allowed rapid recovery in a mission-critical environment.

- Served as the senior escalation point for daily router/switch security issues in support of the NOC and R&D Departments. Contributed to the production of reports and postmortems on events and outages related to the job.

- Full project life cycle for enterprise-scale network contingency planning, network configuration, optimization, and redundancy and routing design.

- Configured and maintained routers, switches, firewalls, and load-balancing solutions from Cisco in a web-hosting, mission-critical, $24 \times 7 \times 365$ high-availability environment.

Sr. Network Engineer—Network Operations Center
Metagroup, Cincinnati, OH   July 2000–June 2002

Metagroup manages international call-centers with capacity of 1,500 plus agents. Metagroup partners with best of breed technology providers, including Avaya, Cisco, HP, Dell, IBM, Nortel, and Sun.

- Responsible for configuring, administering, and upgrading PBX equipment (Avaya G3R) and WAN switches (Nortel Passport 7480.)

- Configured new E1s/T1s for voice connectivity between Avaya G3R and Nortel Passport 7400.

FIGURE 18   *Continued*

Ralph Emerson Page 3

- Administered Layer2 switches (Avaya Cajun P332 and Nortel Baystack 470 Switches).
- Administered Lucent wallboard, call reporting, and monitoring software including Wintap, CDR, CMS, BCMS.
- Reduced system downtime by managing vendor relationships with IXCs and LECs during link failures or major problems.

Telecom Engineer   TSC Communications, Denver, CO   July 1999–June 2000

TSC is a joint venture between SBC and Telco, the leading provider of communications solutions and services in Denver. TSC's solution range from converged voice and data networks to customer relationship management (CRM) solutions to unified messaging solutions. Served in a customer support position.

- Successfully installed, configured, administered, and maintained Avaya Definity (PBX) of Prologix, G3Si, G3R, and S8700 versions at major customer sites. Worked with 29,000 ports, 15 EPNs (Expansion Port Networks), and 2,000 extensions.
- Responsible for the presales and postsales support for the design and implementation of call center networks. Played significant role in achieving highest sales and annual maintenance contracts by our team.
- Implemented call routing, call management, and computer telephony integration.
- Worked on VoIP, that is, configuration, administration of IP Media Processor on Avaya Definity, and also configuration and administration of IP hardphones (type 4612D+, 4624D+, and so forth).
- Administered Cisco IGX 8430, and call logging systems, such as NICE and Witness.
- Installed, configured, and administered BCMS and CMS. Upgraded and increased licenses of BCMS and CMS. Worked with Avaya CMS report parameters.
- Provided support remotely to 20 call center sites for administration, maintenance, and health checkups.
- Worked on ACD, CTI, CVCT, IVR, and Avaya Multi Conference Unit Avaya Intuity AUDIX voicemail system.

Education & Training

ITIL Foundation Certified–2006
Master of Science in Telecommunications, State University of New York, Utica, New York, 2001
Bachelors in Engineering in Electronics and Telecommunications, New York University, 1995

FIGURE 18   *Continued*

▶ Network engineering is also a key skill, as is extensive knowledge of standard telecommunication protocols, including SIP, MGCP, RTP, TCP/IP, SS7, SIP, MGCP, and MPEG2.

▶ Additional bonuses: evaluating new technologies, developing project proposals for technology enhancements, and managing the telecom budget.

Experience Section

▶ Provide examples of having lead or assisted on large technical efforts in the deployment of new telecommunication technologies, especially Voice over Internet Protocol (VoIP) implementations, messaging conversions, and video implementations. For each project, describe not only the technology, but also the business benefits that resulted. Include benefits you personally brought to the projects, such as team leadership.

▶ Provide a range of projects you have experience in to demonstrate your breadth and to get the most possible hits. In addition to the big projects, include some of the standard job responsibilities, including monitoring network performance, capacity planning, troubleshooting, moves/adds/changes (MACs), administering corporate mobile phones and PDAs, auditing telecommunication billing, performing equipment and services cost comparisons, and serving as escalation support.

▶ Highlight any planning, analysis, design, implementation, and support responsibilities. These can include documentation of configuration details, standard operating procedures, and training materials. (See Figure 11-18.)

Index

A

abilities. *See* skills and abilities
accomplishments, communicating importance of, 71–72
achievement statements, developing, 69–70
acronyms, incorporating into résumés, 14
action words
    combining with adjectives, 92
    including in cover letters, 95
adjectives
    advisory about use of, 92
    combining with action words, 92
    to describe self as "people person", 27
    describing personal qualities with, 91
    including in profile statements, 25
alignment of text, considering for résumés, 38
application developer résumé
    profile and experience sections of, 176
    sample of, 177–178
application developer with experience cover letter, 107
applications skills, including on résumés, 61, 64
architect résumé
    profile and experience sections of, 181
    sample of, 182–183
ASCII résumé, creating, 45

B

blogging, obtaining hands-on experience through, 137
bold fonts, using, 32
bullet points
    convenience of, 88
    including in Summary of Qualifications sections, 72
business systems analyst résumé
    profile and experience sections of, 184
    sample of, 185–187
buzzwords
    including in cover letters, 95
    including in online résumés, 47, 49
    maximizing effectiveness of, 151

C

Canadian web site, Monster web site for, 44
Career Builder web site, 44
career changes
    justifying in interviews, 167
    making transition to management, 129–130

masking previous employers during, 126–129
setting realistic expectations for, 123–124
transitioning skill sets in, 124–126
career objectives, defining for college graduates, 112–113
career progression, reflecting on résumés, 8–9
certifications
    including on résumés, 18, 30–31, 121–122
    résumé layout for candidates with, 34–35
CIO (chief information officer) résumé
    profile and experience sections of, 188, 190
    sample of, 191–192
clichés, avoiding on résumés, 25
college attendance without degree, reflecting on
    résumés, 29–30
college graduates. *See also* degrees
    defining career objectives for, 112–113
    defining experience of, 114–116
    résumé layout for recent college graduates, 33–34, 110
    training potential of, 113–117
    uncovering practical experience of, 116–117
    use of skills-based résumés by, 117–119
college hires, maximizing salaries of, 18
communication skills
    demonstrating in interviews, 161
    importance of, 11–12
companies, researching, 14, 94, 163–165
ComputerJobs web site, 44
Computerwork web site, 44
confidence, importance to getting noticed, 4
consultant résumé
    profile and experience sections of, 188
    sample of, 189–190
coursework
    demonstrating learning through, 114–116
    including or omitting, 34
cover letters. *See also* sample cover letters
    avoiding mistakes in, 97
    call to action section of, 96–97
    e-mailing, 98
    getting to point in, 95
    highlights of, 109–110
    hooking employers with, 94
    including action words and keywords in, 95
    introduction section of, 95–96
    length of, 95
    projecting self as ideal candidate in, 110

cover letters (*Cont.*)
    purpose of, 94
    recommendation letters, 102
    reflecting personality and key accomplishments in,
       109
    revealing positive aspects of self in, 95
    self-promotion section of, 96
    thank you letters, 102
    thank you section of, 97
    T-letters, 98, 100
Craig's List web site, 44
customer service, importance of soft skills to, 11

D

data architect job title, connotations of, 6
database administrators, desired skill level for, 15
database development skills, including on résumés, 60
database administration skills, including on résumés, 63
dates, including on résumés, 33
DBA (database administrator) résumé
    profile and experience sections of, 193
    sample of, 194–195
degrees, compensating for lack of, 29. *See also* college
  graduates
descriptors, maximizing on résumés, 92
desktop support specialist résumé
    experience section of, 196
    profile section of, 193
    sample of, 199–200
development manager job title, connotations of, 7
development skills, including on résumés, 58–59, 62–63
Dice web site, 44
dining interviews, engaging in, 169–170
director of IT
    sample job listing for, 75
    sample résumé for, 76–77
documentation specialist job title, connotations of, 6
dressing for interviews, 163

E

educational history
    including on résumés, 18–19, 29–31
    incorporating with certifications, 18
    lack of, 133
    maintaining relevance of, 151
electronic résumés. *See* online résumés

e-mail. *See also* online résumés
    receiving for relevant job postings, 46
    sending cover letters by, 98
e-mail addresses, including in headers, 24, 156
e-mail attachments, sending résumés as, 46
employers
    criteria for hiring IT professionals, 9–10
    customizing résumés for, 151
    customizing résumés to, 151
    hooking with cover letters, 94
    masking previous employers, 126–129
employment history
    dates and gaps in, 33
    listing, 68
enthusiasm, demonstrating in interviews, 162
experience history
    being honest about, 27
    compensating for minimal amount of, 34–35
    completing, 54
    defining for college graduates, 114–116
    expectations related to, 14–15
    including on résumés, 31–33
    maintaining relevance of, 151
expertise, developing, 139
extracurricular activities and achievements, including
  on résumés, 36, 155

F

faux pas to avoid
    burying top qualifications, 150
    demonstrating humor in résumés, 156
    emphasizing age, 152
    exaggerations that backfire, 154
    highlighting trivial skills, 153
    inappropriate e-mail addresses, 24, 156
    including high school graduation date, 156
    including personal interests or information, 155
    including reasons for leaving positions, 153
    including references, 156
    including salary history, 155
    incorrect résumé layout, 153
    job titles unrelated to IT, 151
    listing job responsibilities without detail, 153
    long or wordy résumés, 154
    making generic objective statements, 150
    mismatches with job descriptions, 152
    omitting keywords, 151

omitting studies in progress, 152
outdated extracurricular activities, 155
relative to displaying technical skills, 28
sending additional materials, 156
sending generic résumés to all employers, 151
typos or spelling mistakes, 154
unfriendly formatting for electronic résumés, 152–153
unprofessional résumé appearance, 154
unrelated experience or education, 151
using personal pronouns, 155
weak job titles, 151
Figures. *See* sample résumé content
firings, dealing with, 134, 167
flexibility, demonstrating in interviews, 161
fonts
    selecting, 37
    using, 32

G

gatekeepers. *See* recruiter interviews
getting noticed. *See* standing out
GPA (grade point average), including or omitting, 29
graduates. *See* college graduates

H

hands-on experience
    getting at training centers, 136
    getting from online labs, 139
    getting through on-the-job training, 136–137
    at home, 137–139
    through blogging and RSS feeds, 137
hardware skills
    including on résumés, 55, 61
    obtaining at home, 137
header, information included in, 24
helpdesk analyst job title, connotations of, 6
helpdesk analyst with minimal experience cover letter, 105
helpdesk skills, including on résumés, 64
helpdesk specialist résumé
    experience section of, 196
    profile section of, 193
    sample of, 197–198
hiring managers
    addressing cover letters to, 94
    building rapports with, 19–20
hiring requirements, matching, 8–9

hits on online résumés, checking, 49
Hot Jobs web site, 44

I

IEEE (Institute of Electrical and Electronics Engineers, Inc.) web site, 147
IET (Institution of Engineering and Technology) web site, 147
IIBA (International Institute of Business Analysis) web site, 147
illegal questions, watching for, 170–171
image
    controlling in order to stand out, 5
    projecting with job titles, 6
information architect job title, connotations of, 6
Information Technology (IT). *See* IT (Information Technology)
informational interviews. *See* networking interviews
infrastructure architect job title, connotations of, 7
infrastructure engineer job title, connotations of, 6
infrastructure engineering skills, including on résumés, 64–65
infrastructure specialist résumé, profile and experience sections of, 201, 204
"-ing" constructions, replacing on résumés, 88–91
Internet security analyst
    sample job listing for, 80–81
    sample résumé for, 82–83
internship experience
    including for college graduates, 117
    including on résumés, 33
interview process, dynamics of, 160–161
interviewers
    common questions asked by, 164–167
    posing questions to, 168
    preparing for meetings with, 163
interviews
    demonstrating skills in, 161–162
    engaging in dining interviews, 169–170
    engaging in phone interviews, 169
    following up on, 171
    illegal questions posed in, 170–171
    preferred days for, 161
    preparing for, 162–163
    redirecting, 166
    writing thank you letters related to, 102

IT (Information Technology), competitiveness of, 4
IT certifications, web site for, 18
IT employment, statistic related to, 4
IT Jobs web site, 44
IT manager résumé
    experience section of, 201
    profile section of, 196
    sample of, 202–203
IT managers
    hidden challenges for, 19–20
    sample job listing for, 78
    sample résumé for, 79
IT positions
    demand for, 7
    top candidates for, 10
IT professionals with experience, laying out résumés for,
  35
italics, using, 32
IT-job search engines, consulting, 8
itSMF (The Service Management Forum) web site, 147

J

job ads. *See also* sample job listings
    interpreting, 14–15
    tailoring résumés to, 13–14
job boards, consulting, 44
Job Circle web site, 44
job descriptions, matching résumés to, 152
job search engines, consulting, 8
job searches
    automating online, 46
    notifying others of, 144
job skills and responsibilities, tailoring to job ads, 13–14
job titles
    checking online postings for, 8
    emphasizing, 151
    including on résumés, 7–8, 32
    interchangeability of, 7–8
    maintaining relevance of, 151
    optimizing on online résumés, 49
    projecting image with, 6
job web sites, 44, 47. *See also* web sites
job-hopping, common occurrence of, 123
jobs. *See also* on-the-job experience
    dealing with few jobs, 133
    dealing with multiple jobs over short period, 131–133

K

keywords
    including in cover letters, 95
    including in online résumés, 47, 49
    maximizing effectiveness of, 151
knowledge, demonstrating for college graduates,
  114–116

L

layoffs, dealing with, 134, 167
leadership, importance of soft skills to, 11
learning, demonstrating for college graduates,
  114–116
leaves of absence, justifying in interviews, 167
locations of past employment, including on
    résumés, 32

M

management, challenges to, 19–20
management positions
    making transition to, 129–130
    Technical Skills sections for, 68
management skills, including on résumés, 65–66
margins, setting for résumés, 38
meeting facilitation, importance of soft skills to, 11
messaging systems engineer job title, connotations of, 7
Monster web site, 44
MS skills learned from college courses, 114–116
MS Technical Skills Inventory worksheet, 55–66
multimedia specialist résumé
    experience section of, 211
    profile section of, 204
    sample of, 212–213

N

network engineer résumé
    profile and experience sections of, 201, 204
    sample of, 208–210
network engineers, desired skill level for, 15
network operating system skills, including on résumés,
  62
networking
    initiating, 144
    through professional associations, 147
networking cover letter sample, 100–101

networking interviews
communicating in, 146
ending and getting more names from, 146
objectives of, 145
requesting meeting for, 145
work involved in, 146
networking skills, including on résumés, 55–58
new-media/web-designer skills, including on résumés, 59–60

O

online labs, getting hands-experience from, 139
online résumé forms, using, 46–47
online résumés. *See also* e-mail; résumés
checking hits on, 49
formatting properly, 152–153
including keywords in, 47
optimizing, 49–52
renewing, 49
on-the-job experience. *See also* jobs
emphasizing, 133
getting, 136–137
operating-system skills, including on résumés, 55, 61–62

P

pages allocated to résumés, limiting number of, 37
paper, selecting for résumés, 37
paper certifications
including on résumés, 18, 30–31, 121–122
résumé layout for candidates with, 34–35
PAR (problem, action, results), quantifying skills with, 69–70
past skills, considering inclusion on résumés, 36
PC maintenance technician job title, connotations of, 7
PC technician with no experience cover letter, 104
PDA skills, including on résumés, 55
"people person," characterizing self as, 26–27
people skills
getting training in, 12
importance of, 11
personal interests and information, excluding from résumés, 155
personal qualities, describing with adjectives, 91
phone interviews, engaging in, 169
PMI (Project Management Institute) web site, 147
presentation, importance of soft skills to, 11

problem histories
lack of formal education, 133
layoffs and firings, 134
missing years of work, 131
multiple jobs over short period, 131–133
problem-solving, importance of soft skills to, 11
productivity, reducing time to, 16
professional associations, web sites for, 147
profile statements, including in résumés, 25–26
programmer versus software engineer, 6
programmers, desired skill level for, 15
project management, importance of soft skills to, 11
project manager résumé
profile and experience sections of, 211, 213
sample of, 214–215

Q

QA specialist without experience cover letter, 108
QA tester experience, including on résumés, 67
qualifications
emphasizing, 150
including in résumés, 24–27
Qualifications section, creating, 72–74
quality assurance skills, including on résumés, 65
quality assurance specialist job title, connotations of, 7
quality assurance specialist résumé
profile and experience sections of, 216
sample of, 217–219
questions
asked by interviewers, 164–167
illegal examples of, 170–171
for interviewers, 168

R

Really Simple Syndication (RSS) feeds, obtaining hands-on experience through, 137
recognition of good work, reflecting on résumés, 71
recommendation letters, obtaining, 102
recruiter interviews
attending, 160
getting past, 168–169
references, presenting, 39–41
references document, separating from résumés, 156
responsibility, demonstrating in interviews, 162
résumé faux pas. *See* faux pas to avoid
résumé forms, using online forms, 46
résumé information, focusing on relevance of, 36

résumé sections
    educational history, 29–31
    experience, 31–33
    header, 24
    key qualifications and profile statement, 24–27
    technical skills, 27–29
résumés. *See also* online résumés; sample résumé content
    chronological organization of, 31
    conceptualizing, 36
    creating ASCII résumés, 45
    layout of information on, 33–35
    maintaining consistency of, 31–32
    placing in portfolios for interviews, 162
    posting online and following up on, 46
    scanning, 48
    sending as e-mail attachments, 46
    tailoring to job ads, 13–14, 74
    updating, 18
    use of skills-based résumés by recent college
        graduates, 117–119
RSS (Really Simple Syndication) feeds, obtaining
    hands-on experience through, 137

S

salaries, maximizing for college hires, 18
salary history
    discussing in interviews, 166
    omitting from résumés, 33, 155
salary negotiations, engaging in, 166–167
sample cover letters. *See also* cover letters
    application developer with experience, 107
    helpdesk analyst with minimal experience, 105
    networking cover letter, 101
    networking letters, 100–101
    PC technician with no experience, 104
    QA specialist without experience, 108
    skills-based cover letter for career changer, 127
    thank you letter, 103
    T-letters, 100
    traditional cover letter, 99
    web page designer with referral, 106
sample job listings. *See also* job ads
    director if IT, 75
    Internet security analyst, 80
    IT manager, 78
    systems administrator, 84

sample résumé content. *See also* résumés
    application developer, 177–178
    architect, 182–183
    business systems analyst, 185–187
    career change with transitioned skill set,
        125–126
    CIO (chief information officer), 191–192
    consultant, 189–190
    DBA (database administrator), 194–195
    desktop support specialist, 199–200
    for director of IT, 76–77
    director of IT position, 76
    do's and don'ts, 41
    educational history sections, 18–19
    effective résumé for recent college graduate,
        120
    experience section, 67
    hands-on experience, 140
    helpdesk specialist, 197–198
    ineffective résumé for recent college graduate,
        119
    for Internet security analyst, 82–83
    for IT manager, 79
    IT manager, 202–203
    multimedia specialist, 212–213
    network engineer, 208–210
    online-résumé formats, 50–52
    paper certification, 122
    project manager, 214–215
    quality assurance specialist, 217–219
    references document, 40
    security specialist, 221–222
    skill-based IT résumé, 32
    skills and qualifications summary, 12
    skills-based résumé for career changer,
        128–129
    for systems administrator, 85–87
    technical profile, 28
    technical skills, 29
    technical writer, 224–226
    telecommunications specialist, 227–229
    web application developer, 179–180,
        205–207
    white space, 38–39
scanning résumés, 48
security analyst job title, connotations of, 7

security analyst résumé, profile and experience sections of, 220

security specialist résumé, sample of, 221–222

self-direction, importance of soft skills to, 11

selling, importance of soft skills to, 11

skill progression, reflecting on résumés, 8–9

skill sets
    demonstrating for management positions, 130
    transitioning during career changes, 124–126

skill-level expectations
    for database administrators, 15
    for network engineers, 15
    for programmers, 15

skills. See also transferable skills
    demonstrating in interviews, 161–162
    marketing, 10–12
    quantifying with PAR (problem, action, results), 69–70
    selling benefits of, 9–10
    soft skills, 11–12
    uncovering, 69

skills and abilities, identifying, 54

skills and qualifications summary, example of, 12

skills-based résumés
    use by recent college graduates, 117–119
    using, 32
    using in career changes, 124

"So what?" technique, applying, 71–72

soft skills
    getting training in, 12
    importance of, 11

software engineer experience, including on résumés, 67

software engineer job title, connotations of, 6

software engineer versus programmer, 6

software skills
    enhancing, 139, 141
    obtaining at home, 138–139

spelling, correcting, 28, 49, 154

standing out
    by controlling image, 5
    by understanding management challenges, 20

statements, including in Summary of Qualifications sections, 72–73

statements about self, including in résumés, 25–26

storage architect job title, connotations of, 7

Summary of Qualifications section, creating, 72–74

systems administrator
    sample job listing for, 84
    sample résumé for, 85–87

systems analysis skills, including on résumés, 65

T

talents and skills, uncovering, 69

team orientation
    demonstrating in interviews, 162
    importance of soft skills to, 11

technical capability, demonstrating in interviews, 161

technical skills
    identifying, 54–66
    including for management positions, 68
    including on résumés, 27–29, 67

technical trainer job title, connotations of, 7

technical writer résumé
    profile and experience sections of, 223
    sample of, 224–226

technical writing skills, including on résumés, 64

technician positions, making transition to management, 129–130

technological passion, demonstrating in interviews, 161

technological references, updating, 28

telecom skills, including on résumés, 60–61

telecommunications analyst job title, connotations of, 7

telecommunications specialist résumé
    profile and experience sections of, 223, 230
    sample of, 227–229

thank you letters
    sample of, 103
    sending after interviews, 171
    writing, 102

time to productivity, reducing, 16

T-letters, writing, 98, 100

traditional cover letter sample, 99

training
    including on résumés, 18
    potential for recent college graduates, 113–117

training centers, receiving hands-on experience at, 136

transferable skills. See also skills
    applying to career changes, 124–126
    examples of, 17
    value of, 16

typos, avoiding, 154. See also spelling

U

user interface designer job title, connotations of, 6

V

virtual machines, creating with VMWare, 139
VMWare, creating virtual machines with, 139
vocabulary. *See* action words; word lists
volunteer experience
  getting, 136–137
  including on résumés, 33

W

weaknesses, responding to in interviews, 165
web application developer résumé, sample of, 179–180, 205–207
web page designer with referral cover letter, 106
web sites. *See also* job web sites
  Career Builder, 44
  ComputerJobs, 44
  Computerwork, 44
  Craig's List, 44
  Dice, 44
  Hot Jobs, 44
  IEEE (Institute of Electrical and Electronics Engineers, Inc.), 147

IET (Institution of Engineering and Technology), 147
IIBA (International Institute of Business Analysis), 147
IT certifications, 18
IT Jobs, 44
itSMF (The Service Management Forum), 147
Job Circle, 44
for jobs, 44
Monster, 44
PMI (Project Management Institute), 147
professional associations, 147
soft skills training, 12
VMWare, 139
web-designer/new-media skills, including on résumés, 59–60
web-development skills, including on résumés, 63–64
white space, using on résumés, 37–38
word lists, consulting for use with résumés, 88–91
words. *See* action words; keywords
work, missing years of, 131
work/experience history. *See* experience history
worksheets, using to identify technical skills, 54–66

Y

years of experience, expectations related to, 14–15